ONLY FOOLS
★★★ and ★★★
HORSES

ONLY FOOLS

★★★ *and* ★★★

HORSES

The Story of Britain's
Favourite Comedy

GRAHAM McCANN

CANONGATE

Edinburgh · London

This paperback edition published in 2012

First published in Great Britain in 2011 by Canongate Books Ltd,
14 High Street, Edinburgh EH1 1TE

1

www.canongate.tv

British Library Cataloguing-in-Publication Data
A catalogue record for this book is available on
request from the British Library

ISBN 978 0 85786 056 9

Typeset in Bembo by Palimpsest Book Production Limited,
Falkirk, Stirlingshire

Printed and bound in Great Britain by Clays Ltd, St Ives plc

In memory of John Sullivan

Contents

PROLOGUE

Ever tried.
Ever failed.
No matter.
Try again.
Fail again.
Fail better.

DEL BOY: *All the things that we've ever got out of life have come from my intelligence and my foresight.*
RODNEY: *Well, I'm glad somebody's owned up!*

The yellow van. The little man with the flat cap and gift of the gab. The taller, younger man with the permanently puzzled expression. The deals, the dreams, the scams and the calamities. The grand chandelier crashing to the floor. The gap where the bar flap should have been. The repeated affirmation that 'This time next year, we'll be millionaires!' These are just a few of the things that come to mind when we think of the great British sitcom *Only Fools and Horses*. Surely only a twonk, a plonker, a wally or a dipstick would fail to rub their hands together, when thinking of this show, and exclaim 'cushty', 'lovely jubbly' or perhaps even '*joie de vivre*!'

Only Fools and Horses is one of those sitcoms whose appeal transcends mere cult comedy fandom and engages with all of those who appreciate good acting, good writing and good television. Many sitcoms simply arrive, amuse and then fade away, providing us with nothing more than a pleasant but evanescent distraction. The special few, however, creep deep into our consciousness, capture our imagination, engage our emotions and never, ever, let us forget them. *Only Fools and Horses,* like *Hancock's Half-Hour, Steptoe and Son, Dad's Army, Fawlty Towers* and a few others, has earned its place in such a pantheon.

Only Fools and Horses was the real deal. All of us knew of characters like Del Boy and Rodney Trotter, and most of us also knew of one or two people like Grandad and Uncle Albert, and Trigger, Boycie and Marlene. The life that they lived in and around that high-rise council flat at Nelson Mandela House in Peckham seemed authentic as well as funny. We watched the show not to escape from reality but rather to be entertained by it. As with all of the finest British sitcoms, it was a case of the British laughing at certain defining characteristics of the British.

Only Fools made us laugh at our amateurishness (the Trotters are 'self-unemployed' salesmen who try to flog a strange range of faulty goods), our parochialism (most things strike them as exotic whenever they venture a mile or two outside of Peckham), our dogged nostalgia (Del's for his mother, Grandad's for his youth, Uncle Albert's for the war and Rodney's for the promise engendered by his precious two GCEs) and our adamantine and ineluctable preoccupation with capital and class (one way or another, with unshakeable belief in the principle of 'he who dares, wins', Del is determined to drag his family up the social ladder). It also tapped into that inexhaustible well of contrariness – mixing idealism with cynicism, producing bubbles of pretension that are then rudely pierced and popped just as soon as they appear on the surface – that has driven so many British partnerships from Falstaff and Prince Hal to Lennon and McCartney and beyond ('I've got to admit it's getting better'/ . . . 'It couldn't get no worse'[1]). With one man gazing up hopefully at the stars and the other one glancing down anxiously at the gutter, Britain's traditional comic–drama dynamic was re-enacted all over again. 'We're fifteen minutes from the West End and fifteen minutes from London,' declares Rodney brightly from within the confines of their tower block council flat. 'Yes,' comes the sardonic reply, 'and fifteen minutes from the ground.'

The success of the show was, and continues to be, extraordinary. It attracted huge audiences during its 22-year run, making it the most-watched British show of two consecutive decades, eventually reaching a peak at 24.3 million – still a record for an episode of a UK sitcom.[2] It also won numerous awards, including three 'Best Comedy Series' BAFTAs. It was voted 'Britain's Best Sitcom' in a major BBC poll[3] and came forty-fifth in the British Film Institute's list of the 100 Greatest Television Programmes.[4] It has been sold to many countries throughout the world (including Australia, Belgium, Bosnia, Croatia, Cyprus, Greece, Republic of Ireland, Israel, Malta, Montenegro, New Zealand, Pakistan, Serbia, Slovenia, South Africa and Spain) and it continues to inspire spin-off shows and frequent weeks and weekends of repeats on various satellite channels.

What is, if anything, even more extraordinary is the enduring affection that the programme still commands. A remarkable number of people remain eager to watch the old episodes, discuss them, savour them and cherish them. A whole new generation is now discovering them and delighting in them. An older generation is finding new reasons to re-visit and re-view them. Even in a culture that is now, at its broadest and most prosaic, so robotically and neurotically restless and forgetful, there is still a strong fondness for a sitcom that ended, as a series, in 1991, and then reappeared for the last time as an occasional special in 2003. It came as no real surprise, therefore, when a 2008 OnePoll survey found that *Only Fools and Horses* was the television series that Britons would most like to see return to their screens.[5]

The sadly premature death of the show's gifted creator, John Sullivan, on 23 April 2011, dashed such hopes definitively, but also underlined how keenly so many people still care about the greatest of his numerous achievements as a writer. Included among the countless warmly respectful obituaries and encomia about the man himself were many words of praise for *Only Fools and Horses* in particular. The critic, writer and broadcaster David Quantick, for example, remarked that 'anyone seeking to write comedy who is even only slightly aware of sitcom's lineage' would be well advised to study the show and 'see how it is done by a master of popular, populist, intelligent and witty comedy'; the BBC's Creative Director, Alan Yentob, praised the 'beauty' of the programme's scripts and predicted that 'the Trotter family would provide enjoyment, tears and laughter for generations to come'; and another of Sullivan's fellow writers, Maurice Gran, said of *Only Fools* that 'the richness of characterisation, and indeed the number of vivid characters, leaves most other sitcoms looking sparse and under-populated'.[6]

A substantial celebration of this remarkable show, therefore, is something that it richly deserves, but, nonetheless, it needs to be done in the right spirit. Great sitcoms, in this day and age, remain available at the flick of a switch. There is thus no need to retrieve them via an elaborate and painstaking excavation. What *is* worth attempting, however, is to reach out to those – probably the vast majority – who simply watched the episodes when they first went out and then, when the show finally ended, moved on before the ubiquitous repeats could wear out what had always been most welcome. These are the people who still have an appetite to awaken.

What an appropriate celebration *should* seek to do, therefore, is to revive the old inclusive enthusiasm for the show. A great comedy programme is something to treasure because it brings so many of us together in pleasure.

Only Fools and Horses is a particularly important comedy show to celebrate, because it not only engaged with us as a nation but also with the sitcom as a genre. While reflecting, and sometimes responding to, our various fashions, follies and foibles, the show also explored and challenged what a sitcom is supposed to be and should strive to achieve. It was, in its own sly little way, a revolutionary show, as well as a very funny one.

The story of this sitcom's evolution is thus actually a story of real risks and worries and great triumphs and achievements. It is a story of a brilliant team of hugely talented individuals working together incredibly hard to realise a very special dream. It is a story of ordinary viewers finding something on the screen that genuinely impressed, amused and moved them. The endless loop of repeats, well-intended though it is, can sometimes distort or obscure most or even all of this rich and remarkable story. That is why it is worth going back to the beginning, and seeing it unfold all over again through a fresh pair of eyes.

This book, therefore, will aim to remind the broader audience of how it came to fall in love with *Only Fools and Horses*.

The experience of discovering, following and being fascinated with the show will be reanimated by telling the full story of this sitcom's eventful life, and how it became such a positive and pleasant part of the lives of those who watched it.

CHAPTER ONE

This Time Next Year

Répondez s'il vous plaît.

It is September 1980. This time next year . . .

This time next year, a writer called John Sullivan will begin a labour of love, a producer/director called Ray Butt will commence an extraordinary adventure, a trio of actors named David Jason, Nicholas Lyndhurst and Lennard Pearce will take on the roles of their dreams and a brand new sitcom entitled *Only Fools and Horses* will start to enrich a great comic tradition. Nothing seemed inevitable back in September 1980, but, this time next year, something will arrive on British television that will end up being seen as very special indeed.

In 1980, however, the immediate future, to many British people, seemed bleak. The new Prime Minister, Margaret Thatcher, was busy reassuring her monetarist minions that she was most definitely not for turning. After wrongly attributing her implausibly tolerant initial sentiments ('where there is discord, may we bring harmony . . .') to the medieval theology of St Francis of Assisi (they actually came from an obscure 1912 French prayer), and wrongly associating her modern amoral economics with the eighteenth-century moral philosophy of Adam Smith (she favoured the free market for its own sake; he favoured it because he believed good and decent people would not abuse it), she proceeded to brand any colleagues who possessed more logic but less blinkered conviction than her as 'wet', and set about causing as much discord as seemed politically possible. There were bitter industrial disputes and violent riots, rising inflation and falling factories, and, while two million or so freshly 'unfettered' Britons remained miserably unemployed, self-interest was celebrated at the expense of civic virtue. Council tenants were invited to buy their own homes, so even if they were stuck on a low social rung they could at least console themselves with the thought that they now owned a tiny splinter or two of the ladder, and a few individuals who feared being stuck in dead-end jobs began to buy into the dubious entrepreneurial dream of class-free upward mobility, but in any other sense most ordinary working people were left alone to deal with the mounting mood of despondency and desolation.

British comedy failed, for a while, to be of much help. The Prime Minister herself had wasted no time in demonstrating that she had no real sense of humour (even before her election triumph in 1979, when handed a light-hearted line – 'Keep taking the tablets' – to mock her Labour rival James Callaghan's likening of himself to Moses, she attempted to 'improve' the joke by saying 'Keep taking the pills' instead[1]), and many in the comedy industry seemed to respond to such tin-eared forays into funny business by losing their own invaluable talent to amuse.

While most of the old bow-tied brigade now appeared more energised by the prospect of playing a round of golf than they were by the challenge of making people laugh, and several much-loved but ageing greats (including Morecambe & Wise, The Two Ronnies and Tommy Cooper) had already slipped into a slow but inevitable decline, the only notable sign that a younger generation of comics might one day be ready to take up the reins was the recent arrival on television of the mildly irreverent sketch show *Not the Nine O'Clock News*. Not even sitcoms – so often the most humorously attuned to their times – seemed quite ready to engage with the start of the Thatcher era.

Some hugely popular and critically praised sitcoms had come to an end in the second half of the 1970s: *Dad's Army* and *Porridge* in 1977, *The Good Life* and *Rising Damp* in 1978, and *Fawlty Towers* in 1979. As the 1980s approached, the genre, slouching down somewhere between the humdrum and the ho-hum, was suddenly looking more than a little jaded.

'For the past couple of weeks,' one frustrated TV critic remarked, 'I have, in the line of duty, been sampling as many of the current crop of comedies as a body, if not mind, could bear without actual pain. I thought I might offer a considered survey of the scene, but in the name of charity, I've given that up. A critic cracking at one unlovable comedy risks sounding like a sledgehammer of pompousness descending on a lark's egg, but with a list a dozen long . . .'[2] A few new series were starting – most notably *To The Manor Born* and *Terry and June* in 1979 – but they seemed much safer, and more self-consciously and exclusively middle-class, than most of their illustrious predecessors. The great British sitcom was in danger of falling dramatically out of fashion.

All of this, however, was soon to change. All that it would take was a certain combination of talents and ambitions, this time next year.

The writer who would change things was John Sullivan. The producer/director was Ray Butt. The actors were David Jason, Nicholas Lyndhurst and Lennard Pearce.

John Sullivan was a somewhat stocky but rather shy and softly spoken scriptwriter who, by 1980, suddenly found himself at an unexpected crossroads in his career. After working hard to establish himself at the BBC by shaping a popular sitcom, he was now facing his first real professional crisis.

Born John Richard Thomas Sullivan in 1946 to an Anglo-Irish, Kentish-Corkish family based in the south London district of Balham ('Gateway to the South', as Peter Sellers' legendary cod-travelogue dubbed it), he had experienced an upbringing that, as he would later put it, was almost clichéd in its working-class character. His father, also named John, was a plumber by trade, and his mother, Hilda, worked occasionally as a charlady. They shared a small terraced house in the rough and tough area of Zennor Road with another family, and made do with such basic amenities as an outside lavatory and an old tin bath hanging up in the yard.

School struck John Jnr as an unwelcome and irrational distraction from both his early love of football and his mounting impatience to get out in the world and start earning a regular wage. The challenge of the eleven-plus examination therefore came and went without ever threatening to shake him out of his educational apathy. Feeling fated to become mere factory fodder, he reasoned that there was no real point in trying. The only 'encouragement' to at least appear to study, as far as Sullivan and his friends were concerned, was the prospect of avoiding a gym shoe being slapped across the backside and a piece of chalk hurled sharply at the head. His nascent gift for using his imagination was limited in those days to twisting the truth in the classroom: selling freshly tailored lies – cash up front – to those pupils in urgent need of plausible excuses to tell the teachers. It was only in 1958, when Sullivan reached the age of twelve while at Telferscot Secondary Modern School in Radbourne Road, that he finally started taking an interest in something academic: English Literature.

The reason for this was that he found a new young teacher – Jim Trowers – who stopped making English Literature seem remotely academic. The Geordie-born Trowers looked somewhat unconventional – his hair was a little longer than the norm, he wore a patch over his right eye (which he would sometimes pretend to take out and clean) and seemed full of nervous energy – and, mercifully for Sullivan and others, he taught unconventionally, too. Instead of the robotic 'read, absorb and regurgitate' method employed by previous teachers, which had bored young Sullivan to tears, Trowers took each story and read it out to his pupils, adopting a range of voices and tones and rhythms to bring all the scenes and characters to life. Suddenly, for Sullivan (who had grown up in a home that contained just two books on its shelves – The Bible and a guide to the football pools), literature made sense – and, more than that, it started to matter. Dickens' *David Copperfield* sparked a real interest in English as a subject, and in writing. The mid-twentieth-century schoolboy found himself enthralled by colourful descriptions of areas, social groups and characters that were very familiar to him. Dickens became his favourite author, and Sullivan had something other than football to look forward to in his school day.

Structured and paced for the old shilling monthlies, Dickens' cleverly episodic stories had the kind of social scope, and humour, that engaged Sullivan's youthful imagination. Each fiction seemed to offer a broad range of characterisations that captured the full richness and complexity of the Victorian social hierarchy. In *Bleak House*, for example, level after level was acknowledged and explored: there were the lofty Dedlocks in their West End mansion; lesser landowners like Mr Jarndyce and members of older professions such as the lawyers Mr Tulkinghorn and Mr Vholes and the doctor Allen Woodcourt; figures from the middling classes that included the northern ironmaster Mr Rouncewell, the campaigning Mrs Jellyby, the shop owner Mr Bagnet and the moneylender Mr Smallweed; the marginal types, such as the detective Inspector Bucket, the rag-and-bone man Mr Krook and the shooting gallery man Mr George; the servants, ranging from the superior housekeeper Mrs Rouncewell down through the ladies' maids to the poor dogsbody Guster; and, at the bottom, the manual workers, Neckett the sheriff's officer, and the inarticulate and homeless crossing-sweeper Jo White. No part of the community seemed excluded or overlooked; no aspect appeared under-appreciated. Such fictions struck Sullivan as powerful, plausible and persistently vivid visions of real life: 'Dickens wrote about areas I knew in London; although the writing dated back to the early 19th century, I felt this guy knew where I'd been and I began realising just how special his books were.'[3]

Sullivan's sudden interest in such literary works was soon spotted by Jim Trowers, who was intrigued by the kind of work that the boy was now producing. 'I gave the class an essay to write,' the teacher would recall. 'I said to them: "You have the Epsom races. Write me a short piece from any aspect at all. You know, perhaps one of the bookies, or someone laying a bet." And they all did this. Except John Sullivan. He wrote it as though he were one of the horses running the race. Which I found absolutely fascinating.'[4]

In spite of this belated academic enthusiasm, however, Sullivan still chose to leave school three years later, aged fifteen, without sitting for any qualifications. This was the norm among working-class families, where the pressure to contribute to the family's income often outweighed any sense of individual aspiration. Staying on to sit for O levels was still largely a middle-class privilege.

Rather than being forced straight into one of the local factories, Sullivan found his first job instead working as a messenger for the news agency Reuters, in Fleet Street, in the autumn of 1961. A few months later, after a brief spell helping out in the company's photographic department, he reverted to being a messenger once again, this time at the new and very *à la mode* advertising agency of Collett, Dickenson, Pearce & Partners (CDP), a small but rather glamorous *Mad Men*-style outfit based in Howland Street, west central London, where the likes of future filmmakers David Puttnam and Alan Parker would soon be making a name for themselves (the former as an accounts executive, the latter as a copywriter) alongside the advertising *wunderkind* Charles Saatchi. In 1963, at the age of seventeen, Sullivan, attracted by the prospect of increasing his weekly wage from £3.50 to £20, was persuaded to join his old school friend Colin Humphries cleaning cars for a local second-hand car dealer. He and Humphries then went on to try their hand at selling cars themselves, but Sullivan soon realised that he was not suited to the vocation and drifted off to work for Watney's Brewery in Balham instead.

It was here during the mid-1960s, stacking crates in a large and noisy hall, that he first started to consider pursuing writing as a more fulfilling kind of career. One of his co-workers was another old school friend called Paul Saunders, with whom he shared jokes and funny stories during the many boring periods of inaction. In January 1968, Saunders told his friend that he had recently read an article in the *Daily Mirror* about Johnny Speight: the famous working-class boy from Canning Town who grew up to write grittily realistic and socially aware plays, and then the hugely successful and notoriously controversial sitcom *Till Death Us Do Part*, and, as a consequence, was now winning prestigious awards and commanding a fee of around £1,000 per script.[5] Sullivan was intrigued, and so, when Saunders suggested that they should try to follow in Speight's footsteps ('*We're* funny guys. *We* should have a go at this and earn a load of money!'[6]), he agreed, and promptly went out to buy an old typewriter from a local second-hand shop called The Treasure Chest.

For the next two months, the two young men worked on an idea – involving an old soldier whose pride and joy was the traditional gents' public lavatory that he ran, but who is now faced with competition from a brand-new modern rival down the road – and, when they felt it had developed satisfactorily, sent off a sample script to the BBC. Three more months passed, while the two young men packed beer crate after beer crate and dreamed of emulating Johnny Speight with his Rolls-Royce, big house in the country, champagne, cigars and glamorous celebrity lifestyle. Then a reply finally arrived: 'We are not looking for this kind of material.'

The brusque rejection sapped the spirit of Saunders, who decided to dream about doing something else, but Sullivan was undaunted: He had discovered that he enjoyed the process of writing and therefore continued to write and work on scripts: 'I so enjoyed the process of inventing characters and writing the dialogue that it just became a hobby. It kept me off the streets, and I didn't spend too much money on beer, because I was just writing every evening. And I suppose the dream was that, yes, I still hoped I could get into this business.' Drawing from his own experiences, he based his plots and characters on themes and people that he knew and set them in familiar, local locations. One idea revolved around a family called the Leeches, who fiddled to keep feeding off the State; another featured a football team that always failed to find the winning formula. As soon as each sample story was completed, he sent them off to the BBC and waited patiently for a letter of acceptance. When all that he received was a rejection slip, he simply rewrote the script and sent it straight back in. 'Sometimes I'd change the titles, sometimes I'd even change my own name, to try to fool them'.[7] He refused to accept defeat.

Working-class heroes continued to offer him hope as the 1960s edged towards their end. Apart from Johnny Speight, Sullivan could also look at Ray Galton and Alan Simpson – two other hugely gifted writers from very modest London backgrounds who had reached the top of the profession (and whose 1962 pilot episode of their sitcom *Steptoe and Son*, which had featured bright comedy mixed with raw emotional drama, had dazzled Sullivan when he first watched it) – along with such inspired musicians and lyricists as the Muswell Hill-born Ray Davies of The Kinks and the Chiswick-born Pete Townshend of The Who, and, right at the heart of the decade's pop culture, Lennon and McCartney of The Beatles were continuing to confound Britain's old class prejudices. 'I can remember lying in bed and hearing one of their songs, "From Me To You", playing down the street,' Sullivan would recall fondly about the so-called Fab Four. 'I'd never heard anything like it before, it was such a different sound. I'll always remember thinking: "Aren't the Americans clever." I automatically assumed that any new sound, anything good, originated from the States, so when I found out that they were four working-class boys from a few hundred miles up the road, I was really inspired.'[8] It was still possible, Sullivan kept telling himself, in spite of the old social bias; there was still a chance for an 'ordinary' young man from Balham to make it big via the uses of literacy.

While the challenge of writing continued to inspire him, however, the dull routine of the day job continued to bore him, so he left Watney's and, for want of another way to earn a regular wage, went to work with his father as a trainee plumber. It did not take long for him to realise that he had made a great mistake: he had no real interest in plumbing and was consequently careless, causing frequent floods.

Determined to find a way to better himself before it was too late, he resolved to teach himself some of the things that he had allowed to pass him by during his days at school, devouring books on a wide range of subjects and trying his best to broaden his knowledge. He also continued to write in his spare time, still hopeful that, one day, an idea would spark something genuinely special. As what he called a 'brain exercise', he would open newspapers on random pages (just like he had heard that John Lennon had done prior to conjuring up such songs as 'A Day In The Life') and pick out a story to use as source material for a script. The ambition remained unabated.

He was still labouring as a maintenance plumber while striving to develop as a writer when, in 1972, he met an attractive young secretary called Sharon in the upmarket Chelsea Drugstore pub (mentioned, rather ominously, in the Rolling Stones song 'You Can't Always Get What You Want') on the King's Road. They got on well, and started dating, but Sullivan went out with her a few times before daring to mention his dream of exchanging his tool kit for a typewriter. Sharon was earning more than he was at the time, but, in spite of any misgivings she might have felt, she continued seeing him and listening to his writerly ambitions, and, two years later, they married.

Sullivan – now living with Sharon in a two-roomed council flat at Rossiter Road in Balham – kept up his strategy of bombarding the BBC with sample scripts, and refused to be disheartened by any rejection letter that came back: 'I used to drive past the BBC's TV Centre in west London and I used to look at it like a castle that I had to somehow or other breach.'[9] One day, he came up with an idea for a sitcom that really captured his imagination: an unemployed young man from south London who had convinced himself that he was a dangerous revolutionary and the self-appointed leader of the 'Tooting Popular Front'.

'I knew it was my best idea yet,' said Sullivan, who had known such a character in a local pub (The Nelson Arms) who was always spouting radical political clichés while never seeming to do anything remotely practical. During an era in Britain when there seemed to be a bewildering array of Marxist, Western Marxist, Marxist–Leninist, Trotskyist, anarchist, anarcho-syndicalist, revolutionary socialist and neo-communist splinter groups arguing angrily amongst each other, and it almost seemed *de rigueur* for students to decorate their walls with blood red Che Guevara posters while parroting some or other type of clumsy political jargon (a fashion mocked with great relish by *Private Eye* via the umming and erring character of 'Dave Spart'), the relevance of the comic theme was abundantly clear. Calling his proposed sitcom *Citizen Smith*, Sullivan worked hard on the sample script – believing that its topical revolutionary theme had real potential – and then pondered the most appropriate strategy for submitting it. Knowing that the script represented his best work yet by far, his greatest fear was rejection, and what he would do if it failed to work out.

Determined not to squander this opportunity, Sullivan considered his options as carefully as possible and concluded that his best chance would be to adopt a Trojan Horse-style strategy: get a very basic job at the BBC, learn from within how the organisation functioned and then seek out a suitable patron. He thus applied to the Corporation, on 19 September 1974, and, much to his surprise, was not only invited for an interview but subsequently (on 18 November) given a position in the props department at Television Centre. Feeling emboldened by his good fortune now that he was finally inside the 'castle', he soon engineered a move to scene shifting, which brought him closer to the actual business of filming, and started studying who did what on the set.

One evening, as he went about his usual duties, a colleague pointed out someone – a tall, stick-thin, chain-smoking individual – who was deemed to be very special indeed: Dennis Main Wilson. The name, at least, was well-known to Sullivan, as indeed it was, at the back of their minds, to millions of other comedy fans. Dennis Main Wilson was the name that had been heard, as producer, at the end of countless popular radio shows, including *Hancock's Half-Hour* and *The Goon Show*, and was the name that appeared at the conclusion of some of the BBC's most admired television sitcoms, including *The Rag Trade*, *Sykes and A . . .* and *Till Death Us Do Part*. He was one of the Corporation's most experienced, influential, outspoken and independent-minded producer/directors, having worked there since the early 1940s and battled long and hard to keep the meddling 'management' a safe distance away from himself and the talent. The running joke among some of his colleagues was that he was rarely to be seen without sporting two pairs of glasses – one on the bridge of his nose and the other pair, one containing beer and the other one whisky, in his hands – but nobody doubted his passion for programme-making.

Sullivan knew, immediately, that this was a man who, if he liked a new idea, would really fight for it to reach the screen. Somewhat intimidated by the double-barrelled name and what seemed from a distance to be a brash and brusque 'RAF officer' sort of manner, the would-be scriptwriter was anxious about making contact with such an eminent broadcasting figure, but, eventually, he plucked up the courage to sneak into the crowded BBC bar – where Main Wilson was known to go through the daily lunchtime ritual of sipping half a pint of bitter followed by a small glass of Bell's whisky – and make himself known. 'I said, "I thought I'd introduce myself, my name's John Sullivan, because we're going to be working together soon."'[10] Main Wilson, understandably, thought Sullivan would be working on one of his shows, but, upon discovering that this props man was actually proposing a script, was sufficiently impressed by the sheer gall of Sullivan's approach to offer some friendly advice and encouragement over a drink.

Main Wilson was a good choice as a potential patron. Born in Dulwich and grammar school-educated, he remained, at least by the traditional standards of the BBC, something of a maverick (acutely suspicious of authority since the war, when one of his jobs was writing satirical anti-Nazi propaganda for broadcast all over Europe, he empathised instinctively with the workers on the studio floor no matter how high he rose up the TV hierarchy), and he rather enjoyed the unpredictability that came with the more unconventional of creative spirits. This, after all, was the man who had won the trust and respect of the likes of Spike Milligan, Tony Hancock, Eric Sykes, Peter Sellers, Marty Feldman, John Fortune, Barry Humphries and Johnny Speight. He was no romantic – having been through a hard war, he was realistic to the verge of seeming cynical – but he seized on anything and anyone that struck him as genuine and lifted his spirit.

He had been the one, for example, who in the late 1940s had responded to an audition from a young scriptwriter/stand-up named Bob Monkhouse by eschewing the standard BBC marking system and simply sending on a memo that said: 'WOW!'[11] He had also been the one who, early in the 1960s, had spotted the potential in a modest production exercise by a trainee director called Dick Clement (who had co-written a comic story with his friend Ian La Frenais), and thanks to Main Wilson's enthusiasm and energetic support the project ended up growing into *The Likely Lads*. Writers always fascinated him and, when he found good enough reasons to have faith in them, he became their finest and fiercest ally.

Main Wilson's immediate advice to Sullivan was for him to sharpen his skills and heighten his profile by going off and attempting to write sketches for shows such as *The Two Ronnies*. Sullivan did as he was told, and, once he had some material (revolving around two Cockney blokes – Sid and George – chatting in a pub), he took advantage of the fact that he was currently working on the set of *Porridge* by slipping the scripts to Ronnie Barker. The following week, Barker called Sullivan over, asked him if he thought he would be able to come up with any more material, and then arranged for him to be put on a contract. The budding scriptwriter was suddenly in business.

The Sid and George sketches would become a familiar ingredient in the rich mix that made *The Two Ronnies* so entertaining. Featuring several themes and conceits that anticipated Sullivan's later work (malapropisms, such as, 'You don't like birds, you're illogical to feathers, ain't you?'; slyly sardonic put-downs, such as describing the point of human existence as 'something to do, I suppose'; and a succession of dubious deals, including the duck sold as a racing pigeon, the hamster passed off as a 'day-old Labrador pup' and a digital timepiece described as 'an Elizabeth I wristwatch'), the routines bubbled with comic promise. What was also already evident was Sullivan's delight in drawing together two characters, and drawing out two personalities, through dialogue:

SID: You back, George?
GEORGE: No, no, I'm still down there, Sid.
SID: Eh?
GEORGE: What you're staring at now is one of those uncanny encounters of the third division, see, probably due to the time warp on the A33 between Croydon and the coast.
SID: Eh?
GEORGE: 'Course I'm 'ere!

Sullivan was soon submitting material not only to *The Two Ronnies* but also to shows hosted by the likes of Dave Allen, Les Dawson and Barry Took. Like such fellow budding sitcom writers as David Renwick (*One Foot in the Grave*) and David Nobbs (*The Fall and Rise of Reginald Perrin*), Sullivan first learned to write for an ensemble of actors by contributing to these kinds of programmes. Obliged to supply precisely timed lines as well as sharply structured sketches, some of it bespoke for certain performers and some of it left hanging for anyone to pick up off-the-peg, he was learning his craft at a rapid rate.

It was not long after this first set of *ad hoc* commissions began that Dennis Main Wilson, impressed by Sullivan's progress, encouraged him to start working on his idea for a sitcom. Greatly excited, Sullivan promptly took two weeks' leave and went to his in-laws' home in Crystal Palace, where he locked himself away and laboured until he had a proper pilot episode fully scripted. Meeting once again in the BBC bar, Main Wilson speed-read it in twenty minutes and loved it, and, as he later recalled, resolved there and then to make the project happen:

> I said 'I'll buy it,' even though the scene had changed, and I wasn't in a position to buy officially. But under my old thing I would have been, so sod it, 'I'll buy it.' If [the BBC don't want it] I'll bloody sell it to ATV or something. And I bought it and luckily our Head of Comedy in those days was Jimmy Gilbert [. . .] and I bashed into his office and said 'Read that!', and anybody who works in light entertainment and is a boss, poor devil, the number of scripts that come in, even if they're filtered by script editors . . . But I said to Jim, 'Read that, not at the top, not at the bottom of the thing – now! We'll be in the bar.'[12]

Gilbert – well used to his old friend's passionate attitude, and already impressed by Sullivan's efforts for *The Two Ronnies* – read it, then sought out the two men in the bar and agreed that the *Citizen Smith* script merited inclusion in the next series of *Comedy Special* (the successor to *Comedy Playhouse*, the BBC's traditional showcase for testing the audience reaction to promising sitcom pilots – and the birthplace of, among several other memorable shows, *Steptoe and Son* and *Till Death Us Do Part*). 'I actually liked the script so much,' Gilbert would recall, 'that I immediately asked John for a back-up script, just to make sure that he would be able to maintain the quality, and that turned out to be equally good, so I then went straight ahead and commissioned a whole series before the pilot had even gone out.'[13]

The commissioning process – in stark contrast to the painstakingly slow and neurotically over-elaborate procedures favoured by today's major broadcasters – was remarkably simple, straightforward and quick. 'In those days,' Gilbert explained, 'if you were a head of a department at the BBC, and you wanted to make a programme and get some facilities, you just walked upstairs. I went up to see the Controller of BBC1 and told him I'd got this splendid script. So he got his planner in to see if there was space and get some money out of the budget. And that was it. The whole thing was fixed.'[14]

Sullivan – celebrating with an expensive round of drinks – could hardly believe what was happening. After years of sending in scripts and waiting in vain for something positive to happen, his latest idea was now being fast-tracked into production. A mere six weeks later, on 12 April 1977, the first episode was broadcast on BBC1.[15]

Directed by Ray Butt (a genial but industrious Londoner whose previous projects included *The Liver Birds, Last of the Summer Wine, Are You Being Served?, Mr Big* and *It Ain't Half Hot, Mum*) and starring the up-and-coming actor Robert Lindsay as the workshy radical 'Wolfie' Smith, and Lindsay's then-wife Cheryl Hall as his sweet-natured and far more conventional girlfriend Shirley, the pilot went well and a complete series was promptly commissioned. Also featuring Mike Grady as Wolfie's woozily religious flatmate Ken, Anthony Millan as their fearful fellow-suburban guerrilla Tucker, and Peter Vaughan and Hilda Braid as Shirley's parents (and with a theme song – 'The Glorious Day' – written by Sullivan), the show went on to prove itself a considerable success, building up a solid following over a run that would last for four series from 1977 to 1980.

As a sitcom, it stayed loose and light – the storylines tended to stick to a very small and predictable range of topics, usually involving bungled protests and brushes with the law, and the characters never really acquired any depth or drive – but, at its heart, was the engagingly Walter Mittyish figure of Citizen Smith himself, the sheep in wolf's clothing who fooled no one except himself:

WOLFIE:　We in the Tooting Popular Front are massing our forces ready for the big push!

SHIRLEY:　How many of you are there?

WOLFIE:　*Ha!* How *many?* How many fish in the sea? How many stars in the sky?

SHIRLEY:　How *many*, Wolfie?

WOLFIE:　Six.

Brightly written and nicely played, the character struck a contemporary chord, especially with younger viewers, and kept people interested and entertained even when the plots started to pall. Without inspiring any critic to hail it as a classic, the majority of those who previewed and reviewed it treated the show with a fair measure of warmth and affection, and came to see plenty of potential in John Sullivan as a sitcom writer. As he prepared to move on to his next project, therefore, the future seemed excitingly bright.

It was in 1980, however, that Sullivan suddenly found himself in trouble. After bringing his first sitcom to a satisfying close, his initial idea for a second one – *Bright Lights*, about a naive northern boy who comes to London in search of glamour and excitement – was scrapped at the planning stage and then he also lost the next one that he wrote before it had even reached the screen.

It was called *Over the Moon*, and was about a hapless football manager trying in vain to turn a lower-league football club into the next big thing. A pilot episode had been recorded on 30 November in a studio at Television Centre, and, although one or two who saw it had misgivings about its potential (Jimmy Gilbert, for example, felt that, compared to the first edition of *Citizen Smith*, 'it hadn't worked out so well'[16]), it was well enough received internally for the BBC to commission an initial series of six episodes. Sullivan was very optimistic about its prospects: the cast – which included Brian Wilde (best known at the time for playing the permanently befuddled prison officer Mr Barraclough in *Porridge*) as the manager and George Baker (a familiar face since becoming a British movie star in the 1950s) as his chairman – looked strong, the producer/director was Sullivan's friend and old *Citizen Smith* colleague Ray Butt, and the situation itself – dealing as it did with the old-style working-class milieu of pre-Premiership football – was something that Sullivan knew well, and loved sufficiently to make it seem plausible as well as funny. It therefore came as a shock when, just as he was in the middle of writing the fourth instalment, the call came from Ray Butt that Bill Cotton, the then-Controller of BBC1, had returned from a trip overseas and promptly cancelled the commission.

The explanation Butt was given was that, as the Corporation had previously committed itself to making a brand new sitcom about a boxer (*Seconds Out*, starring, ironically, Robert Lindsay), it was decided that one comedy with a sporting theme was quite enough for the time being, so *Over the Moon* was dropped like a sick parrot. It was disastrous news for John Sullivan, because he and his wife had just had a baby and taken out a mortgage on their first house in Sutton, Surrey. Only under contract at the BBC for one more year, the future, financially, suddenly looked ominously bleak.

While the scriptwriter and his erstwhile producer/director busied themselves with finding a solution to the problem, three actors were facing their own challenges as 1980 moved towards its end. David Jason was still searching for the role that would establish him once and for all as a *bona fide* star; Nicholas Lyndhurst was looking for the chance to advance his fledgling career; and Lennard Pearce, having been in the business for the best part of fifty years, was finally pondering the possibility of retirement.

David Jason, at the time, was by far the best known of the three performers, but in 1980, after being touted for years as a big star in the making, he was still regarded by many as nothing more than a top-class support act. Although his thick dark hair was sometimes disguised with a variety of coloured wigs, his diminutive stature (5feet 6inches tall), large and dark orbital eyes and wide thin-lipped grin were familiar to many viewers after seeing him in numerous supporting roles, but some still responded to his presence in the credits with the question, 'David *who?*'[17]

Born David John White on 2 February 1940 (sadly his twin brother, Jason, lived for only two weeks), he came from a similar working-class background to that of John Sullivan. His father, Arthur, was a fish porter at Billingsgate Fish Market. His Welsh mother, Olwen, was a charlady. The family home was a small terraced house in Lodge Lane in Finchley, north London.

He was always a gifted mimic, and found it easy to amuse his family and friends with impersonations of popular radio stars, but acting only became important to him after he took part, at the age of fourteen, in a school play about the English Civil Wars. Grudgingly standing in for an ailing classmate, he appeared as a cavalier and, much to his surprise, loved the experience and, after it was over, resolved to remain on the stage by joining a local amateur dramatic society.

He left school at fifteen, and tried to honour his parents' wishes by training for a trade, working first as a mechanic and then as an electrician. His real ambition, however, was to make acting his proper profession, and he spent his spare evenings treading the boards in amateur productions. He received his first notice in July 1955, when a local drama critic named W.H. Gelder spotted his potential and praised his performance in the Incognito Theatre Group's production of the St John Ervine play, *Robert's Wife*. Further reviews by Gelder appeared in the *Barnet and Finchley Press,* including one that applauded David's efforts for another local amateur dramatic group, The Manor Players: '[T]he extraordinarily precocious schoolboy by David White, looking like a young James Cagney, and playing, though only 16, with the ease of a born actor [was] possibly the high-light of the evening, which was bright enough in all conscience . . .' Gelder would also write that the young actor was 'one of the comparatively few amateurs whom I could conscientiously recommend for the professional theatre'. The critical plaudits delighted the amateur actor, who saved all of Gelder's reviews and made sure that they did not escape his parents' attention.[18]

By his early twenties, David was working during the day as an electrician alongside his old friend Bob Bevil for a company the two men had set up called B & W Installations, but, even though the business started to do quite well, he never stopped listening and looking out for a serious chance to perform. The opportunity finally arrived in March 1965, when his elder brother Arthur, who had himself started acting professionally, was offered a part in the popular BBC police drama series *Z Cars*; in order to accept, Arthur had to abandon a forthcoming engagement (to play the minor part of a coloured butler called Sanjamo) in a play – Noel Coward's *The South Sea Bubble* – at Bromley Rep in Kent, but, before dropping out, he recommended David to the director, Simon Oates.

The recommendation worked: after watching David in an amateur production, Oates judged him a 'stunningly talented' actor and signed him up.[19] Thrilled to be given such an opportunity, David promptly surrendered his share in B & W Installations and made his professional debut as an actor on 5 April 1965 at Bromley Rep. He followed this with a few more minor engagements before returning to the repertory company on a twelve-month contract. It was here that he served his theatrical apprenticeship, submitting himself to the discipline of Rep's rapid rotation of roles, tones and themes. Always a very private man ('The only person who knows me,' he would say, 'is me'[20]), as well as a very driven one, he submerged himself in his work, relishing the opportunity to concentrate on each distinctive characterisation.

After Rep, Jason acquired an agent – Ann Callender, the

wife of the BBC producer/director David Croft, who was based at The Richard Stone Partnership – and adopted the stage name of Jason (possibly in honour of his late brother, although he once claimed that it was prompted by his fondness for *Jason and the Argonauts*) after discovering that there was already a 'David White' on Equity's books. He then proceeded to work in a wide range of plays and summer seasons.

His first major break on television arrived in 1967, when he became a regular member of the new ITV children's comedy show *Do Not Adjust Your Set* alongside the future *Monty Python* stars Eric Idle, Michael Palin and Terry Jones and the versatile character actor Denise Coffey. Overseen by the producer Humphrey Barclay (who had been recruited specially from the BBC with the brief of creating a bold new brand of 'adult' comedy shows for youngsters), *Do Not Adjust Your Set* was, for the time, an intriguingly adventurous and imaginative sketch show that mixed silliness with surrealism to appeal beyond the normal audience for its modest tea-time slot. Among Jason's regular contributions was his role as Captain Fantastic, a comically British bowler-hatted and moustachioed super-hero drawn into a succession of darkly slapstick situations. His very physical Buster Keaton-style performances helped distinguish him from his more reserved co-stars, and won him not only a sizeable youthful following but also some encouragingly positive reviews in the newspapers.[21]

After the show ended in 1969, Jason went on to appear in a wide range of other productions, including another ITV tea-time comedy show in 1970 entitled *Two Ds and a Dog* (in which he was reunited with Denise Coffey, playing a couple of eccentrics called Dotty Charles and Dingle Bell who, with their dog Fido, travel around in search of adventures), a short stint in the daily ITV soap *Crossroads* (playing an increasingly unpredictable gardener), and a few one-off episodes of such shows as *Randall and Hopkirk (Deceased)* and *Doctor in the House*. He also joined the large team of contributors to the long-running BBC Radio 4 satirical news series *Week Ending*. Rather more significantly, he was given a regular role – or, more accurately, range of roles – in LWT's *Hark at Barker*.

Hark at Barker was a sketch show, running from 1969 to 1970, that first brought Jason into the orbit of Ronnie Barker. Like Jason, Barker had started out in Rep, acquiring his technique and exploring his range by accepting each new weekly challenge as the conveyor belt of productions rolled on. He represented to Jason just how far an actor like him could go in his profession: the rather portly Barker had never been leading man material, but his versatility, intelligence, discipline and wit had enabled him to become a very popular, in-demand and critically admired performer, who was now regarded as a star in his own right. The two men soon saw in each other a kindred spirit, became good friends, and worked extremely well together on the screen.

Encouraged by his association with Barker, Jason then went on to win his own first starring vehicle in the 1974 ITV slapstick-spy spoof *The Top Secret Life of Edgar Briggs*. Although it was actually a very patchy affair – sometimes inspired, sometimes falling flat – and it struggled to compete for viewers in the ratings, the programme brought him easily the most positive publicity of his career so far, with the *Daily Mirror* describing him excitedly as 'the talk of the comedy world' and quoting his director, Bryan Izzard, as predicting that he 'is going to be a great star'.[22] He followed this in 1976 with another starring vehicle for ITV entitled *Lucky Feller*, which cast him as a woman-shy man called Shorty Mepstead who was still stuck at home with his mother and his much more confident elder brother, but this programme, too, failed to capture the public's imagination and faded quietly away after a solitary series.

Here was the nagging problem for David Jason: he was, by this time, sufficiently well known to attract plenty of media attention for his new projects, along with quite a few predictions about his imminent ascension to 'overnight star' status, but the projects and promises continued to come and go without that final big breakthrough being made. Indeed, by the middle of the decade, the optimistic articles were already beginning to sound somewhat hollow. His most vocal champions in the press were starting to sound unsure, with *The Stage* newspaper capturing their growing sense of frustration, disappointment and impatience when it declared: 'Somewhere there is a writer whose ideas Mr Jason can execute to great effect, but they have not yet met.'[23] In a ruthless profession where timing is often thought to be everything, the actor was fast reaching the stage in his career when his image as one of the 'next big things' was in serious danger of seeming outdated.

The most significant thing that happened in 1976 was his recruitment, in a supporting rather than a starring role, in a new BBC2 sitcom that reunited him with Ronnie Barker: *Open All Hours*. Deeply respectful of his more experienced, and more famous, friend and fellow performer, Jason was happy to serve as his sidekick, playing the put-upon and quietly desperate little Granville to Barker's big, tight-fisted, lustful and stuttering shopkeeper Arkwright. The chemistry between the two performers seemed effortlessly engaging, and the show, gradually attracting more and more viewers, would run on well into the next decade. It added greatly to Jason's popularity, while seeming to suggest that, by this stage in his career, he had found his level as, to put it bluntly, a superior kind of support act.

Although he continued to be offered, and sometimes accepted, the odd starring role of his own, the moment never seemed right to finally realise his full potential. The most successful of these ventures was almost certainly *A Sharp Intake of Breath*, which lasted for four series over four years, starting from 1977, on ITV. Playing yet another likeably 'ordinary', somewhat whimsical, figure named Peter Barnes (and ably supported by a good cast that included Jacqueline Clarke, Alun Armstrong and Richard Wilson), the show performed very well in the ratings and he received another flurry of favourable reviews, without, once again, threatening to become one of the small screen's iconic comic figures.

By 1980, therefore, David Jason was in real danger of being pigeonholed, albeit reluctantly, as the nearly man of great British comic acting: the splendid character actor who, due to bad luck rather than lack of talent, had lost out when it came to landing the career-defining roles. He still wanted to break through, and he certainly still deserved to break through, but, to be harshly realistic, time seemed to be fast running out.

Nicholas Lyndhurst, in contrast, had many years ahead to fulfil his own great potential, but he, too, was looking to move on at the start of the new decade. Tall and skinny and aged just nineteen, he was eager for roles that allowed him to be something other, and more, than yet another stereotypical boy or son.

Born in 1961 in Hampshire, Lyndhurst had first stepped on to a stage at the age of six, when he played a donkey in his school's nativity play ('My only line was "Hee-Haw . . .").

Two years later, he started asking his mother if he could go to drama school, and, when he reached the age of ten, his mother relented and he went off to the Corona Stage Academy, in Hammersmith, west London. 'I was determined to go to this magical place where the teacher was an actor, though I had no concept of what I was aiming for,' he would later explain. 'I didn't believe I'd ever actually open my mouth and have a speaking part in anything. The idea of achieving fame and fortune didn't cross my mind.'[24]

Lyndhurst did start to appear in adverts, but this was primarily to pay for his tuition fees. His first 'proper' television work came in a couple of BBC Schools productions, followed by a number of peripheral non-speaking roles in a variety of mainstream programmes. His debut in a major production was as Peter in a 1974 BBC adaptation of *Heidi*, and he followed this a year later by playing Davy Keith in a BBC period drama mini-series called *Anne of Avonlea* (a sequel to *Anne of Green Gables*).

It was shortly after this, when Lyndhurst was deemed to have reached that difficult 'transitional' phase between juvenile and adult actor, that work started to dry up and his professional future looked uncertain. The only option was to wait and see what, if any, offers arrived, and, fortunately for him, a very exciting one materialised in 1978: the role of Ronnie Barker's young Cockney son in the post-prison sequel to *Porridge*, *Going Straight*. Building on the priceless prime-time exposure that this afforded, he then moved on to win the role of Wendy Craig's gauche teenaged son Adam in the funny if sometimes rather cloyingly bourgeois Carla Lane sitcom *Butterflies*.

By 1980, on the verge of his twenties, he had impressed plenty of critics with the breadth of his portrayals, which had stretched all the way from patted and powdered posh fops to gruff and grungy rough scruffs, but he was, in truth, still in danger of being stereotyped – as far as most of the programme makers were concerned – as the short–shelf–life 'youth' type. He had reached that point in his career where, even if an 'older' role was not yet available, he hoped that at least a better youthful role was open to him that would allow him to settle into the part and start to grow. The range of options, however, seemed slim. All that he could do was wait, and hope, for his best chance to arrive.

The veteran Lennard Pearce, meanwhile, had started 1980 with a nagging feeling of professional *ennui*. He had been through it all – the highs, the lows, the generosity, the pettiness, the pleasure and the pain, the drama and the dullness of the acting business – and he was finally getting tired of it all. He still loved his profession, he still relished the best roles, but, after several years of being obliged to do little more but go through the motions, he was, by 1980, beginning to feel like calling it quits.

Pearce was born in Paddington, London, in 1915. He was a rather dapper and diligent RADA-trained actor who had also experienced the more fluid and informal atmosphere of the wartime show business community as a member first of ENSA and then of the Combined Services Entertainment touring companies. He followed this in peacetime first with a couple of seasons at the Shakespeare Memorial Theatre in Sheffield, and then a fairly lengthy period based at the Empire Theatre in Peterborough as a member of Harry Hanson's Court Players (writing a few plays there himself).

A fairly familiar minor figure in West End plays from the early 1960s onwards, he appeared as the Hungarian phonetician

Zoltan Karpathy, as well as understudied the role of Alfred P. Doolittle (played by Stanley Holloway), in the original London production of *My Fair Lady*, before moving on to have spells at the National Theatre under Sir Laurence Olivier and the Royal Shakespeare Company under Trevor Nunn, as well as shorter and less glamorous stints in various repertory companies (where, amongst many other encounters, he met David Jason at Bromley Rep, appearing with him briefly during the mid-1960s in a production of Richard Brinsley Sheridan's *The Rivals*).

Mixing with the likes of such up-and-coming talents as Albert Finney, Derek Jacobi, Maggie Smith and Anthony Hopkins, he contributed – albeit most often in minor roles – to numerous theatrical successes during the best years of his stage career. Pearce never really established himself on television, however, but did appear in the odd minor role in such notable productions as the BBC's groundbreaking docu-drama *Cathy Come Home* (1966), as well as one-off episodes of *Crown Court, Dixon of Dock Green, Dr Finlay's Casebook, Play for Today, Coronation Street* and *Sykes*.

Always a heavy smoker, and – as a consequence – having struggled for many years with a weakened voice, he had also started to experience problems relating to balance and concentration while appearing mainly in stage plays during the 1970s, thus shaking his confidence in playing in front of an audience. Over-worked, increasingly worried about how he could make ends meet and now drinking rather heavily, he was at a very low ebb in his life. 'I hadn't had a break from acting for 35 years,' he would later explain. 'People were trying to evict me from my flat, and I drank a bottle of whisky every night. I looked gaunt – a skeleton, absolutely ghastly.'[25] In 1980, after being diagnosed with critical hypertension and put on seven different types of medication for the rest of his life, he turned teetotal and contemplated, at the age of sixty-five, retiring from the profession and leading a much more leisurely existence.

This, then, was where the relevant figures were at the start of the new decade: Sullivan and Butt reeling from the cancellation of their new project, and Jason, Lyndhurst and Pearce dissatisfied, to varying degrees, with the current state of their acting careers. None of them knew it, in the autumn of 1980, but, this time next year, each one of their professional lives would seem much more exciting – and the British sitcom would start seeming genuinely relevant once again.

CHAPTER TWO

He Who Dares

'Cos where it all comes from is a mystery . . .

Early in 1981, John Sullivan and Ray Butt sat in a London pub and wondered what they should do next. Their new sitcom had been aborted. Time was running out. Something had to be done. Quickly.

The pub in question was The Famous Three Kings, on the corner of North End Road and Talgarth Road – a place where Butt often liked to go for a quiet drink and a think. After the pair had sat there for a while and moaned about the decision to axe *Over the Moon*, they tried to distract each other by moving on to other, less troubling, matters, exchanging anecdotes about the many things that they had in common in their backgrounds. Both of them, for example, came from working-class families in London (Sullivan's in the south, Butt's in the east), and had grown up in a similar kind of milieu, so they talked about some of the places and people that had made a mark on their memory.

As they flitted from one colourful story to the next, something came up that struck the two of them as, just possibly, the seed of another sitcom. It centred on that traditional *laissez-faire* location, the local market.

As a teenager, Sullivan had worked for a brief time informally on a Saturday stall in the small but busy Hildreth Street

Market in Balham, and had been fascinated by all of the 'characters' there who competed for the customers' cash. It had seemed like a modern-day version of a street scene from Dickens: a busy, colourful, richly diverse array of individuals, each one with his or her own personal style and strategy. Some were loudmouthed bullies, others were artful charmers and a few were engaging or hapless amateurs, but all of them contributed to the powerful theatricality of the social event.

Butt knew exactly what Sullivan was discussing, because he had similar memories: his father, for example, had returned from serving in the Second World War, pooled what money he had with that of a friend to buy an old NAAFI wagon and then started a small business selling ice-creams on Roman Road Market in Bow. Butt himself had spent some time there as a youth working alongside a very memorable street market trader: none other than the future comic icon Tommy Cooper.[1]

As they compared and contrasted experiences, they found one figure in particular loomed large in both of their memories. 'We discovered that our favourite character was the fly-pitcher,' Sullivan later explained. 'He's always funny, always a lad, and he was only there for half an hour, because he had to get away quickly before the market inspector came. You can have a good laugh with them, then they're gone. You barely knew their names but they seemed like friends.' The air of casual mystery that surrounded them had always struck Sullivan as particularly intriguing: 'You never seemed to see them anywhere: where do they come from, where do they go?'[2]

The fly-pitcher seemed like the most audacious natural performer: either working with one or two Jimmy James-style sidekicks, or, more bravely, on his own, this figure went out into the street each morning ready to take on the world, no matter how much ammunition, or brummagem merchandise, was currently at his disposal. Living on his wits, the *al fresco* entertainer treated the market place as his stage, the standing crowd as his audience, and the act of selling as an art. Words washed over those who watched and listened like great tidal waves, drowning out any critical thoughts before they could bob up and catch their first breath. Like the British equivalent of America's old lapel-grabbing huckster, the fly-pitcher simply would not let you go until you had bought what he sold.

They grew into their game. Some came to rely on a 'shill' (a collaborator who poses as a customer in order to dupe innocent bystanders into participating) and others remained honourably solo, but all had to learn how people reacted to different phrases, gestures, gags and gimmicks. If he did well, he would return the following day, and maybe even stay on for a fairly regular run, but if he did badly he would slip away to find another unofficial venue. The overlap with show business was obvious; the fly-pitcher was the open-air echo of the doughty old Variety star. Max Miller sold gags; his modern day equivalents sold cheap pairs of tights, portable CD players, pop-up toasters and china plates.

The thought dawned on both Sullivan and Butt more or less immediately: this character could work brilliantly as the catalyst for another sitcom. The context of the black market seemed to fit the early Thatcher era in Britain rather smartly, with countless stories already being circulated in the media about dodgy would-be entrepreneurs attempting to exploit the confusion that came with deregulation to make fast and fluid fortunes, and the fly-pitcher in particular suddenly appeared emblematic of the new breed of working-class free riders. Butt, Sullivan later recalled, was quick to advise his friend to test this project's potential: 'Ray said: "Why don't you have a crack at that?"'[3]

Sullivan went home from the pub that afternoon with a renewed sense of enthusiasm. The ideas were suddenly coming together, quickly, and he knew what he wanted to do with them. He wanted to write the kind of vivid and rich sitcom that really engaged with contemporary life instead of evading it. He was eager to write something that cut through the clichés about ordinary working-class life – especially the life in his native London – and write about the community from the inside. He wanted to explore, for example, the ambiguity of the black market ('When I was a kid the black market fed and clothed us a lot better than the Common Market does now') and depict a more balanced view of the contemporary cultural mix ('In the pubs where I drink, there are people of all races and they're not at each other's throats. If there's a fight, it's between two drunks, not between racial antagonists').[4] Sullivan's London was the pubs, clubs and tower blocks – working-class, multi-racial and vibrant. He realised that he could write about such an environment with real authority, capturing the key details with a high degree of realism and sensitivity as well as plenty of playfulness and humour.

As far as the situation of the sitcom was concerned, he elected to set it in Peckham, because it was an area of London that he knew well, and it was also, in those days, one of those multi-racial, high-crime areas of the city that seemed redolent of the current confused social mood. Among some of the recent reports in the newspapers, there had been one about a high-profile clash between the National Front and the Anti-Nazi League, monitored by 3,000 police, outside one of the area's many derelict houses,[5] as well as countless other stories and opinion pieces relating to instances of urban decay, vandalism, arson attacks, robberies and muggings. More positively, the district had also become known for its role as a centre of underground dance, rock and reggae music (championed by a group of squatters, based ironically enough at a former DHSS building in Collyer Place, who dubbed themselves 'The Dole House Crew'), thus acting as a catalyst for the many diverse elements of urban and travelling culture then under threat from restrictive laws.

More specifically, John Sullivan wanted to focus on one of Peckham's cold and drab-looking brutalist tower blocks that seemed to loom high in the skies as sad and lonely relics of an outdated architectural vision of the future. Most of them erected in the early 1950s, they had elevated countless working-class people physically while the social world below kept them stuck in the basement. By the start of the 1980s, many of these so-called 'streets in the sky' were under attack not only for their ugliness but also their insalubrity (Sir John Betjeman, for example, branded them 'inhuman things'[6]), and their image as incubators of alienation and social unrest had become notorious.

'In those days,' Sullivan later explained, 'I had a lot of mates who lived in tower blocks. The lifts never worked and you always had to walk up to the seventeenth floor to get them to go to football. One of the things I wanted to say in it was: The lifts don't work in council blocks. Will somebody do something?'[7] The man who had been so engrossed by the comedy and drama of Dickens now saw the chance to emulate that social and literary spirit within a sitcom that tapped straight into the *zeitgeist*. While the likes of *Terry and June* fussed about inside their strangely timeless and placeless suburban abode, this show would find humour in the grit and the graft of the here and now.

As far as the comedy of the sitcom was concerned, it had to seem organic. Sullivan wanted the laughs to come more from the quality of the characters than from the quantity of the one-liners. All of the great sitcoms that he admired had proceeded in this subtle, truthful manner: Galton and Simpson's *Hancock's Half-Hour* and *Steptoe and Son*, for example, had worked hard to draw humour from within the individuals and their relationships rather than merely from a few funny things they were given to say, and even Johnny Speight's more overtly topical and dialogue-driven *Till Death Us Do Part* still tried to lock the laughter into the logic of a particular life. Unlike lazily traced stereotypes or clumsily constructed caricatures, these keenly observed comic creations seemed real enough to belong to the complex community within which all of the audience existed. It was this thoughtful precision and attention to detail that had helped make the likes of Anthony Hancock, Albert and Harold Steptoe, and Alf Garnett seem so strongly iconic for the culture and society of their time. It was this achievement that John Sullivan was now so eager to emulate.

He was getting particularly excited about the potential of the central character of the fly-pitcher. Dubbing him Derek 'Del Boy' Trotter ('I'd worked with a guy called Trotter, while Del was one of those names I loved, like Del Shannon'[8]), he proceeded to draw on his memories to add some flesh to the basic fiction.

One of the specific inspirations for Del was a man Sullivan had known called Chicky Stocker. He was a hard and often aggressive working-class Londoner, but always took great care over his appearance and was fiercely loyal to other members of his family. It was this 'tough and tender' combination that served as the template for Derek Trotter. Sullivan also drew on a couple of other characters he had observed in the car trade, who used to flash their gold signet rings, wave wads of borrowed money around and buy other people drinks that they often could not really afford.

A more general idea that the writer dreamed up for Del was to make him a kind of verbal jackdaw, complementing his readiness to collect a wildly disparate range of commodities with a penchant for accumulating a similarly bizarre bricolage of exotic-sounding phrases. As Sullivan later explained:

By then we were part of the European Community and I noticed all the products you bought, whether they were British or foreign goods, had ingredients and other bits of information written in different languages. I regarded Del as an entrepreneur, also someone who thought of himself as worldly wise, yet he was living within his own personal society with people who weren't. I thought he'd most probably read, for example, a foreign statement on the back of a pair of tights and used it to try and impress people, not realising what it actually meant, and the fact that he was impressing no one.[9]

Del already seemed real to Sullivan, but the writer wanted to find a way to constrain the figure in order to keep him from straying beyond the boundaries of this particular sitcom. At a time when the Government's Employment Secretary was urging people like Del to 'get on their bike' in search of better prospects, Sullivan had to ensure that this particular character would stay put in Peckham.[10] He wanted to root the free rider within some kind of family unit.

The decision was taken, therefore, to 'trap' him, emotionally, inside his situation. Just as the young and socially aspirational Harold Steptoe, for example, had been stuck with his old-fashioned working-class father, Albert, so Del needed to be fastened tightly to his own flesh and blood. After toying with the idea of linking him to a cousin (which, on reflection, did not seem intimate enough), he was given a dependent younger brother, Rodney, and an otherwise isolated and semi-helpless grandfather.

Rodney was inspired mainly, once again, by Sullivan's own memories of real-life figures:

I knew a couple of guys. One is a fellow who works for me now, a mate of mine from my old street; he's got a brother who's about twelve years older than he is, and the brother has naturally guided him and led him and looked after him. And I knew another set of brothers, the same situation. And my sister is fourteen years older than I am, so as a kid she was never like a normal sister, she was kind of an auntie. It took me until I was twenty to really take her as a sister. I thought, I can do it in a way that he's got this kid brother: the mother dies, and he brought him up. People will look on him as a hero because he didn't let the kid go into care or an orphanage, he brought him up. Even though he's a bit of a toe-rag, Del, and he'll sell you an iffy thing, he brought that kid up, so that's a great sound basis for a sympathetic man.[11]

Sullivan also remembered a boy in his class at school who later 'went round acting like he was Einstein' because he had just passed two GCEs. This undying pride in a couple of humble O levels thus became the foundation of Rodney's own chronically friable *amour-propre*.

In order to tie this odd couple more closely together emotionally, Sullivan came up with the more detailed 'back story' that their father had deserted them a long time ago and their mother had died when Rodney was aged just three, leaving Del to act partly as older brother and partly as a surrogate parent. Sullivan then added an older, semi-detached observer to the mix: Grandad. The older character provided a view of life that stretched from the end of the First World War, rooting the younger Trotters and taking the edge off the vicissitudes of their lives with his stoical 'seen-it-all' armchair view.

The next step, as he developed the potential sitcom, was to invest this trio with their own distinctively, and believably, dynamic relationship. He not only had to draw them together; he also, crucially, had to find a reason to keep them together.

Sullivan proceeded, therefore, by making sure that each figure kept bouncing off the others: Del had been forced to grow up quickly – probably too fast – and his responsible side was tempered with boyish enthusiasms and ambitions; Rodney was young but socially aware, matching himself against his older brother and finding his own way within Del's waning parental authority. One had to feel obliged to take notice of the other. Grandad, meanwhile, was there as the one who would keep the other two feeling young while providing them with a sense – albeit unreliable – of historical perspective. Combined, the three ages gave the situation a sense of balance.

Preparing to record his initial impressions on paper, however, the writer struggled for a while to conjure up his pilot script. 'I don't look forward to that first day when you sit down,' he

would explain. "'We're off!' That's the worst day of the lot.'
He thus had to find unconventional ways to make the project
progress: 'That idea of just "Page 1" is a killer, and I advise
everyone I ever talk to who wants to write, if you start on
Page 1 and it's not working, well, go to Page 30. Start anywhere.
Just start, start getting a flavour, start getting a taste of the thing
for yourself.'[12]

Easing himself slowly into this fresh comic world, therefore,
he accumulated the corroborative details: various biographical
notes were composed about the late mother and the absent
father; Del Boy's formal full name was recorded as 'Derek
Edward Trotter', and Rodney's was 'Rodney Charlton Trotter'
(the middle name coming from his mother's love of Charlton
Athletic FC); Grandad was provided with an eventful past with
plenty of potential for rambling anecdotes; the humble Peckham
tower block was awarded the topically worthy name of 'Nelson
Mandela House', given twenty-six levels, and the Trotters were
installed in a tiny flat on the twelfth floor; their living room
was decorated with cheap and cheerful wallpaper, an assortment
of tacky bric-à-brac and boxes of dodgy merchandise; the title
coined for their unofficial and unregistered company was
'Trotters Independent Traders'; and everyone was given a vocabulary rich in contemporary Cockney slang. There were also
three basic places planned for where these characters would
most often move about and interact: the flat, the pub and the
market.

Sullivan also felt certain that he wanted Del Boy, in particular, to embody the strangely ebullient mood that some
members of Britain's *lumpenproletariat*, in spite of the many
widespread social and economic problems, were now exhibiting.
'In London, at least,' he would later explain, 'there was this

incredible tidal wave of confidence for the future, and I wanted to write about it, because no one at the BBC or on TV was writing about it then.'[13] This defiantly upbeat spirit, in short, would supply the sitcom with its heartbeat: no matter how bleak or shambolic the circumstances might be, Del would always remain convinced that, 'This time next year, we'll be millionaires.'

With some of the background now settled, Sullivan's attention moved on to the foreground. Action had to happen. The important thing was that it had to happen primarily due to the nature of the characters rather than purely through the power of the plot; viewers had to keep coming back mainly because of the comic potential they could see in the key personalities. Del had to be pushing and pulling, Rodney had to be pausing and pondering, and Grandad, sitting lazily in the middle, had to be equally unconcerned and unconvinced by either side's position. Any particular storyline that followed would thus proceed from strong personalities and plausible problems rather than anything laboured and contrived.

The more that Sullivan contemplated the kind of schemes and scams that this trio might pursue, the more promising the project seemed. As he began to write the first few scenes and exchanges of dialogue, he already felt convinced that he could conjure up something that would strike an audience as not only funny but also engagingly real.

A couple of weeks after that initial conversation in the pub, therefore, it was an optimistic John Sullivan who turned up at Ray Butt's office at Television Centre with a completed draft script for the new sitcom whose working title had been *Readies* ('People like Del never dealt in cheques or credit cards; everything had to be ready cash, so the title seemed to be appropriate'[14]) but had now been given the more unusual and hence eye-catching name of *Only Fools and Horses* (a phrase that Sullivan felt captured Del Boy's outlook on life very neatly). Butt read it, liked it and sent it on to the BBC's then-Head of Comedy, John Howard Davies.

Davies (a tough, imaginative and very experienced programme-maker who had produced and/or directed such hugely successful comedy shows as *Monty Python's Flying Circus, The Goodies*, *Steptoe and Son*, *The Good Life* and, most notably, *Fawlty Towers* before rising up the ranks as an executive) read it, quite liked it, but sent back a memo saying that he doubted that the script would work as an opening episode. In spite of his misgivings, however, Davies saw enough potential in the basic idea to go ahead and commission enough scripts for a full series, although there was still no firm guarantee at this stage that the project would end up on the screen.

Davies's decision might have had something to do with the fact that, as Sullivan was still under contract, it made sense to at least keep him working for his wages. More positively, however, Davies was also shrewd enough to note that there were some encouraging signs that, all of a sudden, Sullivan had arrived with the right idea at the right time.

In terms of popular music, at least, London's working-class themes and scenes had not received so much telling attention since the era of The Kinks in the late 1960s. Upminster's Ian Dury and the Blockheads, the Deptford-based band Squeeze and Camden Town's Madness had all come to prominence at the end of the 1970s with a succession of clever, playful and colourful songs about local characters and their culture (including Dury's Essex-born 'Billericay Dickie', who 'ain't an effing thicky'; self-styled Jack the Lad 'Clever Trevor', who protests that 'things have got read into what I never said till me mouth becomes me head which ain't not all that clever'; and – in 'This is What We Find' – DIY expert Harold Hill, who 'Came home to find another gentleman's kippers in the grill/So he sanded off his winkle with his Black & Decker drill'[15]). The self-styled 'rockney' music of Chas & Dave was another recent phenomenon, with such hits as 'Gertcha' and 'Rabbit' bringing other old Cockney phrases back into fashion. After years of American-accented preoccupations and pronunciations, therefore, a growing number of British songwriters and performers were looking to London for inspiration.

More pointedly, as far as any proposed television project was concerned, there was also a new show on ITV that featured a working-class London milieu and was beginning to build a large and loyal audience: a comedy–drama written by Leon Griffiths called *Minder*. First broadcast in the autumn of 1979, *Minder* followed the fortunes of Arthur Daley, a dapper but devious 'importer–exporter', and Terry McCann, his young and dimmer-witted bodyguard and sidekick, as they pursued a variety of get-rich-quick schemes in a colourful black-market environment. Its growing popularity augured well for a sitcom that promised to tap into the same kind of contemporary context.

Within a matter of a few more weeks, Sullivan had written the rest of the episodes and completed the series, and Butt took them to the BBC. John Howard Davies and other senior executives at the Corporation – most importantly the Head of Light Entertainment Jimmy Gilbert – were broadly satisfied with what they read, and they gave the green light for the show to go into production.

Gilbert, however, although he found the scripts 'really very funny indeed',[16] still had one specific reservation he wanted resolved: he did not like the title of the show. It sounded, he said, far too odd and too obscure. 'John actually gave me the impression that, originally, it had mainly been Ray Butt's idea,' Gilbert would later recall. 'I suspected that John would still have preferred *Readies*, but he was now standing up strongly for the new name. I just told him that I wondered if *Only Fools and Horses*, as a title, would really mean that much to the viewers.'[17]

Sullivan had actually used the phrase 'Only Fools and Horses' once before, as the title of an episode of *Citizen Smith* (the third episode of the third series, broadcast on 27 September 1979), and was now adamant that it was ideal for his new sitcom. He liked the traditional expression 'only fools and horses work', and the delicate irony of Del spending all hours of the day engaged in the tough and tricky business of not working.

Once again, the genial but extremely diligent Jimmy Gilbert reacted with scepticism. 'What does it *mean*?' he asked Sullivan. 'Oh, you know,' the writer replied, 'it's a London saying.'[18] In fact, after the doubtful Gilbert (who had heard of a similar saying – 'Only birds and idiots fly' – during his days in the RAF) had asked around, it was discovered that the origins of the phrase were contentious: some claimed that it dated back to the late nineteenth century in Australia, where a notoriously unscrupulous Sydney-based racehorse owner called Jim 'The Grafter' Kingsley was said to have coined the term, while others argued that it had originated during the same era in American vaudeville and then crossed over the Atlantic via visiting music-hall performers. The phrase had actually first started popping up in British newspapers a little earlier in the Victorian era

(*The Morning Post*, for example, reported in 1857 on a court case in York in which several men, on trial for a local burglary, had been seen buying a great deal of beer in a pub with gold sovereigns, boasting: 'only fools and horses work'[19]), and by the middle of the twentieth century it was being cited as a relatively familiar saying.[20]

None of this did much to reassure the Head of Light Entertainment. The key point, as far as Gilbert was concerned, was that it would probably puzzle quite a few people in Wick.

This, according to John Sullivan, was the Edinburgh-born Gilbert's litmus test for anything that struck him as in danger of appearing obscure: as some of his family hailed from in and around the northern Scottish town of Wick, and he associated the place with good, wholesome, commonplace British tastes, he supposedly reacted instinctively to anything out of the ordinary by exclaiming, 'But will they understand it in Wick?'[21] Gilbert objected to *Only Fools and Horses*, therefore, because he doubted that the title would stand up to scrutiny from the good citizens of Wick. Gilbert himself would later clarify his position *apropos* 'the myth of Wick':

I used to have in my office a photograph which I'd taken as a joke. Because we used to go up to Caithness to a farm near Wick, where my wife comes from, and there was a broken-down crofthouse there, which had tinkers in it. And it really did look an absolute wreck. But out through the roof was the biggest television aerial you've ever seen! So I took a photograph of it, put it on display in my office, and, if there was ever something proposed which I knew was not going to be universally approved of or understood, I used to show them this photograph and say: 'He's paying his licence fee too!' So that's how the 'Will they understand it in Wick' stories came about. It was just a light-hearted way of getting people to think a little bit harder about their audience.[22]

Sullivan was sufficiently rattled by this reaction to propose as an alternative title *Dip Your Wick*, which he knew, as Jimmy Gilbert was a Baptist with a pronounced aversion to smut, would go down as badly as possible. 'I almost got the sack on that one,' Sullivan later recalled.[23] Among the other, serious suggestions that the team went on to consider, the most popular title was probably *Big Brother*, but that ended up being rejected because of the possible association with George Orwell's *1984*. Time was now pressing heavily, and Sullivan was due to meet Jimmy Gilbert and John Howard Davies at the start of the following week to agree on a definitive title, so he spent the weekend trying hard to come up with something that sounded right to him as well as right for them.

He typed and Tipp-Exed but still ended up drawing a blank. Some invaluable advice arrived shortly before the meeting from Gareth Gwenlan, another experienced executive producer in the BBC's Comedy department, who had heard of the *Only Fools* idea and was eager to offer, discreetly, his support. 'I told him to say he wanted to use [*Only Fools and Horses* as the title],' Gwenlan would recall, 'and they would need to think of something else if they didn't like it.'[24]

It worked. Sullivan sat down, shrugged his shoulders, said his mind was a blank and passed the buck across to Gilbert and Davies. The two executives exchanged glances, somewhat anxiously, and realised that neither had anything constructive to say, so they then said to Sullivan: 'OK, you can have it.' After several weeks of haggling, therefore, the team went back to the future: the show was going to be called *Only Fools and Horses* after all.

The last obstacle had been overcome. Everyone was now committed to pushing the project on.

The sense of relief, mixed with excitement, was immense. After suffering the crushing disappointment of seeing *Over the Moon* cancelled at such a late stage in the planning process, John Sullivan and Ray Butt could now celebrate the fact that a new sitcom was about to be created. The next stage, however, would be crucial: they would have to ensure that it was properly cast.

CHAPTER THREE

If You Want The Best 'Uns . . .

Très bien ensemble.

The most promising of sitcoms can be compromised at the casting stage. The wrong actor in the right role (or the right one in the wrong role) will ruin its prospects of realising long-running success.

What makes the casting process so exceptionally hazardous is the knowledge that some of the best sitcoms in British television history, overseen by some of the shrewdest producers, only stumbled on the ideal actors after the supposed first (and sometimes second and even third) choices had dropped out of contention. In the case of *Dad's Army*, for example, Arthur Lowe only came to be offered the chance to portray Captain Mainwaring after first Thorley Walters and then Jon Pertwee had opted not to take on the part, while Warren Mitchell only won the role of Alf Garnett after Peter Sellers, Leo McKern and Lionel Jeffries had passed on the part.[1] Good judgement is essential, but history teaches those who cast such shows that one also needs rather more than one's fair share of good luck.

Ray Butt, in this sense, was facing a formidable challenge – and he knew it. As the man now appointed to produce *Only Fools and Horses*, he was still, by the very high standards of the BBC, a relatively inexperienced figure, so the pressure was on for him to gauge not only quickly but also correctly which of the many risks would be worth running. He was, nonetheless, very confident about his ability to prove himself as a senior programme-maker. Having worked under the likes of such masterful producers as David Croft (for *Are You Being Served?*) and Dennis Main Wilson (for *Citizen Smith*), he believed that he had received an excellent education and now, in the late spring of 1981, felt ready and eager to shape a sitcom all on his own.

Butt, however, was not the only person who expected to contribute to the casting process. Apart from the writer, John Sullivan (who had been consulted about such matters by Main Wilson during the planning for *Citizen Smith*, and now expected to be so again), some of Butt's bosses were also determined to have their say.

It was fairly conventional for certain executives at the BBC to get themselves involved in matters of casting – whether or not their input was expressly requested. This was not merely because of anxiety about how the process was evolving, but also, more pertinently, because many of the key figures high up at the BBC in those days were people who had been programme-makers themselves, knew a wide range of tried-and-tested performers, and could make good and swift use of a long list of top-rated contacts.

When *Dad's Army* was being cast back in the late 1960s, for example, the then-Head of Comedy was Michael Mills, a hugely experienced former impresario and programme-maker who could not resist assuming a hands-on role in the selection of actors, nominating John Le Mesurier for the role of Sergeant Wilson ('He *suffers* so well!'[2]) and insisting on John Laurie to play Private Frazer. He also pushed through the idea of putting

Frankie Howerd into *Up Pompeii!*, and put himself in charge of making *Some Mothers Do 'Ave 'Em*.[3] Mills was simply still too much of a creator and organiser to retreat inside his office and let too many things happen in his absence. The situation had not really changed by the start of the 1980s, when John Howard Davies was the man in charge.

Davies, like Mills, knew all about planning, casting and filming popular comedy shows. The son of the scriptwriter Jack Davies and a former child actor himself (making his debut in 1948 as the eponymous young hero of David Lean's adaptation of *Oliver Twist*), and described by John Cleese as 'a very, very good judge of comedy',[4] he was an authoritative figure who already had an impressive track record for picking the right performers for the right roles. While planning *Fawlty Towers*, for example, he had taken primary responsibility for choosing most of the members of cast (selecting, among others, Prunella Scales as Sybil Fawlty, Andrew Sachs as Manuel and Ballard Berkeley as Major Gowen), and had also brought together the talents that worked so well as a team in *The Good Life*.

Davies, as John Sullivan would later recall, thus wasted no time in making his own views known on how the casting of *Only Fools and Horses* should go: Nicholas Lyndhurst was the actor who was going to play Rodney. Others – including Sullivan – were initially concerned that the middle-class boy from *Butterflies* would struggle to portray a convincing Cockney, but these anxieties would be allayed just as soon as he auditioned.

Lyndhurst was at home, late one Thursday afternoon, when the package of scripts from the BBC landed on his doormat. He was due to go out for a drink with friends, so he put the material to one side, planning to read them the following day. When he returned at 11 p.m., however, feeling somewhat the worse for wear, he glanced again at the covering note and suddenly noticed a line that said: 'Could you come and see us tomorrow afternoon?' Lyndhurst sobered up rapidly from the shock and started speed-reading the first script. It did not take long for him to slow down, relax, start laughing at the dialogue and feel the need to read the second script, and then the third, and then all of the rest. It was about two o'clock in the morning when he finally finished, and he was already in love with the idea of the series.

Reflecting on what he had just read, he thought ahead as to how he might bring the character of the lanky and lugubrious Rodney to life, and some ideas came to him rapidly as he prepared for the imminent meeting. 'I'm six foot plus, and quite awkward and gawky, so I accentuated that for the character,' he later explained.[5] He also drew inspiration from the memory of observing, some years before, the younger brother of one of his friends: 'This young boy was always trying to be older than his years, and so he was always trying to be desperately cool. And he never knew what to do with his hands: he would never stop moving, and the more that he tried to look relaxed the more awkward and gawky he became. And so I borrowed a bit of that.'[6]

He went to the BBC's Television Centre later that morning and read for what he thought was an audition. The reality, however, was that he already had the part. He was going to play Rodney.

The choice of the actor to play Grandad Trotter, however, came about more through luck than judgement, because no one on the production team had an immediate idea as to who was really suitable. Ray Butt knew who he did *not* want for the part: Wilfrid Brambell, because, although he was still an extremely able actor who certainly fitted the bill (and, ironically, Brambell had appeared in the episode of *Citizen Smith* entitled 'Only Fools and Horses'), his association with *Steptoe and Son* remained far too strong to make him a serious contender.

Butt called a theatrical agent he trusted, Carole James, explained the role and invited her to suggest some lesser-known names. She replied that, although there was no one on her own books, she did know of an actor called Lennard Pearce whom she felt was well worth considering. Butt duly booked Pearce, along with several other candidates, for an audition. John Sullivan recalled: 'Lennard came in and he read a bit for us and we just heard that lovely old growly voice of his and when he'd gone I said to Ray, "That's him."'[7]

Pearce, so close to ending his professional career, could not believe his luck. After enduring all of his health and financial problems, he would say, it felt as though he had suddenly been given 'a new lease of life'.[8]

The biggest challenge was casting the part of Del Boy: because he was the character who was going to have to drive the sitcom on, and everyone involved understood how crucial it was to get this decision absolutely right. Ray Butt's first choice was a thirty-one-year-old Scottish-born actor named Enn Reitel. An increasingly in-demand and exceptionally versatile voiceover artist as well as a reasonably artful performer (although not yet established on the small screen, he would go on later in the decade to supply several impressions for ITV's satirical show *Spitting Image*, as well as star in the Clement and La Frenais sitcom *Mog*), he seemed capable of bringing this new character to life. Jimmy Gilbert had wanted the Trotters to really look like 'proper' brothers, and Reitel had a physical similarity to Lyndhurst that therefore made him seem an ideal choice. Butt was forced into a rethink, however, when he discovered via Reitel's agent that the actor was otherwise engaged (filming another comedy series for Yorkshire TV entitled *Misfits*).

An alternative suggestion then came from John Howard Davies. He advised Butt to go and see Jim Broadbent, another up-and-coming actor (of a similar age and height to Reitel) who, rather promisingly, was appearing at the time as a brash car salesman in a Mike Leigh play called *Goosepimples* at the Hampstead Theatre in north London. Butt went, was very impressed, then went backstage and invited Broadbent to play the part of Del. 'He turned it down,' Butt recalled, 'because the play was transferring to the West End. He said he loved the script I'd shown him but didn't think he could give enough concentration and energy to both things at the same time.'[9]

Two other actors were then considered – Robin Nedwell (an already very well-established actor best known for his starring role in the 1970s ITV sitcom *Doctor in the House*) and Billy Murray (an intimidating-looking young Londoner who later found fame as DS Beech in *The Bill* and the crooked businessman Johnny Allen in *EastEnders*) – but neither, after further reflection, was judged to be quite right for the part. The sound of the clock ticking was thus getting louder and louder, and Ray Butt was beginning to panic.

It was soon after this moment of crisis, however, that a degree of good fortune intervened. Butt was sitting in his apartment off the North End Road in West Kensington when, as he watched television one evening, he came across a repeat of an episode of the Ronnie Barker sitcom *Open All Hours*, and was hugely impressed by the performance of Barker's co-star, David Jason. Butt had known Jason for years, and had worked with him before on a 1974 *Comedy Playhouse* pilot episode of a proposed sitcom, called *It's Only Me – Whoever I Am* (a sort of forerunner of the Ronnie Corbett vehicle *Sorry*), about a young man struggling to break away from the control of his powerful mother. Produced by Sydney Lotterby, with Butt assisting him as Production Manager, the pilot ended up on the shelf ('It just didn't work,' said Jason), but it had been an enjoyable programme to make, with Lotterby and Butt joining Jason for regular games of pool each evening at the hotel where they all were staying. The fondness that Butt still felt for the forty-one-year-old actor (who in the past had delighted in mimicking his strong Cockney accent) helped him focus on those scenes in which Jason's gifts as a character actor were allowed to shine, and, as he continued to watch, the connection clicked into place.

The following morning, Butt went into his office at Television Centre and called John Sullivan to tell him about his enthusiasm for Jason. The response from the writer was not what the producer–director had expected. The problem, Sullivan explained, was that Jason's recent work had made him seem so ill-suited to playing the role of the tough but secretly tender-hearted fly-pitcher: 'I'd only seen him in *A Sharp Intake of Breath*, and that was all very slapstick, falling over on the floor, opening the washing machine and all the water coming out. I though that was his style and I was saying that Del had to be sharp, very sharp, tough, an aggressive little guy who has lived in the streets and survived.'[10] There was no great aversion to Jason as an actor, as far as the scriptwriter was concerned;

he was just sceptical as to how closely such a figure could come to matching his mental image of the indomitably doughty Del.

Some sources would later allege that, while Sullivan pondered this proposal, the BBC's Head of Light Entertainment, Jimmy Gilbert, expressed his concern that the decision to give David Jason a sitcom of his own might ruffle the feathers and upset the future plans of his *Open All Hours* colleague Ronnie Barker, who was such a big BBC star at the time that no executive wanted to risk upsetting him in any way.[11] This is incorrect. Barker himself, in fact, not only liked and admired Jason both as an actor and a friend but also saw his colleague as his protégé, and was certainly not the kind of performer who resented seeing younger talents rise up the ladder. Gilbert would also later confirm that he had never expressed any such concerns:

I was pleased when David's name was mentioned. There had been various actors, ever since I became Head of Comedy in 1973, whom I'd wanted to find things for at the BBC. The top five were: Ronnie Barker, Richard Briers, Ronnie Corbett, Leonard Rossiter and David Jason. So I'd been delighted when David Jason joined Ronnie Barker in *Open All Hours*. Then, some time later, his agent at the time, Richard Stone, who was an old friend of mine, told me: 'David would love to do some more *Open All Hours* with Ronnie – he loves it, and loves working with Ronnie – but he would also want us to look for something else, for him, as well.' And I was happy to take that on board. So when David was suggested for *Only Fools and Horses* there was absolutely no resistance from me – quite the opposite in fact – and certainly no anxiety about upsetting Ronnie

Barker, because, after all, Ronnie had been doing the same thing himself, with *Porridge* and other shows, and I knew that he and David were such great friends.[10]

One query that Gilbert did express initially was much easier for the team to dismiss. He had argued that David Jason did not look anything like Nicholas Lyndhurst, so audiences might struggle to suspend their disbelief when watching them playing brothers. Apart from the fact that Gilbert appeared to have forgotten that the BBC had already enjoyed great success in the 1960s with a sitcom – *Sykes and A . . .* – that had relied on the comic conceit that Eric Sykes and Hattie Jacques had been cast to play 'identical twins', he also seemed to have ignored the fact that, as far as this current project was concerned, such a physical mismatch had already been envisaged clearly by John Sullivan in his scripts. 'The whole point,' explained the exasperated writer, 'is that Del and Rodney are actually the only ones who think they are brothers. Everyone else thinks they might well have different fathers. They had to be counterpoints to each other – one tall, one short, one blond and the other dark-haired. They had to look different to each other and at one point when we casting there was even a suggestion that we had one of them mixed race.'[13] The disparity in height was also something that Sullivan had planned in order to prevent Del from appearing unsympathetic: 'In my view, they had to be different. If you had a big, tall Del Boy treating a slightly smaller Rodney the way Del treated his younger brother, people would regard him as a bully. I felt you had to have Del smaller than his brother to get away from the bullying aspect.'[14]

Butt was convinced that Jason was, by this time, the best option, so he sent the actor a script via their mutual friend and colleague Sydney Lotterby (the producer of *Open All Hours*) and, without specifying what role was still to be cast, invited him to respond with his opinions. Jason loved looking through the sample episode – 'I thought it was one of the funniest things I'd ever read' – but was unsure of where, if anywhere, he was meant to fit within this fiction. His first guess was that it might be the part of Grandad, because, he reflected, he had acquired something of a reputation for playing elderly characters. It was true: as early as 1968, when Jason was still only in his twenties, he came close to being cast as the septuagenarian Jack Jones in *Dad's Army*, then portrayed an elderly patient in both a 1969 episode of *Doctor in the House* and a 1971 episode of *Doctor at Large*, as well as a hundred-year-old gardener named Dithers in the 1972 Ronnie Barker sitcom *His Lordship Entertains*, and then in the mid-1970s he appeared once again alongside Barker in *Porridge* as the very elderly inmate called 'Blanco', so he would have been forgiven in 1981 for wondering if he was now wanted for the part of the Trotter boys' grandfather.[15]

Ray Butt clarified the matter when he called to ask Jason to come in and read for the part of Del Boy. Somewhat ruffled by the revelation that he had only come into contention as a 'tail-end Charlie', Jason was tempted to point out politely that, at this stage in his career, he felt he was far past auditioning for jobs. The quality of the script, however, struck him as simply too good to turn down, and, besides, the character of Del Boy seemed to be the role for which he had been waiting throughout his career. After being asked to play a long succession of losers and lonely misfits, here, at last, was something different: a quick-witted, fast-talking, indefatigably ebullient sort of character who was always the centre of attention. The actor therefore agreed to go in for a meeting, desperate to do whatever was needed to secure himself the job.

Jason was asked to return the following day to read with Nicholas Lyndhurst and Lennard Pearce, because Butt was particularly keen to see how well the three actors would interact. John Sullivan was also present, and, as the session progressed, he was very impressed. The instant rapport, particularly between Jason and Lyndhurst, struck the writer as extraordinary: 'They had this little read and although they'd never met before, it was immediate – just like you see it now. They both went into their characters. It was incredible. They had this wonderful chemistry. David was perfect all along and I didn't realise just how perfect he was for the part.'[16] The impact of the read-through was overwhelming; Butt and Sullivan simply turned to each other and nodded.

The decision was made there and then, and all three actors – Jason, Lyndhurst and Pearce – were duly confirmed as part of the cast. The Trotter family had been formed.

This, however, was only one aspect of the casting process. While the search for these three key actors had been going on, Ray Butt had also been busy selecting the first few supporting players. The two ostensibly minor characters requiring the most careful casting, because – if played well – they had the most potential to evolve into regular figures, were Del's permanently dazed-looking roadsweeper friend Trigger, and a competitive local second-hand car dealer with misguided pretensions to social superiority called Boycie.

Ray Butt spotted a potential 'Trigger' (RODNEY: 'Why do they call him Trigger? Does he carry a gun?' DEL: 'No, he looks like an 'orse!') when, a few months before, he had gone to see a West End play (a comedy by Stanley Price starring Penelope Keith and Peter Jeffrey) called *Moving*. Butt had actually chosen to go there in order to assess the suitability of Billy Murray to play the part of Del, but, once he started watching the action unfold, he found himself drawn instead to another actor in the cast: Roger Lloyd Pack.

Born in Islington, London, in 1944, and educated at Bedales public school in Hampshire, Lloyd Pack – the son of the film and theatre character actor Charles Lloyd Pack – was an experienced RADA graduate who had already appeared in numerous television programmes (ranging from the critically acclaimed Quentin Crisp biopic *The Naked Civil Servant* in 1975 to an episode of the popular crime series *The Professionals* in 1978) as well as a steady procession of theatrical productions. Butt, who had worked with the actor's father, looked at this tall and thin figure on stage with his long and lugubrious face and thought he was 'just right' to play Trigger: 'So I met with him, we had a chat, and he accepted the part.'[17]

Casting the character of the shady and snide second-hand car dealer, Boycie, did not take the team too long, either. This was partly because the character was not envisaged originally as a definite regular in the show, and partly because both John Sullivan and Ray Butt soon agreed that the actor best suited to playing him – and perhaps pointing to his full comic future – was John Challis.

Born in Bristol in 1942 and then brought up in south-east London and educated at Ottershaw independent school near Woking in Surrey, Challis had started his adult life as a trainee estate agent before committing himself to an acting career. Moving on to enjoy a spell with the Royal Shakespeare Company as well as making countless television appearances in shows ranging from *Coronation Street* to *Doctor Who*, he was, by 1981, a very experienced and versatile performer well respected within the profession, even though his name remained relatively unfamiliar to the average viewer at home.

Sullivan and Butt had worked with him a couple of years before, when he appeared as a police inspector in an episode of *Citizen Smith*, and Sullivan, in particular, had been so impressed with his performance that the writer had promised the actor he would find something else for him to do in a future project. Challis had heard such things many times before, taking each one with a pinch of salt, so he was surprised when, in April 1981, he received a script from Ray Butt inviting him to take on the part of Boycie.

Challis had only recently returned from America, where he had worked on a number of plays and enjoyed the experience so much that he had been tempted to stay there indefinitely, until a failed romance prompted a sudden change of mind. Resuming his career in Britain, he regarded the *Only Fools* offer as nothing more than a short-term distraction, as, initially, it only involved a single day's shooting on the set. Both Sullivan and Butt, however, were hopeful that Challis would make Boycie seem too good a character to leave behind if the first series proved a success.

Other minor characters were also recruited, but, by this stage, the core of the ensemble was safely in place. With Jason as Del, Lyndhurst as Rodney and Pearce as Grandad, the heart of the new sitcom was about to start beating.

It had been, by the normally very eventful standards of the traditional British sitcom, a relatively painless and problem-free process. True, the casting of Del Boy had lured Ray Butt into embarking on a number of brief detours and diversions, but, after that singular shaky start, the proper aim had been achieved: not only finding the right individual actors, but also, perhaps even more crucially, the right combination of individual actors. The talent, the team and the chemistry were now there, and that made everyone involved so much more confident about all of the other daunting tasks that now had to be attempted.

CHAPTER FOUR

Setting Up

Little acorns . . .

Apart from overseeing the casting, Ray Butt, as the man in charge, still had a bewilderingly complex set of tasks to see through all the way to their completion. Any sitcom producer's 'To Do' list runs to a very long roll indeed, and, as Butt pushed on with the planning for the debut series of *Only Fools and Horses*, the multiple stresses and strains kept on coming. He had assembled a large team of talents and could delegate particular tasks, but the fact remained that, when everything was ready and the time arrived for the production as a whole to be judged, the buck would stop with Butt.

One aspect that required careful attention was the physical look of the show: the costumes, the make-up and the sets. Butt dealt with this by appointing some trusted specialists to help sharpen the sight of the sitcom.

The person enlisted to design the costumes was Phoebe De Gaye. 'I was a young designer,' she would recall, 'in fact I might have been an acting designer, and the job was given to me as a way of trying me out before deciding whether to appoint me as a full-blown designer. I can't remember exactly, but I do know inexperienced designers were often tried out on sitcom pilots.'[1] Even though *Only Fools* was her first major project in control of this area, she felt that she had proven herself as an assistant on numerous other BBC productions, and was delighted to get her chance to stamp her own mark on a show.

Researching the types and trends that might help to find the right look for the characters, she went out into London, photographing those figures – such as the flashily dressed men who strutted about in used-car showrooms – who struck her as potential templates for decorating the likes of Del Boy. She also visited a warehouse off the North Circular that contained a startling array of gaudy Gabicci shirts, as well as a shop near Marble Arch that sold cut-price suits so shiny and badly made that they creased as soon as one touched them. Adding a selection of similarly cheap and tacky clothes and trinkets from Shepherd's Bush market and Islington's Chapel Market, and a few other items from the BBC's own stockroom, she then proceeded to age a number of them artificially (especially those earmarked for Grandad), using cheese graters, soap and sandpaper to register the right degree of wear and tear.

She also spent time with the main actors, taking them to sample some of the styles she had spotted, and discussing with them her ideas for each character's wardrobe. David Jason, as a famously strong-minded performer who always had his own ideas about the people he played, was probably the greatest challenge for the young designer, as he resisted a number of her suggestions – including her desire to see Del Boy sporting suitably fashionable permed hair – but she also relished his eagerness to examine and exchange ideas.

Jason's primary inspiration for how Del should appear was a character he had encountered during his time as a jobbing electrician. Back when he and his partner were struggling with their company B & W Installations, they decided to try to drum up business via a mailshot, sending out hundreds of letters to local builders, plumbers and contractors, and one of the first recipients to respond was an Eastender called Derek Hockley.

Hockley was a contractor who had recently added Ind Coope Brewery to his list of clients. Although he was one of countless wheeler-dealers in the area, what struck Jason most about the man was the stark contrast between his down-to-earth attitude and his self-consciously dapper appearance. He had short, neatly parted hair and a small and precisely pruned goatee beard, and was always very well turned out with a clean and immaculately pressed shirt, a sharp suit, highly polished shoes, a camel-hair coat and plenty of eye-catching gold jewellery. Unable to shed his old gorblimey Cockney accent, he took obvious pride and pleasure in what he regarded as his new sartorial elegance.

Hockley's firm belief in the axiom that 'clothes maketh the man' thus became a major element in Jason's interpretation of what made Del Boy tick, but the actor also drew on his memories of numerous other young men on the make to give the character a suitably confident swagger. 'I'd seen it so many times with guys who fancy themselves,' Jason later explained. 'They develop a body language that is supposed to impress the birds I suppose. It's like a signal that says, "I'm the business, look at me, I'm the cat's whiskers, I've got style, I've got class."'[2] One other thing that he took from Hockley and some of his colleagues was a strangely bumptious little mannerism that involved twitching his neck as though his collar was slightly uncomfortable: 'I've no idea what it means,' Jason said, 'but lots of them do it and it's a bit intimidating.'[3]

Collaborating with Jason, Phoebe De Gaye gradually pieced together the key ingredients to dress Del ready for action. John Sullivan's original vision of the character as a medallion man with a sovereign ring on every finger was revised to make him a slightly more reserved, but almost as tacky, figure with a fake gold chain around his neck, a couple of rings on his fingers and a chunky bracelet dangling from his wrist. She also chose a wide range of injudicious colour combinations, tailored some trousers that were 'tight over the bum' and pliable at the front for the onset of a paunch, and, following another unconventional shopping expedition, found him the perfectly imperfect patchy sheepskin coat along with a patterned flat cap.

Lyndhurst and Pearce also had De Gaye to thank for assembling a basic wardrobe for their characters. She decided to dress Rodney (whom she described initially as 'tall, dingy and droopy') in an old pair of blue jeans, some cheap and grubby T-shirts or limp woollen V-necks and a green camouflage combat jacket she had found in the BBC Costume Department, and then added a Palestinian-style scarf selected from Shepherd's Bush market. The key idea for Grandad was that he should look as though he could not be less bothered about his appearance, with the top of his head almost always covered (even indoors) by a dirty-looking old hat, and part of his pyjamas mixed up with his other layers of clothes. In order to give his specially aged outfits an additional 'crusty' look, she daubed them with Vaseline, make-up and even a few bits and pieces of real food.

While De Gaye was designing the costumes, Pauline Cox was planning the make-up. A very experienced BBC make-up artist, with a track record that included programmes ranging from *The Morecambe & Wise Show* to the 1978 adaptation of *Wuthering Heights*, she did not take long to sketch out her visions of the key characters.

She wanted Del to sport the kind of long sideburns that seemed to suggest a man who smelt of Brut aftershave and cheap hair oil, but David Jason, once again, proved resistant to the idea, so she decided instead to settle for giving the character a slight but shiny-looking quiff. Having worked with Nicholas Lyndhurst before on *Butterflies*, she knew him well and was quick to find the right pasty powdering for Rodney's callow face. Lennard Pearce, though sixty-six, needed to look a little older and much coarser, so Cox drew some thin red spider veins on his cheeks to lend him a weather-beaten appearance, and put greasepaint under his eyes to resemble pouchy bags.

As the characters thus came into sight, so, too, did the actual sets. Tony Snoaden was the production designer who was piecing together the various places in Peckham. His research had begun when he went with Ray Butt to view a row of three more-or-less identical twenty-storey tower blocks near Kew Bridge in south-west London, and another, even scruffier, set just off Bollo Bridge Road, north Acton, in the north-west of the city. Butt said that these were the kind of ugly constructions he thought would serve as models for Nelson Mandela House, and so, after studying the exteriors, they went inside one of the empty apartments and Snoaden made some notes. The tower block that would be shown at the start of each episode was one from north Acton.

When it came to creating the set for the Trotters' flat, he paid close attention to John Sullivan's existing scripts, which included such unusually specific descriptions as the following:

The room should reflect their style of business. Nothing is permanent. The settee and two armchairs are from three separate suites as the other pieces were used as make-weights in various other swaps. There are three TV sets; one colour, one black and white, and one with its back off awaiting repair. There are a couple of stereo music centres standing one on top of the other. Various video games, talking chess games, etc., litter the room. Their phone is one of the ornate 1920s type with separate ear-piece on an alabaster base. The décor is clean but gaudy. Dozens of clashing patterns. It should look like the start of a bad trip.[4]

Acting on such suggestions, Snoaden kept firmly in mind the knowledge that the family had no real taste at all, so he went for the most vulgar and idiosyncratic décor that he and his colleague Chris Ferriday (the BBC's Props Manager) could find. He covered the walls in a melancholic shade of beige paper and carpeted the floor in what resembled a mixture of mud, sugar and honey, and, as he recognised that this was supposed to be an all-male environment, filled the scruffy living room with an incoherent selection of unlikely objects, including old car wheels, ice buckets, reproduction paintings, a Pirelli calendar, forgotten holiday souvenirs, an ugly wrought-iron guitar, piles of yellowing newspapers and creased magazines, a few empty beer bottles and a wide variety of unsold items of stock. There also had to be a large and diverse range of tables, because the Trotters were the type who were prepared to sell everything – even the table on which they ate their meals.

The initial inspiration for that other locus of activity, The Nag's Head, came from a pub near Chapel Market in Islington called The Alma, which Snoaden spotted during the early days of visiting filming locations.[5] The traditional-looking Victorian frontage seemed ideal, and, once inside, looking at the rather dull and downbeat drinking areas, he realised that 'the layout was almost like a studio set, which meant I could virtually copy the actual layout'.[6]

Arguably the most important physical item of all – the battered Reliant Regal Supervan III – was something insisted upon by John Sullivan. It was to be Del Boy's equivalent of Pinocchio's nose: the taller the tales that he told, the smaller this silly vehicle would seem. No matter how many times he would boast about how, this time next year, he and his family would be millionaires, they would all still have to squeeze back into the truth of the situation: that tiny yellow van. The make was arrived at through a quick process of elimination: the more sporty options were rejected in favour of a far more functional vehicle with enough space to carry the Trotters' miscellaneous merchandise, and the fact that it was a three-wheeler struck Sullivan as symbolic of the Trotters' incomplete lives – even their van had something missing. The 'New York–Paris–Peckham' slogan on the side of the van was inspired by the 'New York–London–Paris' line on a packet of Dunhill cigarettes, and would serve as another unwitting reminder of just how little the business has really achieved.

Chris Ferriday found the right model, in the right stage of deterioration, at a specialist prop vehicle supplier called Action Cars in Harrow in Middlesex. The BBC rented it for the first series, but would go on to hire several more because their chassis kept giving out and none of them were worth repairing.

Surveying all of these actions and initiatives as each week went by, Ray Butt was very pleased with how the visual aspect was developing, but there were still other matters to which he needed to attend. The sitcom's characters and structures needed to be shot for the screen, so more support was needed both on the studio floor and up in the production gallery.

He was assisted here, as with many other aspects of the process, by his production manager, Janet Bone. An old colleague from *Citizen Smith*, Bone was busy scouting for suitable location sites as well as supervising the schedule, but she also helped Butt assemble the rest of his technical staff.

The very reliable and experienced Bill Matthews was brought in as cameraman (he had previously worked on such sitcoms as *The Liver Birds*), two more former members of Bone and Butt's *Citizen Smith* crew, Dennis Panchen and Don Babbage, were installed as sound recordist and lighting director respectively, and John Jarvis (whose credits included a period working on *The Goodies*) was enlisted as film editor. Their immediate task was to spend the next few weeks filming all of the exterior scenes required for the entire series, before returning to Television Centre to record the studio sessions.

Ray Butt was meant to have taken control of the actual direction himself, but he hurt his back (slipping a disc) just after location shooting began early on in May and was rushed off for what would prove to be a profoundly frustrating three-week stay in Charing Cross Hospital. At the very last moment, therefore, a replacement needed to be found. Gareth Gwenlan stepped in to oversee the first day's schedule, but, as a busy figure elsewhere within the BBC, he was unavailable to continue (although he would carry on helping out with the production as a whole), so John Howard Davies contacted Martin Shardlow to take over the directorial duties for the remainder of the location shooting and then the studio recordings.

Shardlow was in the process of setting up for another project, so he was somewhat startled to find himself uprooted and moved on so suddenly. When all of the scripts and the location schedule were sent to him in his office at Television Centre, he had a brief amount of time to read and assess them, used a few of Janet Bone's photographs to complete a very basic shooting script, and then found himself straight out on the streets filming the relevant scenes. Once the combination of shock and disorientation had faded, Shardlow started to enjoy the experience, relishing the opportunity to play such a major part in what soon came to seem like a thoroughly promising project. 'After a bit,' he would recall, 'Ray was able to turn up for the technical runs, and things like that, but on the whole he left it to me.'[7]

John Sullivan, meanwhile, was watching much of this activity from a greater distance than he would, ideally, have desired. 'Dennis Main Wilson was all for [me playing an active role in the production process],' he would later remark. 'He was all for me coming to editing and everything, being heavily involved, and being on filming, and he talked to me an awful lot. Ray Butt was less so. He was protecting his area more.'[8]

Sullivan did at least know that, even *in absentia*, Martin Shardlow would still be properly apprised of his opinions as to how each episode should be shot, because, very unusually, those opinions were already included in all of the scripts. 'When I joined the BBC,' the writer explained, 'I never knew how to lay a script out; I didn't know what was expected. So the first thing I wanted was a script, but what I realised years later was that I had a director's script, a shooting script, which had all the reaction, so that was the habit I got into: "Cut to reaction, cut to reaction." When I saw other writers' work I

realised they didn't do it. But that's how I write.'[9] Such unconventional input was a source of some reassurance for Sullivan,
but it did little to dispel the feeling that his influence on the
project as a whole was still not as strong as it could, and should,
have been.

One particular cause of his frustration was the show's opening
theme tune. Sullivan had always been a keen music fan – 'As
a kid, I was always writing songs'[10] – and, when Dennis Main
Wilson had encouraged him to write 'The Glorious Day' for
Robert Lindsay to sing at the start of *Citizen Smith*, he had
snapped at the chance. When it came to making *Only Fools
and Horses*, therefore, Sullivan came up with a new song that
he thought would be ideal:

> *Stick a pony in me pocket*
> *I'll fetch the suitcase from the van*
> *Cos if you want the best 'uns*
> *And you don't ask questions*
> *Then, brother, I'm your man.*
>
> *Where it all comes from is a mystery*
> *It's like the changing of the seasons*
> *And the tides of the sea*
> *But here's the one what's driving me berserk*
> *Why do only fools and horses work?*[11]

The problem was that no one else – and certainly not the
producer – seemed to agree about the song's appeal. 'Ray Butt
didn't particularly like it,'[12] Sullivan later complained.

It was a great disappointment for the writer, therefore, when
Butt decided instead to ask the doyen of television theme tune

composers, Ronnie Hazlehurst, to come up with something more suitable for *Only Fools*. Having either written or arranged the music for such sitcoms as *The Likely Lads, Not in Front of the Children, Are You Being Served?, I Didn't Know You Cared, Last of the Summer Wine, The Other One, Some Mothers Do 'Ave 'Em, The Fall and Rise of Reginald Perrin, Butterflies, Yes Minister* and *To the Manor Born*, as well as collaborated with John Sullivan on *Citizen Smith*, he seemed the obvious choice to create a theme for this new show, but his finished effort – a 'jolly' tune featuring a swooping pub piano, a hyperactive bass guitar and jaunty saxophones – struck many who first heard it as something more appropriate for a cheap ITV game show than a carefully crafted BBC sitcom. 'John hated it,' Ray Butt later admitted. 'I hated it. It just wasn't right.'[13] Unfortunately, however, Butt was still incapacitated at the time with his slipped disc, and, with time fast running out, there seemed no option but to go with what they had.

More positively, the music was set to be accompanied by an opening title sequence created by the talented Peter Clayton, whom Butt had hired as his graphic designer. After discussing the nature of the sitcom with his producer, Clayton had proceeded to go out on to the London streets and take pictures of those places that he felt were most evocative of the environment envisaged for the Trotters: a busy market, the inside of a pub, a large second-hand car lot, a scruffy-looking wine bar and a couple of run-down tower blocks. He then devised an animated sequence that saw each actor's name arrive on a piece of paper shaped like a bank note, which flapped on, peeled back and flew off the screen, symbolising the vicissitudes of the fly-pitcher's existence, getting hold of cash only to see it slip swiftly away again. In order to introduce each character's distinctive personality as quickly as possible, Clayton took some stills of Del Boy (smiling cockily while waving around a wad of cash), Rodney (pulling out his empty pockets and looking puzzled) and Grandad (sitting down munching idly on a pie), added an establishing shot of the rust-ridden Reliant Regal parked outside the building, and then, in the painstaking way that was necessary in those pre-computer graphics days, linked them all together frame by frame via a rostrum camera.

Not everything was progressing smoothly, but, in general, good advances were being made. All of the work behind the scenes had provided the production with a very solid bedrock. The time was now fast approaching for the most telling signs of the preparations to loom more sharply into view.

The momentum really grew most rapidly at the start of June, when the location work had been completed and all of the shows were due to be recorded in front of a studio audience. This was the stage when everything had to come together to make the sitcom ready for the screen.

The intensive weekly schedule for the cast and crew consisted of the following: Tuesday was when the cast read through the script and then worked with the crew 'blocking' the key action (assessing, for example, where the actors and cameras should be positioned for certain scenes, gestures and dialogue); Wednesday and Thursday saw the actors move from script to memory as they continued to develop their performances; Friday functioned primarily as a technical run-through for Butt and his team; and Saturday involved two more run-throughs as the various sets were put up, followed by a relaxing trip to the pub. The process reached its climax on Sunday, beginning at 10 a.m. with a 'stagger through' of the scenes on the set (allowing the actors to get accustomed to each physical area while the director considered what if any changes needed to be made to the shooting script), which was followed at about 4.30 p.m. by a full dress rehearsal, and then at 7.30 p.m., after a break for dinner, the latest episode was recorded in front of the studio audience.

Butt chose Sunday as recording day because, as he later observed: 'You tended to get better audiences, perhaps because it was the weekend.'[14] He sought to further improve the mood by hiring the indefatigably ebullient Felix Bowness, probably the most experienced warm-up man in the business at the time (as well as a sitcom performer in his right, most notably as former-jockey Fred Quilly in *Hi-de-Hi!*), to keep the public entertained during the inevitable breaks and delays between scenes and technical set-ups. With this and everything else now finally in place, Butt felt, it was time for all of the hard work to pay off: the series was ready to start.

The very first episode of *Only Fools and Horses* was duly recorded on Sunday, 7 June 1981. Entitled 'Big Brother', it needed, as all pilot programmes do, to set the appropriate tone by finding the right fine balance between information and entertainment, introducing the characters and context while getting plenty of laughs from the action.

It began inside Nelson Mandela House, in the lounge, with Grandad (his hat still on his head) slumped in his old easy chair as he leads a life of soft-slippered leisure; he is watching not one but two television sets (both of them tuned to the same channel), enthusing wheezily about how good an actor 'that Sidney Potter is' because he 'always plays the black fella'. Rodney, meanwhile, is stretched out on the settee, checking the company accounts with the help of a pocket calculator. As he argues with Grandad over whether the actor in question is really Sidney Potter or Sidney Poitier, Del Boy (dressed in a tomato red top and cheap battleship grey trousers) saunters out from one of the bedrooms, declares that the star in question is actually Harry Belafonte and starts admiring himself in the mirror: '*S'il vous plaît, s'il vous plaît*, what an enigma. I get better looking every day! I can't wait for tomorrow!'

His smug mood is spoiled once he spots that his younger brother is recording the accounts and thus providing evidence for the tax man. 'Well, there you are Grandad: a lot of people told me I was a right dipstick to make my brother a partner in the business, but this only goes to prove how bloody right they were. You dozy little *twonk*, Rodney!' Rodney, however, is unrepentant: 'Don't worry, if the tax man comes, I'll eat it. This is the only way I can keep a check on you, Del. I'm sure you're cheating me in some way – I just can't figure out how.'

The perceived slight prompts Del to resort to invoking the memory of their late mother: 'It's any excuse with you, innit, eh? What d'you think about poor old Mum, then, eh? Do you know that she was thirty-nine when she fell for you? For the first three months of her pregnancy you were treated as an ulcer. And to this day I sometimes think the original diagnosis was correct! Look, eh? Come on, what sort of bloke do you think I am, eh? Cheat me own brother? Come on, Rodney, I told you before haven't I, eh? It's everything between you and I split straight down the middle: 60–40.' Rodney, though still a little puzzled, is more or less placated by this explanation, and Del proceeds to defend the *modus operandi* of Trotters Independent Traders: 'Look, so we don't pay VAT. We don't pay income tax or national insurance. On the other hand, we don't claim dole money, social security, supplementary benefit, do we, eh, eh? The Government don't give us nothing, so we don't give the Government nothing – right? What you complaining about?'

The two brothers go off to their local pub, The Nag's Head, but it is clear that Rodney, slouching at the bar, is still unhappy about the future that Del envisages for him as a self-employed free-rider:

RODNEY: Do you realise we've always had something missing in our lives? First we was motherless, then we were fatherless, and now we're flogging one-legged turkeys from a three-wheel van.

DEL: Little acorns . . .

RODNEY: What, you got one of them missing as well, Del?

DEL: No! Marks and Spencers started off with a barrow.

RODNEY: At least they had four wheels!

Del is defiant, eager to romanticise the life of the 'He who dares, wins' wheeler-dealer, ducking and diving while revelling in the sheer unpredictability of it all. Rodney, however, confesses that, seeing as he has his two GCEs, he is contemplating getting a proper job. Startled, Del wastes no time in reminding him that he went on from this modest academic success to get himself expelled from Basingstoke Art College after a mere three weeks after being caught 'with the biggest reefer this side of Marrakesh,' and will therefore find it all but impossible to pass any interview: 'No, no, I'm afraid not, Rodney. At the ripe old age of twenty-three, you are a social leper. Society has placed you in the darkest corner of its deepest cellar to grow moss and be forgotten about. Still, never mind, eh? *Viva la France* as they say in Rome. No need to get depressed!'

Rodney's dark mood is hardly improved when Del's old mate Trigger arrives and, for some unknown reason, calls Rodney 'Dave'. When, however, the younger brother is dispatched to get in another round of drinks, the older brother proceeds to boast about him to Trigger: 'Very clever kid, you know, my brother. Yeah, got two GCEs: one in Maths, one in Art. You wanna see him when he writes a letter. Some of the words he uses!'

Trigger, though impressed by the news that the words are 'long ones', is more concerned to pass on some merchandise: twenty-five shiny-looking executive briefcases. Rodney, returning to the table, is distinctly unimpressed ('Plastic?'), but Del is dazzled ('Old English vinyl!'). Trigger assures Rodney that the police are not looking for these items, although he admits that he is keeping them hidden under the table because 'You never know when they're gonna start looking for 'em, do you!' This is good enough for Del, who starts haggling hard in spite of being hampered by his naive brother's honesty:

TRIGGER: To you, Del Boy, £17 each.
DEL: You know what happened to the real Trigger, don't you? Roy Rogers had him stuffed!
TRIGGER: All right, then – fourteen.
DEL: Fourteen? Leave it out! Five.
TRIGGER: Twelve.
DEL: Six.
TRIGGER: Ten.
DEL: Nine.
TRIGGER: Eight.

DEL: Done!

TRIGGER: *[To Rodney]* That's the way to do business, Dave!

DEL: *[Taking out a pocket calculator]* Right, okay Trig, let's work that out. That's eight times 25 equals . . . 175, okay?

RODNEY: 200.

DEL: *What?* No, no, Rodney, no, no, *no.* The calculator says 175, all right?

TRIGGER: *[Puzzled]* Yeah, but he's got GCEs in Maths and Art!

DEL: So what does that prove – he can paint by numbers? Look, Trig, I mean, this is a *calculator,* innit, eh? You know what I mean? Look – calculator says 175! You can't argue with a calculator can you, you know?

RODNEY: Give it here. *[He grabs the calculator]*

DEL: Rodney . . .

RODNEY: 25 times eight equals . . . 200 – see?

DEL: Oh, yeah! Look at that. I must have got my finger stuck on the button, yeah.

RODNEY: *[Triumphantly flexing his fingers]* Pianist's fingers, Del.

DEL: *[Scowling]* Yeah! Yeah, you wanna look after them, Rodney – they break very easily . . .

Back at the flat, Grandad is moaning about food (he asked Rodney to buy him an emperor burger but Rodney claimed he could only afford a humble cheeseburger) while the new stock sits unsold. Del is deflated when, upon calling his mate Dougie Sadler, the owner of a local stationer's shop, he discovers that not only has Dougie recently had twenty-five executive briefcases stolen from his premises, the items in question were also faulty, as the locks lack a combination and can only be opened by professional safe crackers. Rodney cannot wait to say 'I told you so,' and when Del tries to defend his self-image as an entrepreneur ('The French have a word for people like me') Rodney snaps back ('Yeah, the English have got a couple of good 'uns an' all!') and all of his festering sibling resentment spills out:

RODNEY: You make my life a misery, you do!

DEL: Here – oi, just a moment! What was that last remark about me making your life a misery?

RODNEY: Yeah, well, you do, Del, with your over-bearing, over-protective manner!

DEL: Let me remind you, Rodney, that you were a six-year-old little nipper when God smiled on Mum and made her die! Two months after that Dad packed his bags and left us to fend for ourselves. It was *me* that kept us together, nothing to do with Grandad! He was an out-of-work lamp-lighter waiting for gas to make a comeback! I grafted 19 to 20 hours a day to put groceries on that table – all right, it wasn't always double legal – but you ate the finest food that was going!

RODNEY: All you ever give me was TV dinners and convenience foods! If it wasn't frozen or dehydrated we didn't eat it. If you'd have been in charge of the Last Supper it would have been a takeaway!

This was the scene when *Only Fools and Horses* really came alive. The fine writing of John Sullivan and the powerful and plausible acting of Jason and Lyndhurst gelled so well to produce the kind of character comedy–drama that elevated the sitcom far above and beyond the more formulaic examples of the genre. Having been inspired as a young man by the emotional, as well as the humorous, tensions evident in the 1962 pilot edition of *Steptoe and Son*, Sullivan was now emulating that rare effect as he drew the audience deeper into the close but complicated sibling relationship that was to form the very essence of the new show:

RODNEY: Del, look, don't get me wrong, I'm, I'm grateful . . .

DEL: I don't want your gratitude – ungrateful little git! I don't know what is the matter with you, Rodney. Sometimes I hesitate to tell people that you're my brother!

RODNEY: Well, I always say I'm your social worker!

DEL: Do you mind telling me exactly what it is that has made your life a misery?

RODNEY: Well, you've always treated me like a child, ain't you? I was the only sixth former in my grammar school who wore short trousers!

DEL: Yeah, well, I got 'em cheap, didn't I?

RODNEY: But I was *FIFTEEN*, Del! I was growing hairs and things! My legs looked like Italian foot-ballers'! And you'd never let me do anything on my own, would you? You even had to help me with my GCE studies!

DEL: You passed in two subjects.

RODNEY:	I failed in the other eight, Del! I mean, you *embarrass* me, that's why I never bring women home!
DEL:	Oh, you know some women do you? Cor, that's a turn up for the book! The only bird I've ever heard you mention was old Shanghai Lil from the art college in Basingstoke. Even then you had to drug her before you could get your leg over!
RODNEY:	No, I didn't!
DEL:	What – you didn't drug her or didn't get your leg over?
RODNEY:	You're *suffocating* me, Del! I'm getting out of this house! I'm going to prove to you I can survive on my own! I'm going to the pub!
DEL:	What – to prove you can survive on your own?
RODNEY:	No, to get legless! I don't *NEED* you no more Del! I don't need you for *NOTHING!!*

The impact of Rodney's dramatic exit is spoiled somewhat when he has to come back in, mumbling awkwardly, to borrow a note from Del, but then he leaves again without uttering another word. 'I think he's very much like you, Grandad,' Del sighs. 'What, dignified in defeat?' asks Grandad. 'No,' mutters Del. 'A ponce!'

The denouement of this opening episode would lack the dark drama of Sullivan's *Steptoe and Son* template (that pilot had ended with Harold trying but failing to break away from the family business, collapsing in tears as he sensed how tightly his life remained tied to that of his irascible old father), but, in a tamer way, it would again echo the earlier show in the care it takes to underline the trapped relationship that Del and Rodney share. After the younger brother bids to escape while his sibling sleeps by packing his rucksack and planning to hitchhike to Hong Kong, where he hopes to start a new life with his now-deported love Shanghai Lil, he is then dragged back to the flat to face his fate.

The scene begins the morning after Rodney's emotional departure, with Del still preoccupied with the problem of how to shift his permanently locked briefcases. When Grandad informs him that Rodney has gone, Del is sceptical ('He'd never reach Hong Kong. He has trouble finding Clapham!'), but Grandad insists that the young boy seemed serious ('He's very determined').

Obliged to get on with business as usual, Del leaves in the hope of selling his troublesome briefcases, but, after six days of fruitless sales patter, he returns to the flat with the stock still stuck on his hands. As he argues tetchily with Grandad about yet another faulty item, both of them are surprised when a scruffy and unshaven Rodney walks in. In an awkward exchange, Rodney claims that he got as far as the South of France before homesickness pulled him back to the 'raw and savage beauty' of the environs around Nelson Mandela House. Del listens patiently before passing Rodney back his passport.

Rodney is infuriated that, once again, his big brother has made him look the proverbial plonker, but Del is in a conciliatory mood:

RODNEY: It must be wonderful to be you, Del – to always be right!

DEL: I know. It gets a bit embarrassing at times. I'll
            tell you another thing shall I Rodney? You
            said that I would never get rid of them brief-
            cases.

RODNEY: And you did, didn't you, Del?

DEL: Yes, I did. I chucked the bleedin' lot in the
            river!

The two brothers laugh together about all that money lost, and a brave trip to St Tropez that actually got no further than a doss house in Stoke Newington. It is clear, as the episode ends, that they are back together again, and off down the pub.

As the credits rolled on the monitors and the studio audience applauded, the mood among the cast and crew was extremely positive. The acting had been uniformly excellent, with a wonderfully lively Jason, artfully awkward Lyndhurst and slyly amusing Pearce looking immediately at home in their respective characters, and the direction (with plenty of fast-paced cuts between two-shots and close-ups to draw the viewer swiftly into the family dynamics) was admirably precise, understated and effective. John Sullivan's script, in particular, had been very impressive, with some of the most flowing, funny and apposite dialogue heard in a new British sitcom for many years, indeed reminiscent at its best of Galton and Simpson in the way that it blended comedy and pathos with such unforced assurance. The view, both down on the studio floor and up in the production gallery, was that this 'first night' had been a great success for the team as a whole.

When the lights went out and all of those involved made their way home, the sense of relief, and cautious optimism, was palpable. After months of planning, pressure, hopes and fears, the show – their show – was finally up and running. With five more episodes to record between 14 June and 11 July, there was still much to do, but spirits were now soaring. *Only Fools and Horses* would soon be on the screen.

CHAPTER FIVE

Slow Business

No money back. No guarantee.

There was no noisy fanfare, no great fuss, when *Only Fools and Horses* finally arrived on British television in the autumn of 1981. Like most other sitcoms of the period before TV pre-publicity veered so wildly to the opposite extreme, the show was left to build up an audience largely by word-of-mouth alone.

The *Radio Times* did provide it with a brief and perfunctory preview, describing the premise as concerning 'two brothers living with their granddad in a south London flat and existing off shady deals,'[1] but otherwise the apparent media indifference was overwhelming. If *Only Fools* was going to succeed, it was certainly going to need some good luck.

The first episode, 'Big Brother', was broadcast on Tuesday, 8 September at 8.30 p.m. on BBC1. The competition, in that three-channel terrestrial era (the launch of Channel 4 was still a year away), consisted of a sober documentary on BBC2 about the then-French President François Mitterrand and, over on ITV, the latest instalment of a popular big budget drama series, *The Flame Trees of Thika*. *Only Fools* fared reasonably well in such circumstances, attracting a fairly healthy initial audience of 9.2 million,[2] but its debut was overlooked by most of the reviewers in the national newspapers. Probably the most favourable comments from among the few regional critics who bothered to discuss the new sitcom came from Stephen Biscoe in the *Yorkshire Post*, who praised the 'earthy' quality of the three main characters and noted 'more than a touch' of *Steptoe and Son* in the tone of the show.[3]

It was a similar story for all of the subsequent episodes during the first series: watched by modest but reasonably solid audiences (averaging just under 8 million,[4] which paled in comparison to the 17 million or more who tuned in each week to view that year's most popular sitcom, *To the Manor Born*[5]), and ignored by most of the reviewers. Such a mediocre performance was frustrating for all concerned, because the shows themselves contained plenty of comic promise.

Apart from the splendidly impressive opening episode, highlights included the first appearance of the braying used car salesman Boycie in 'Go West Young Man' (an episode that also underlined Del Boy's desperately deluded desire to dazzle people with his own peculiar 'pot-pourri' of French and other foreign phrases picked up from the dubious packages he imports from Europe); some deftly rendered moments of pathos in 'The Second Time Around' when Del's vulnerable side is shown as he feels a failure with women; and a nice early example in 'A Slow Bus to Chingford' both of gawky Rodney's gaucheness when he invites a potential new girlfriend up to the flat ('Janice . . . get your bra off') and Grandad's disarmingly detached docility ('It wasn't me, Del Boy, it was me brain'), along with a fine example of the classic British idealism/cynicism dialectic when Del announces that he has had a vision in which he saw himself standing proudly on the penthouse balcony of a skyscraper office block, with the initials of his company emblazoned at the top of the building in giant neon lights – only for Rodney to point out that 'Trotters Independent Traders' spells out 'TIT', causing a deflated Del to give up and go home.

More so than any individual episodes, however, what proved most compelling about this first series was the quality of the characters and how well they were portrayed. Although Sullivan's scripts seemed to lack any real pattern from week to week, with some of them (such as 'Cash and Curry') so heavy on plot that the dialogue seemed a little too light, and others (such as 'The Russians Are Coming') similarly imbalanced in the opposite way, thus supplying the series with plenty of variety at the expense of coherence, the simple and constant charm and clarity of the three main characters kept those who watched on a weekly basis richly entertained.

The last episode in the series, 'The Russians Are Coming', was probably the most audacious of all at tapping the potential of the comic trio of Trotters. Following in a great sitcom tradition stretching from *Hancock's Half-Hour*'s 'Sunday Afternoon At Home' (in which the fact that 'nothing happens' becomes the basis for all the humour) through to *Dad's Army*'s 'Asleep in the Deep' (where events force the platoon to interact within the minimal space of a flooded room inside a pumping house) and then on to other singular sitcom episodes, 'The Russians Are Coming' saw John Sullivan confident enough about his characters to confine them within a similarly claustrophobic context, eschewing most of what could pass as a proper plot in favour of showcasing the pure interplay of personalities.

Drawing on the current anxieties about the prospect of nuclear war (prompted by the sharp decline in US–Soviet relations following the latter's invasion of Afghanistan back in 1979), the episode sees Del buy a pile of old bricks which Rodney soon realises is actually a prefabricated nuclear fall-out shelter. While the business-blinkered Del is keen to sell the property on for a fast profit (and possibly buy himself a flash 'Rollox' watch with the proceeds), the more politically aware Rodney is adamant that they should build it for themselves just in case Peckham ends up being earmarked for a quick shower of Strontium-90. Still sceptical but a little alarmed, Del is prepared to go along with the protection plan, and, after dismissing Grandad's preferred location for the shelter – the New Forest – as impractical for heeding the four-minute warning, the trio decide to set it up much closer to home: on the roof of Nelson Mandela House.

It is here, inside the newly constructed container, that the three men sit and interact, with one personality bouncing off the other as the dialogue goes on. Del, for example, clashes with Rodney over the meaning of war, with Del's working-class Thatcherite bullishness contrasting with his younger brother's more liberal and critical outlook:

RODNEY: That is typical of a ruthless little mercenary like you, innit?

DEL: What do you mean: 'ruthless mercenary'? *I'm* not a ruthless mercenary! Who is it goes round the estate at every Christmas time making sure all the old people have got enough to eat and drink?

RODNEY: Yeah, and who was it, during the Brixton riots, drove down in the van selling paving stones to the rioters? I mean, what did you think they were going to do with them, eh? All run off home and start building patios?

DEL: Mine is not to reason why, mine is but to sell and buy! No, anyway. Anyway, I know a lot of them youngsters down in Brixton and their trouble is frustration. Yes, you see, modern society has denied them the birthright of a war!

RODNEY: Oh, I don't believe you! You saying war's our birthright?

DEL: Oh yes – yes it is! For century after century, you see, every generation of British youth has been guaranteed a decent war! Well, that's sort of, you know, raw, 'Over the top, chaps!' you know, 'Try that one on for size, Fritz!' I mean that sort of courage is obsolete. Because the next war's gonna be fought by computer programmers. See, that's what's frustrating the modern youth! You can see them any day down the amusement arcades, you know, they're doing their National Service on the space invaders. Yeah, but that sort of *real* war that I'm talking about, you know, Errol Flynn leading the gallant 600 into the Valley of Death. John Mills marooned in a dinghy, it's Kenneth More refusing to let a little thing like no legs get him down. It's a glorious, valiant, war, that!

It is at this point, really for the first time in the entire series, that Grandad, snapping angrily at Del's callow romanticism, is moved to make his own views heard, and what he says shows how this sitcom has the potential to deal with emotional and sensitive issues as well as light-hearted comic themes:

My brother George was at Passchendaele. Nigh on half a million Allied troops *died* there, all for five miles of *mud!* I was at King's Cross station when his regiment come home after the armistice. Most of them was carried off the train. I saw men with limbs missing, blind men – men who couldn't breathe properly 'cos their lungs had been shot to bits by mustard gas! While the nation celebrated, they was hidden away in big grey buildings, far from the public gaze. I mean, courage like that could put you right off your victory dinner, couldn't it? They promised us homes fit for heroes, they give us heroes fit for homes!

Rodney shows his own immaturity by interrupting Grandad to say that he would never wear a British military uniform on principle. 'What principle?' asks a suddenly subdued Del. 'Well, on the principle that the Russians might shoot at it,' Rodney replies with an awkward-looking smile. Grandad ignores them and continues:

GRANDAD: The politicians . . . the politicians and the military men used to *con*, you see. They had little lads, youngsters, believing that their country really did need them! D'you know, they used to have little lads of fourteen pretending they was eighteen just so they could fight for their king and country!

DEL: What, and they accepted the little sprogs?

GRANDAD: More often than not . . . My brother George lied about his age.

RODNEY: Pretended he was eighteen?

GRANDAD: No, he *was* eighteen, he pretended he was fourteen! They saw through it though. I think it was the moustache . . .

The clever comic pay-off switched the mood back swiftly to the conventional sitcom lightness, but, nonetheless, Grandad's sombre monologue put down a marker for future episodes. That, the show seemed to be saying, is what this programme – with these characters – can do. These are the places where they can take you.

It seemed a far cry from the one-dimensional frets and fripperies of many other contemporary sitcoms. It seemed rather real, and rather special.

The problem, once the series came to the end of its run on 13 October, was that so few people – not only among the public but also, depressingly, inside the BBC – seemed to have noticed. Even while the episodes were still going out, John Sullivan and David Jason had been sufficiently frustrated by how the show was being promoted – or rather, more accurately, not being promoted – they complained to any and every executive they encountered. The Tuesday evening slot – never a traditionally popular slot for BBC sitcoms, which tended to fare far better on 'feel good' times such as Fridays or over the weekend – was bad enough on its own to nurture the niggles, but the absence of any publicity really rattled all members of the team. It seemed that the show went out without any publicity at all.

The growing suspicion that some people at the BBC considered the sitcom to be in some sense 'beneath' the broadcaster was further exacerbated when, as part of an

ONLY FOOLS AND HORSES

ongoing departmental publicity scheme, the foyer of Television
Centre was decorated with a range of massive images relating
to its current comedy output, and, to Sullivan's great irritation, the only sitcom that appeared to have been omitted
was *Only Fools and Horses*. When he asked about its absence,
he was told that an image was indeed on show, but only
on the sixth floor, where it was rare for anyone other than
bosses and their assistants to spend any meaningful amount
of time.

The team did get to make a seasonal special, entitled
'Christmas Crackers', which was filmed on 23 December and
broadcast five days later, but, once again, the episode – though
full of amusing observations about how tense, dull and tiresome
festive family gatherings sometimes can be – seemed to get
buried in the schedules without any noticeable attempts at
promotion. Attracting a very disappointing 7.5 million viewers,[6]
the experience only encouraged the suspicion that *Only Fools*
was being knowingly neglected by the powers-that-be at the
BBC.

The team felt increasingly that they were an embarrassment
to the BBC, but the then-Head of Light Entertainment, Jimmy
Gilbert, would later challenge such suggestions:

I'd been very surprised at how slowly it started, that's true,
but, then again, that'd happened often enough in the past
with other shows for you to hold your nerve and keep
faith. *Dad's Army, Last of the Summer Wine, Fawlty Towers* –
they all started quite slowly. So, at the time, I was very
disappointed – as anyone in my position would have been
– that *Only Fools* wasn't doing better, but I don't think
there was any despondency or anything like that. And,

speaking for myself, I certainly didn't want to 'hide the show away'. That would have been counter-productive and crazy! I really liked the show.[7]

It did nothing to discourage such suspicions, however, when the Head of Comedy, John Howard Davies, kept bumping into the writer and telling him 'I liked that other idea of yours . . .' – which Sullivan took as a sign that Davies was looking to drop the sitcom and steer him off in another direction. By the time that the series was over, therefore, and the so-called 'BBC silence' commenced, he harboured serious fears that the show was about to be axed: 'I started thinking that someone didn't want the show to continue so they decided to suffocate the baby at birth.'[8]

Eventually, the festering feelings of resentment, irritation and anxiety about the show's treatment and possible cancellation led to Sullivan and Butt arranging a meeting with John Howard Davies early in 1982. The executive proceeded to surprise them, very pleasantly, by making it clear that, regardless of his own misgivings, he was committed to them making a second series of seven episodes and also another Christmas special – 'The BBC, in those days, was patient,' Davies would say, 'and always tried to give sitcoms time and room to germinate, grow and develop properly and fully.'[9] He also assured them that he would ask the then-Controller of BBC1, Alan Hart, to move the next series to somewhere more favourable in the schedule. The troublesome issue of publicity remained largely unaddressed, and would thus continue to be a cause of concern, but Sullivan and Butt were still hugely relieved, as they left Davies's office, to know that the project would now have another chance to succeed.

Both men felt sure that they could do things to make the second series much more effective than the first. Sullivan, for example, now knew enough about the actors to tailor the characters to their particular talents.

'I did the first series of *Only Fools and Horses* without a pilot,' Sullivan later explained, 'so I wrote six episodes blind, not knowing who [the actors] were. Then we got David Jason and Nick Lyndhurst and made a few adjustments. Once I'd seen that first series, I was writing for them. You aim towards the strengths of the actor. You can hear the voice, see the face, see David's eyes, his looks, and Nick's open mouth. So a lot of the time Del would say something, and I'd just write: "Cut to Rod", knowing full well Nick would give you the most wonderful expression and you'd get a great big laugh on it.'[10]

Ray Butt was similarly confident about pushing the programme on. Now fully recovered from his back problems, he resumed full responsibility for direction as well as production, and concentrated on finding ways to fine-tune the programme. In most aspects, however, he was already very satisfied with how things were and could not wait to reassemble his team and start making more episodes: 'I just used to say, "Do it, boys",' he would recall. 'It was the easiest job in the world. I've always said I was lucky being paid good money to go out to work and laugh. It was an easy job thanks to the quality of the scripts and the calibre of the actors.'[11]

A few minor changes were made to the look of the show. The sets were slightly revised and rebuilt. The Trotters' lounge – which seemed somewhat dull and shadowy during the first series – was given a little more depth and brightened up, with the curtains (previously always closed) drawn open and the studio lighting increased to give the set a sharper, more accessible and traditional sitcom atmosphere. Some external scenes were now to be illustrated via a stop-action sequence of stills in order to lend the show a more playful and faster-paced element. Further work also went into the costumes associated with each key character: Del was given a set of monogrammed shirts, Rodney acquired a ska-style skinny tie and mix-'n'-match suit for more formal occasions and Grandad was allowed to look even scruffier than before.

John Sullivan, meanwhile, added a little more depth to each character's personality. Del would remain just as tough and tricky on the outside, but some of his inner frustrations would now be glimpsed on such occasions as when he laments the fact that he is still stuck inside 'a Lego set built by the council'. Rodney, though still gullible enough to play straight into the hands of those who see him as a 'plonker', would start harbouring even greater moral misgivings about his brother's 'He who dares, wins' policy, while his admission that he feels cheated that he lost his mother when he was so young would further underline his sense of bewilderment and vulnerability. Grandad was already too set in his ways to be changed significantly, although Sullivan would find the odd reason to shake him out of his sedentary lifestyle and invest him with a little more edge and energy.

The writer, in general, was greatly encouraged by the fact that all three of his main actors were already so supportive of his long-term ambition to explore the more delicate areas of each character's emotional map and balance the light with the shade. David Jason, in particular, had started urging Sullivan from a very early stage to trust in his own instincts about drama as well as comedy. 'He kept pushing me,' Sullivan would recall. 'He'd say things like: "Don't ever be frightened to write anything, just go with it." I remember telling him that I'd like to write more about emotions and have some pathos in the scripts, which I'd tried out before but found I'd scared actors off because they wanted to play everything with a smile. But David kept saying: "Push the barriers and go as far as you want." That was a tremendous help to know that I didn't have to feel embarrassed about it; I could write something and know full well that the actor was behind it one hundred per cent.'[12]

One further thing that helped bring a sense of authenticity both to the scripts and the performances was the fact that, at the heart of the production, were three men – Sullivan, Jason and Butt – who shared the same sort of working-class London background. 'There was a tremendous amount of empathy between us,' Jason would confirm. 'Time and again, John would bring dialogue into the script that we'd used when we were lads, that wasn't heard any more. I'd read a line in a script and that would spark off another one in me, either that my father had said or we had said as kids.'[13]

In another move to accentuate the London sound as well as the look, Butt and Sullivan managed to persuade John Howard Davies to let them replace Ronnie Hazlehurst's original, somewhat anonymous and anodyne, theme tune with Sullivan's own more distinctive effort, on the grounds that the new version would at least explain the significance of the title. It was also agreed that the closing credits would be better served by another song that Sullivan had composed called 'Hooky Street':

We've got some half-priced cracked-ice
And miles and miles of carpet tiles
TVs, deep-freeze and David Bowie LPs
Pool games, gold chains, wossanames
And at a push
Some Trevor Francis track-suits
From a mush in Shepherd's Bush, Bush, Bush, Bush

No income tax, no VAT
No money back, no guarantee.
Black or white, rich or broke
We'll cut prices at a stroke

God bless Hooky Street
Long live Hooky Street
C'est magnifique Hooky Street
Magnifique Hooky Street, Hooky Street. . .

The plan was to enlist the services of Chas & Dave, with the assistance of Ronnie Hazlehurst, to record the songs. Sullivan had even described the theme tune, in his original script, as sounding like 'Chas & Dave-style rockney'. The problem was, however, that the duo had recently made a breakthrough in terms of chart success with a more romantic sort of song entitled 'Ain't No Pleasing You', which had reached Number 2 in the UK during March 1982 and thus launched them on an unprecedented international promotional campaign. When Butt tried to contact them, therefore, they were on tour abroad and proved to be frustratingly elusive.

The singer and pianist Chas Hodges would later explain: 'We were in Australia at the time and "Ain't No Pleasing You"

was still in the charts in England and it had just got to Number
1 in Australia. And, quite rightfully, our manager said, "I think
I should say yes, you'll do it if you write it." But they said,
"Oh, it's already written," so we said, "OK, we'll pass.'"[14]

John Sullivan was hugely disappointed – not just because
he felt the song suited them so well but also because he knew
that their involvement would have been invaluable in helping
to promote the show: 'That was a bit of a choker because if
they'd done our theme that might have gone to number one,
too.'[15] The writer was then greatly surprised by how calmly
and pragmatically Ray Butt (later described by Sullivan as a
'clever sod') responded to the setback: 'He said, "Don't worry.
Come down to the studio, we've got someone." So I've gone
to Lime Grove, we'd had a couple of drinks, and I said: "Who
is he?" He said: "It's you, mate." I said: "I can't do that!" Anyway,
nine lagers later, I'm in there, and I did it. And I told my wife:
"Oh, Ray got some pub singer in.'"[16]

When location work on the new series began early in April
1982 (the same time that the Falklands conflict between
Argentina and Britain broke out), Butt, Sullivan and the rest
of the team were full of enthusiasm for all of the hard but
light-hearted work ahead. Apart from the obvious camaraderie
among the crew, the key members of the cast, too, were clearly
attuned as a talented troupe.

Lennard Pearce, for example, could not quite believe his
luck to be part of such an enjoyable show after coming so
close to calling time on his career, and his easygoing nature
and excellent professionalism had quickly endeared him to
everyone involved. David Jason and Nicholas Lyndhurst had
also struck up a near-instant friendship that further enhanced
their obvious on-screen rapport. Both of them were the kind

of men who eschewed the 'show business' lifestyle (with Jason preferring to lose himself in such hobbies as renovating vintage motorcycles, and Lyndhurst favouring outdoor sports), but both of them enjoyed working hard – and playing hard – on the set. 'When I read a script,' Lyndhurst would say, 'I know how he is going to play a scene and say a line and I'm sure he knows in advance how I'm going to play my lines. So there are no big surprises when we get together. We just get on terribly well.'[17] A sign of how high morale now was occurred when the actors started to tease not only each other but also, at times, the rest of the team as a whole.

During the first week, for example, while based at Studland Bay near Bournemouth in Dorset, the crew heard what sounded like a blazing row break out at lunchtime between David Jason and Nicholas Lyndhurst in the Winnebago that they shared. Suddenly, after the shouting had grown louder, the door flew open and Lyndhurst marched out, barking expletives at Jason as his co-star responded by bleating something equally offensive back in his direction. As the rest of the team, waiting around for their lunch, stood about looking mortified, messages were sent off to John Sullivan, who was back in London, urging him to come as soon as possible and do what he could to smooth things over. Just before he set off, however, he received another call to say that Jason and Lyndhurst – after a few more tense hours of apparent antipathy – had collapsed in a fit of giggles and admitted that the whole thing had been a hoax.

Another cathartic prank during location work took place on the occasion of Nicholas Lyndhurst's twenty-first birthday, on 20 April. In keeping with his unassuming personality, he had told few of his colleagues about the personal significance of the date, but was still somewhat disappointed when not a single person mentioned anything about it, let alone bothered to buy him a present. Lunchtime came and went without the arrival of a birthday cake, but, when shooting for the day was over, he set off expecting to share a drink with the rest of the film unit at the hotel bar. Once again, however, he was left disappointed, as everyone seemed to have made prior engagements and hurried off elsewhere for dinner.

When David Jason eventually came down from his room, Lyndhurst was sufficiently frustrated to reveal his secret and suggest that they do something – anything – to celebrate the event. Jason expressed surprise and immediately offered to buy his young friend a drink. Jason then proposed playing a practical joke on Lennard Pearce by sneaking down to the gym – which was being used by the unit as a wardrobe room – and super-gluing Pearce's shoes to the floor. As the two of them entered the room, however, Lyndhurst was shocked to find Lennard Pearce, along with all of the rest of the cast and crew, waiting there for him with champagne, flags, banners and piles of presents. He was so overcome that he was close to tears.

Such occasions were welcome distractions during what was a very intense shooting schedule. As was normal for sitcom productions, every external scene for the entire series had to be filmed in that one short space of time, with the actors having to move quickly from one storyline and mood to the next, taking great care to ensure that, when it came to recording the rest of each episode in the studio a month or so later, each link to and from the location footage would look and feel flawless. The levels of concentration thus had to be exceptionally high, and, as a consequence, any brief moments of fun proved invaluable in maintaining a relaxed and positive mood.

Once all of the outdoor sequences had been completed, attention turned to the work still to be done back inside the studio at Television Centre. The technical preparations began, and so did the rehearsals. Encouraged by the location sessions, and excited by the quality of the scripts, the outlook was very good as the production progressed.

The seven recordings commenced on Sunday, 23 May and concluded on Sunday, 27 June. Probably the most surprised member of the studio audience, on that first night, was none other than the wife of John Sullivan, because, when the opening credits rolled on the monitors, she was expecting to hear the 'pub singer' whom her husband had said would be singing the song he had composed. 'When we went into the studio for the show,' he would recall, 'she was in the audience and she said to me she just froze when she heard my voice and she couldn't enjoy the show. Actually, she didn't realise there was an end number as well coming . . . So that was a bad night for her.'[18]

Once again, much to the team's disappointment, the series received barely any promotional help before it was due to reach the screen. The *Radio Times* came up with another throwaway reference, but, other than that, the media attention was minimal. It came as no great surprise to John Sullivan, Ray Butt and all of the others, but it still caused them genuine distress. They really cared about this show, and they believed, if it was given a proper chance, it would succeed.

The first episode, entitled 'The Long Legs of the Law', was broadcast at 8.30 p.m. on Thursday, 21 October. It was, true to John Howard Davies's word, a good slot for a sitcom at a better time of the week – when many viewers' spirits were starting to rise as the weekend was coming in sight – and

hopes were high among those willing the show to start, belatedly, to advance.

The episode concerned Rodney's strange weakness for
women in uniform, which leads him to start dating someone
– called Sandra – who turns out to be a policewoman. Grandad
is horrified because of the Trotter traditions – 'What are the
neighbours gonna say?' – and Del, who has just dumped a box
of knocked-off watches in the flat, is disgusted: 'He's kinky!'
Things get worse when Rodney brings her up to the flat, and
Del spots that he has given her one of their dodgy watches.

The episode – a simple enough but well-told story – was
compromised (not for the last time) by a rather wooden
performance by the guest actor, but there were still some good
moments and numerous excellent exchanges of dialogue. One
clash between Del, Rodney and Grandad was particularly
pertinent in terms of developing the character dynamics:

RODNEY: What have you ever done for me?
DEL: What have I done for you? *I brought you up!*
          I fed you, I clothed you, I picked you up
          when you fell down, I wiped your . . . tears
          away, but most important of all, Rodney, I've
          always been there. I have *always* been there!
RODNEY: *[Embarrassed]* Besides that . . .
DEL: Always used to take you away on holidays
          . . .
RODNEY: Oh yeah – the Costa del Kent! That's right,
          yeah! You used to create therapeutic little
          adventure games, didn't you, like 'Let's see
          who can pick up the most hops today,
          Rodney.'

DEL: Hopping was all we could afford, weren't it, Grandad?

GRANDAD: You've either got a short memory, Rodney, or you're just ungrateful. Don't you remember the time when your little mate, Roy Taylor, got a set of Jacko roller skates for his birthday? You came in crying 'cos you didn't have none. The next day Del Boy brought you in a pair exactly the same as Roy Taylor's!

RODNEY: What d'you mean –'exactly the same as Roy Taylor's'? They *were* Roy Taylor's! His big brother give me a right hiding when he caught me on 'em!

DEL: Yeah, I got him back for you, though, didn't I?

RODNEY: Yeah, fine consolation *that* was, weren't it? I'm sat in me bed with a split lip and an 'eadache!

DEL: All right, all right, then – who paid your fine when you got caught smoking pot?

RODNEY: Yeah . . . well, I could have handled that meself.

DEL: What, 300 quid? Do me a favour, Rodders! I remember when you got nicked for riding your motor scooter without a crash hat. You only got fined five quid and you asked for time to pay!

GRANDAD: You've always been a bad 'un, Rodney!

RODNEY: What? 'Cos I didn't wear a crash helmet?

GRANDAD: I mean smoking mari-jew-arna! You brought a slur upon the family name.

RODNEY: Oh, leave off, Grandad! I'd have to get done for chicken molesting to bring a slur on *this* family's name!

DEL: *Oi! Oi!* That's enough of *that!*

GRANDAD: It's a good thing your mum died when she did 'cos that would've killed her!

Subsequent episodes saw John Sullivan, slowly but surely, broaden the regular range of characters by bringing in a few more supporting characters. First Trigger returned for 'Ashes To Ashes', and then Boycie was reintroduced for 'A Losing Streak'.

The reason for Trigger's initial reappearance was the death of his grandmother, who, it turns out, was an old flame of none other than Grandad Trotter. In a farcical style of plot, Del decides to 'relieve' the slow-witted Trigger of a couple of lucrative-looking family heirlooms, but, after Grandad points out that one of the china urns in question contains the cremated remains of Trigger's grandfather, and Del Boy is persuaded that the contents are indeed what they seem ('How d'you know it's 'im, eh? It's hardly a passport photo!'), the challenge involves disposing of the human detritus.

The reason for Boycie's return was Del's desperate need to make some money so quickly that he gets drawn into a gambling habit. After relying first of all on his mother's 'lucky rabbit foot', and then his Grandad's 'double-headed coin', he ignores his younger brother's anxious admonitions ('You give my arse an 'eadache, Rodney!') and arranges a poker game at his flat. In one of Sullivan's occasional self-contained, Damon Runyanesque yarns (inspired initially by the writer's memories of his own father's gambling sessions), the rest of the action hinges on the game inside Nelson Mandela House, with a nervous Del playing cards against a dazed Trigger and a ruthlessly competitive Boycie.

Roger Lloyd Pack had already established his slyly simple but very effective portrayal of the rather docile Trigger in the previous series. 'I used certain qualities of myself,' he later explained, 'like what my father used to call dumb insolence. Whenever I got into trouble as a boy I'd adopt a blank expression, something I used for Trigger.' His aim had always been to resist the temptation to portray the character as a one-dimensional stooge, so he sought instead to suggest something quirky and perhaps even complex behind those dark and doleful eyes: 'From day one I tried making him believable. He says the most ridiculous things, so finding some truth in the character is where I started. I didn't want to play him stupid, that wouldn't be funny, [so] I played him from his point of view, as if he was intelligent.'[19]

John Challis, meanwhile, now seized on the chance here to bring his own vision of Boycie fully to life. Regarding him as 'a bit of a lord of the manor' figure who revels in the regalia of his occasional financial successes, Challis saw Boycie as a chippy but secretly insecure type, a mock-toff residing proudly inside his mock-Georgian house and parading around the area looking brashly suited and booted.

Boycie's nasally, braying voice was something that came to Challis the moment he read John Sullivan's first few lines: he drew on characters he had met, including a particular man – called Gordon – from the St Margaret's Hotel, Twickenham, to pull together Boycie's uniquely uninformed, but menacing, ennui. Gordon was one of those people who would always turn up in the pub on his own and then start bothering the other customers, volunteering his opinions on a wide range of topics, addressing each assertion with an unnerving air of authority. Challis was drawn particularly to the tragic-comic quality that came with this glibly garrulous man's self-delusion: 'For a long time no one was ever quite sure what he did for a living. They'd say, "What do you actually do, Gordon?" and he'd say, "Well actually I can't really talk about it, suffice to say it's something to do with the electronics business." People then assumed that it must be something top secret, to do with rockets or something. It turned out that he was a travelling salesman selling video recorders and record players. He was a fantasist really but a riveting character who I sort of liked but thought he was ridiculous as well.'[20]

Challis eased back into the show as Boycie with aplomb. One slight problem that David Jason encountered during the same 'A Losing Streak' episode, however, came in the middle of an emotional scene in which he recalled for Rodney how their father had deserted them, leaving him, at the age of sixteen, to defend the remaining family no matter how frightened he might have felt about assuming such responsibility. 'From that day,' said Del, 'I swore that I would never run away from anything in my life. I mean, you know, if a wild lion were to come in here now my old April'd be pouting like a good 'un, but I'd stand me ground!' The problem for Jason was that he did not understand some of the new slang that Sullivan – always eager to make his characters sound contemporary – had introduced.

Jason later explained: 'I had to say to Rodney or somebody, "I was so worried that my old April was pouting like a good 'un," and I said to John Sullivan, "What is *that*?" He said: "It's modern day Cockney rhyming slang."' Jason continued: 'So I said: "What does it *mean?*" He said: "Well, my old April – April in Paris, Harris, Aristotle, Bottle, Bottle and Glass = Arse." So I said: "John, that'll *never* get a laugh!" He said: "Yeah, it will, they'll all know it." So there in front of an audience, I said: "I was so worried that my old April was pouting like a good 'un", and the audience were completely silent. John Sullivan, he was up in the box, he laughed. But that was just one moment I've never forgotten because it did absolutely stop the show – it stopped me and I did warn him. Everybody had to say, "What did it mean?""[21]

The fourth episode – 'No Greater Love' – saw Rodney succumb, yet again, to his romantic obsessions, falling this time for a woman twice his age who turns out to be the estranged wife of a violent convict. When her husband gets out of prison, he soon discovers about the affair and vows to take his revenge, prompting Del, in the first of many acts of big brotherly bravery, to protect Rodney from a certain beating.

It was the next episode in the series, entitled 'The Yellow Peril', that explored the peculiar tensions between the entrepreneurial and sentimental sides of Del's psyche. It began with Del and Rodney sitting in the cemetery, the older brother's arm around the younger brother's shoulder, by their mother's grandly elaborate marble-looking monument:

RODNEY: It's looking a bit tatty nowadays.

DEL: I don't know, it's not too bad. It's bound to
                 be a bit iffy, after seventeen years, innit? I
                 mean, so would you if you'd been standing
                 out there for seventeen years with pigeons
                 and diesel fumes and other mourners stubbing
                 their cigarette ends out on you. I dunno,

maybe you could be right. It could do with brightening up a bit. Yeah, if I added some fibreglass models, of say, an apostle and four cherubims with trumpets, do you think it would alter the effect?

RODNEY: If you added fibreglass models of Snow White and the seven dwarfs you couldn't alter the effect of that!

DEL: Oi, oi, *oi* – don't start getting sacrificial! I don't know what's the matter with you, Rodney, really I don't! You seem to have no sense of occasion. You've no . . . *très bien ensembles*, as the French say. I mean, look at you now, loafing about round your mother's graveside. Don't you feel any emotion?

RODNEY: Now look Del, I didn't know Mum that well, did I? When she died I was just a little nipper-ooni, all odd socks and eczema! Now you feel a sense of personal loss – me . . . I just feel . . . cheated.

DEL: I'm sorry Rodney. I should have realised . . . Our Mum was a wonderful woman . . . She had long golden blonde hair . . . sometimes. Every night you'd see her sitting at the bar in The Nag's Head in her simulated beaverskin, with her rum and pep in one hand, 20 Senior Service in the other. She looked like a *lady* – you know, lots of people mistook her for a money lender!

RODNEY: Really?

DEL: Yeah, straight up! Course, I was a lot younger then and didn't have much money, but every

night she used to send across two or three
pints of light bitter, or whisky if she was flush.
That was Mum . . . Then come about ten
o'clock, she'd look over where I was sitting
and she'd shout, 'Come on, Del Boy, get off
home to bed – school in the morning!' That
was the kind of woman she was, concerned
about our welfare!

The penultimate instalment, 'It Never Rains . . . ', was another
self-contained little story about Del trying to secure himself,
his brother and their grandad a free holiday in Benidorm. They
do end up going there (although it was actually filmed in a
very chilly Bournemouth), but only at their own expense, and
Grandad's improbably eventful past comes back to haunt him
when he stumbles into contact with the local police. Surprisingly
little happens, given the initial possibilities of the scenario
(indeed, if there was a problem with Sullivan's early scripts it
was that they often promised more than they delivered, with
the plot sometimes petering out due to the vast amount of
dialogue), but a rambling anecdote from Grandad at least
allowed Lennard Pearce more screen time than usual in which
to impress.

It was the final episode of the series, 'A Touch of Glass',
that would lift the show to a new level. It would do so not
merely for the high quality of the episode as a whole, but,
even more so, by providing the kind of comic climax that
was destined to be regarded as one of the all-time classic
sitcom moments.

Any sitcom with pretensions to greatness needs one or more
of such moments to help push it up into the pantheon, providing

sharply bright jewels for the comic crown. *Hancock,* for example, had one with 'The Blood Donor' (broadcast on 23 June 1961), when he famously debated with a doctor the wisdom of extracting 'very nearly an armful' of blood from his body. *Steptoe and Son* had one with 'Divided We Stand' (broadcast on 27 March 1972), which saw the rowing Albert and Harold try to move on by co-existing on either side of a hastily made partition. *Whatever Happened to the Likely Lads?* came up with another in 'No Hiding Place'(broadcast 20 February 1973), when Terry and Bob attempted to avoid hearing or seeing the result of a football match until they could settle down to watch the highlights safely on TV. *Dad's Army* secured one of its own in 'The Deadly Attachment'(broadcast 31 October 1973), when Pike, perched up a ladder while guarding over some Germans, was asked by the enemy for his name, prompting Mainwaring to bark, 'Don't tell him, Pike!' *Fawlty Towers* also supplied one in 'Gourmet Night', (broadcast 17 October 1975), when an exasperated Basil gets out and gives his car 'a damned good thrashing,' and, of course, the same show delivered another example in 'The Germans' (broadcast 24 October 1975), when a semi-concussed Fawlty kept failing to avoid mentioning the war.

These moments not only made wonderful episodes seem extra-special; they also went on to pass almost immediately into the public consciousness, prompting light-hearted conversations in the office, school and street and eventually acquiring a kind of adjectival authority in ordinary life. Once such moments are embedded in the memory, they impinge on our impression of, among other things, squabbles with doctors, slips of the tongue and bitter battles with inanimate objects. No matter how serious the occasion might be, a comic echo is audible, and many of us thus feel compelled to liken each particular instance to one of those scenes that we all seem to share.

In the case of *Only Fools and Horses*, the first great moment arrived on Thursday, 2 December 1982, when 'A Touch of Glass' was first broadcast. The action begins at a small country auction, where Del, Rodney and Grandad have gone in the hope of picking up some bargain stock, but depart with nothing but a large collection of wind-up china cats that play 'How Much Is That Doggy In The Window?'[20] Soon after they have set off on the long drive home in their chronically misfiring Reliant Regal, they stop to assist a woman whose car has broken down. Impressed to find out that she is actually Lady Ridgemere, who resides with her husband at the very grand Ridgemere Hall estate,[23] they become even more eager to help.

After towing her car back to the impressive stately home ('Bet you've held a few balls in 'ere, my lady!'), Del overhears the haughty Lord Ridgemere complaining on the telephone about the problems he is experiencing with the company he hired to clean a couple of his Louis XIV chandeliers. Seizing his opportunity, Del 'reveals' that he and his fellow Trotters are in fact specialist cleaners of quality crystal, and offers to give the aristocrat's two precious chandeliers a thorough wash and polish for the cut-price fee of £350. Lord Ridgemere cannot resist, and so, after a quick trip back to Nelson Mandela House to grab some Windolene and superglue, they return to put up the ladders, spread out the sheets and finish the job.

Lord Ridgemere's white-haired and florid-faced butler, Wallace (played perfectly by Donald Bissett), is there to monitor the exercise, but, after he expresses his concerns about Grandad going off with a hammer, a large screwdriver and a spanner to remove some of the floorboards upstairs, Del wastes no time in dismissing such a sceptical presence from the workplace:

WALLACE: Why does he have to remove the floorboards?
DEL: What is this, the International Year of the Wally-Brain or something? Listen, my good man, how do you think that great big heavy chandelier stays up there on that ceiling, eh? It is not by the power of prayer or double-sided sticky tape! There is a long threaded bolt through that chandelier, it goes through a wooden joist and is held in position by a locking nut. Now, in order to undo the locking nut you must first lift up the floor-boards. *Ordre du jour?*
WALLACE: We learn something new every day! If you need me I shall be round at the garages.
DEL: Right. Here – while yer there, give the van a wash, will you?

Now left to their own devices, the trio proceed to the most crucial part of the operation: getting both of the chandeliers down from the ceiling in one piece. While Grandad waits upstairs to undo the first locking nut, Del and Rodney climb the ladders underneath the first chandelier, holding a large canvas bag stretched out between them. With everything safely in place, Del shouts up to Grandad to go ahead and unscrew the nut while he and Rodney wait below to catch the lights when they fall. A couple of twisting noises later, Del and Rodney look up expectantly, Grandad says 'One more turn,

Del,' and then, as the brothers brace themselves beneath the first chandelier, the second chandelier comes crashing down at the other end of the room.

Del and Rodney stare at each other in silence, until Del mumbles redundantly, 'Grandad was undoing the other chandelier.' Rodney mumbles back blankly, 'How can you tell?' Once both of them climb down their ladders and Grandad descends the stairs, Wallace the butler arrives to survey the shocking scene: 'It's *broken!*' Realising that the game is up, Del tells Wallace to get Lord Ridgewell to contact them at home: DEL: 'Oh, by the way, has his lordship got our home address and telephone number?' WALLACE: 'No!' DEL: '*Good!*' With that, they are gone, and the episode ends.

The inspiration for the climactic moment had actually been a true story John Sullivan had been told by his father – a plumber by trade – as an example of why one should always check, and double-check, before attempting anything complicated:

> He told me about the time he was serving his apprenticeship and there was an incident at this manor house. Central heating was being installed in the property. There were two very expensive chandeliers hanging in the house, so for safety's sake they had to take them down. While one chap nipped upstairs to undo the bolts from underneath the floorboards in the room above, the others were up this ladder holding one of the chandeliers. They all said, 'Yeah, we're ready.' The trouble was, the man upstairs undid the wrong chandelier and it crashed to the ground.[24]

His son's reaction to this story was predictable, even though, like the chandelier, it did not go down well with Sullivan

Senior: 'I was on the floor laughing, and he was really angry with me. He said, "Fifteen men got the sack for that!" And of course, he was talking about the times when if you got the sack you could almost starve. So it was very serious to him.'[25]

When Sullivan was having a drink in the BBC bar a few days later with David Jason and Ray Butt, he could not resist retelling the tale, and, immediately, Jason said: 'You've *got* to use it.' Sullivan agreed, but it took him a while to find a plausible reason as to why the Trotters should find themselves in a country mansion. Once this aspect of the storyline had been established, he had to write his script from 'back to front', starting with his ready-made denouement and then adding all of the preliminary events.

Filming the final part of the episode was an unusually tense affair, because everyone knew that, with only one fake but still quite expensive chandelier (made for the BBC by a props company called Trading Post for the sum of about £6,000) to smash, its success hinged entirely upon capturing the most crucial scene in a single perfect take. If anyone made a mistake, or laughed, or the chandelier landed in slightly the wrong place or at slightly the wrong time, the entire episode would be wrecked. One of the designers, Andy Dimond, later recalled the keen sense of anticipation as the scene was about to be recorded:

Waiting on the ground floor were three cameras, ready to film the moment. I sat myself down on the staircase for a grandstand view, then Ray Butt, the director, called 'Action!' and gave the signal for the electrical bolt to fire. We had just a few seconds to the drop and at that moment I turned away. Then I heard the sound of breaking glass followed by 30 seconds of deathly silence. Should I look back? Suddenly people were clapping and mayhem broke out – it had gone to plan.[26]

Ray Butt, who had warned Nicholas Lyndhurst that he would fire him if he laughed and spoiled the scene, reacted to the stunt by turning his back on the actors and stuffing a hand-kerchief into his mouth to stifle any noises. As they looked over at the director from their ladders, all that they could see were his shoulders going up and down, rapidly but silently. Once someone had shouted 'Cut!' Lyndhurst climbed down and took revenge on his director: 'I swore my head off at him!'[27]

The result, on the screen, was a wonderful moment of television – surprising, extraordinarily funny and superbly choreographed. It was one of those sights that made viewers want to think and talk about it the following morning, and, indeed, on countless occasions ahead. *Only Fools*, right at the end of its second season, had genuinely impressed itself on the memory.

The only problem was that not enough people had been watching. A total of 10.2 million had seen 'A Touch of Glass' – the highest so far for the show and the ninth largest audience for BBC1 during that week[28] – but the series as a whole had only averaged just under 9 million (about 2 million fewer than the much-maligned *Terry and June*[29]), and, each week, the show had lost the channel more than a million of the viewers who had been watching the previous programme, the Ronnie Corbett sitcom *Sorry!* The data was a huge disappointment to all concerned. The show did reappear twice at the end of the year – first on 27 December as an eight-minute comic short called 'Christmas Trees' that formed part of a Frank Muir compendium called *The Funny Side of Christmas*, and then as a nicely observed but somewhat downbeat Christmas special, entitled 'Diamonds are for Heather', on 30 December – but that, feared the team, could well turn out to be that.

Everyone involved agreed that the second series could and should have made a much bigger impact at a time when there was relatively little else on show in the comedy landscape to capture the attention of fans and critics alike. The BBC's strongest sitcom of the year, in terms of its performance in the ratings, had probably been the cosily conventional *Last of the Summer Wine* (which was drawing in around 16 million viewers[30]), followed – with painful irony for David Jason – by *Open All Hours* (with a weekly audience of approximately 13 million[31]) and the nostalgic Croft and Perry vehicle *Hi-de-Hi!* (which was averaging about 12 million[32]), while ITV's most-watched example of the genre was a very ordinary edition of *The Benny Hill Show* (which attracted an audience of 17.95 million[33]). The timely and lively *Only Fools and Horses*, in such a comparatively dull and uninspiring context, ought to have shone out and sparkled, but instead, to the bafflement of all those concerned, it had remained stuck in the shadows.

Most of the reviewers had remained unmoved throughout the run, and, once it was over, the internal 'BBC silence' returned, and the future for *Only Fools* looked very bleak indeed. After going out with such a bang, all that were left were whimpers.

A mood of fatalism was fast descending: sometimes, for no apparent reason, not enough of the public takes to a promising new show, it atrophies through indifference and quietly fades away. It appeared to be happening to *Only Fools*. Early in 1983, John Sullivan's agent called him to suggest that it was probably time for him to look around for another project. The dream really did seem to be over.

CHAPTER SIX

The Great Escape

Fromage frais!

John Sullivan was on holiday when it happened. Quite unexpectedly, and very belatedly, *Only Fools and Horses* acquired a proper following.

It resulted from industrial action. There was a technicians' strike at the BBC, and, as several of the current productions ground to a halt and numerous outside broadcasts were disrupted, gaps started to appear in the upcoming schedules.[1] More out of a sense of desperation than of any degree of great faith, one of the many repeats chosen to fill up the airtime was *Only Fools and Horses*.

Beginning at 8.30 p.m. on Tuesday, 5 July 1983, the second series started a repeat run on BBC1 – and, more or less immediately, the episodes ignited a much stronger and broader interest in the show. The ratings – bearing in mind that the shows were repeats and audiences during the summer almost always had a tendency to slump – were encouraging (averaging around 7.7 million viewers[2]), and, as the run went on, both the Head of Comedy, John Howard Davies, and the Controller of BBC1, Alan Hart, felt that they had glimpsed enough green buds of recovery to commission another series.

Ironically, John Sullivan was, by this time, close to completing the scripts for another sitcom: *Just Good Friends* – about the on-off romance of a thirty-something couple, which was set to co-star Paul Nicholas and Jan Francis, and be produced and directed by Ray Butt. At that stage in the summer, however, he was taking a brief break with his family and still licking his wounds over what he regarded as the premature ending of *Only Fools*: 'My wife and I had two kids by then, so we decided to take a caravan holiday in Hastings. I was really down in the dumps.'[3] The success of the repeats thus came as a great surprise: 'One day I went out and bought a *Daily Mirror* and I came back and sat at the table reading it. And they used to give you the Top TV [chart], and suddenly . . . there's *Only Fools and Horses* at number five!'[4] The next episode, he would be thrilled to discover, figured even higher in the list. The public, it seemed, had finally noticed the show. 'God bless whoever decided to schedule them,' he later reflected about the repeats. 'From that moment, the show's popularity increased.'[5]

With *Just Good Friends* slated to make its debut on BBC1 later in the year at the end of September, the prospect of *Only Fools and Horses* suddenly being recommissioned presented Sullivan with something of a headache as far as his writing commitments were concerned, but, nonetheless, he was delighted by the news of its unexpected revival. He was even more pleased and excited when, a short while later, the BBC decided to improve its offer and a fourth series was added. It felt, he would say, as if a degree of security had, at long last, arrived in his professional life: 'If you are from a working-class background and you are fortunate enough to crack this business, until you've actually had that success, you are writing for your money. You write scared almost and you worry about every idea you get, and you tend to think that some of them are just too outrageous, and that can make you think of holding back and doing a nice script that doesn't offend, because your money relies on it'.[6]

Overworked though he was, Sullivan now felt that his old project was valued by the BBC, and a sense of vindication drove him on to do it justice. He wanted to bring in more characters like Trigger and Boycie, write some better and more interesting female characters, and draw out the drama as well as the comedy. He proceeded to write, therefore, with the intensity of a man determined to prove a point. Although he knew that there was barely enough time to deliver the first batch of scripts, he could now plan ahead and do his best to make the sitcom evolve.

Ray Butt – although, like Sullivan, somewhat daunted by the sudden doubling of his workload – was similarly delighted to be back, as producer–director, developing a third series. Quickly putting together another very proficient production team – which this time included Denise Brown as make-up designer, Dinah Collin as costume designer, Ian Hilton as cameraman and Clive Derbyshire as sound recordist, Antony Thorpe as designer and Andy Smith as production manager – he raced through the preparations, reassembled the cast and was ready to start location filming (most of which, in part for reasons of time and convenience, would take place in and around London) on Friday, 2 September.

The third series, rushed through in near-record time, reached the screen at 8.30 p.m. on Thursday, 10 November 1983 with an episode entitled 'Homesick'. The plot revolved around Grandad's supposed concerns about his age, as his complaints about the strain placed on his body by the daily walk up and down the twelve floors of Nelson Mandela House lead to a visit to the doctor's and the recommendation that the Trotters relocate to somewhere on the ground floor. Rodney, having just been made chairman of the Housing Committee, is soon nudged by Del into persuading the housing and welfare co-ordinator to take pity on Grandad and move the family into a much more appealing bungalow in nearby Harrington Road. Things fall apart when the supposedly frail and failing Grandad is spotted up and about puffing on a cigar, and, much to Rodney's embarrassment, the deal falls through.

The first sign of things moving forward, in terms of character development, was Rodney's role in this opening episode. He seemed, right from the start, to be a little more mature and aggressive than the naive and pliable 'plonker' of before, ready – at certain times – to mock his big brother and his mates. Right at the start, for example, he responds sneeringly to Del's boast about the date he has 'blagged' with a waitress from the local Pizza Palace:

RODNEY: How did *you* manage to pull her?
DEL: Well, I read somewhere that women were turned on by men in situations of power. So I told her I was a Euro Minister.
RODNEY: She must be thicker than them pizzas she dishes out!

Later on, in The Nag's Head, he even dares, at long last, to question Trigger about his apparent inability to call him by his proper name:

RODNEY: Trigger – why d'you call me Dave? My name's *not* Dave. My name's Rodney.

TRIGGER: I thought it was Dave!

RODNEY: No, it's *Rodney!*

TRIGGER: You sure?

RODNEY: Yeah, I'm positive! I've looked it up on me birth certificate and passport and everything! It is *definitely* Rodney!

TRIGGER: Oh well, you live 'n' learn. So what's Dave – a nickname, like?

RODNEY: No. *You're* the only one who calls me Dave. Everybody else calls me Rodney, and the reason they call me Rodney is because Rodney is my name!

TRIGGER: Oh well, I shall have to get used to calling you Rodney!

RODNEY: Thank you.

None of Rodney's protestations will result in any increase in respect, and Trigger will continue to call him 'Dave', but his greater readiness to challenge those around him will add a sharper edge to the subsequent exchanges.

His combativeness continued in the (much stronger) second episode, 'Healthy Competition', when he snaps with frustration at still being a mere look-out on a market stall and announces that he is going to set up a rival business to Trotters Independent Traders by teaming up with his old friend and occasional foe, Mickey Pearce. The character of Pearce had previously only been mentioned in certain episodes, but the actor Patrick Murray had been monitored and discussed for two years before finally being cast as a character who was envisaged as a kind of 'Del-lite' type. Ray Butt had noticed the young actor in a television commercial for Pizza Hut and thought he might suit the show's working-class milieu. When he was hired for this episode, he struck up a near-instant rapport with Lyndhurst and the rest of the cast, and settled easily into the comic context.

The other interesting aspect of the episode was another insight into Del Boy's sensitive side. After outwitting Rodney and Mickey Pearce at an auction, and hearing about how Pearce had reacted by abandoning Rodney and slipping off for an unearned break in Benidorm, Del lets his younger brother squirm for a while but then secretly arranges a way for Rodney to save face. He pays a friend to buy the rubbish that Rodney bought at auction, allowing his brother to think that he has proved a point: 'I want him to think that he's been successful,' Del tells his mate. 'I want him to believe that he's proved me wrong. It's important.' The fact that Rodney ruins the ruse by taking his profit and reinvesting it in more of the same worthless stock does not spoil the gesture: the brothers' emotional ties to each other are seen to tighten.

The comic highlight of the whole show came about due to the droll Lennard Pearce's excellent timing of his one significant line. Sitting in the lounge as usual, listening to his two grandchildren arguing, he remains silent as Rodney tries to convince Del that he is still in a position to go it alone as a budding businessman, boasting about his new plans to invest in the self-catering holiday trade. When Del finally interrupts him to ask how he expects to do this with only £200 to his name, Rodney blusters that he is starting out in 'a small way'. It is at this point that Grandad looks up and exclaims, 'What you got – a Wendy house?' The line provoked such a loud and long bout of laughter from the studio audience that it threatened to bring the recording to a halt, and both Jason and Lyndhurst had to resist the temptation to 'corpse' when they struggled to resume their dialogue. After the filming was over, David Jason came back out to meet the audience and joked: 'I'm going to resign. That's it. I don't want to be in this show any more. Do you realise that Nick Lyndhurst and myself have spent twenty minutes in this show working our socks off? Lennard Pearce hasn't said a bloody word in the whole show and he just says "Wendy House" and it gets the biggest laugh I've ever had!'[7] From that point on, the team rated all laughs on a sliding scale of 'Wendys', from a full-blown Wendy, down to a 'sub-Wendy', and then a 'mini-Wendy'.

One thing that seemed very much the same in any series of *Only Fools and Horses*, so far, was the episode that stood out as a slightly jarring, self-contained, shaggy dog-style sort of 'yarn', and, in this third run, not one but two episodes in succession fitted that bill. First, the instalment entitled 'Friday the 14th' flopped in terms of logic even though it generated its fair share of laughter. A strained tale of a salmon-fishing expedition to Cornwall that ends up with Del, Rodney and Grandad being terrorised by a murderous escapee from the local institute for the criminally insane, the episode made little sense. The quality of the dialogue, along with the usual splendid standard of acting, was good enough to generate the requisite number of entertaining moments, but, nonetheless, the story seemed to belong to an entirely different sitcom. The series really appeared in danger of sinking into a rut, however, when the next episode, 'Yesterday Never Comes', arrived with another overly mannered tale – this time about Del almost being 'stung' by a female grifter posing as a 'posh tart' antiques expert. Apart from the fact that, once again, the one-off female character was rendered irritatingly ineffectual and unconvincing by the combination of an under-written role and some painfully wooden acting, the entire episode seemed rushed, awkward and forced as the dialogue took a distant second place to the plot.

Mercifully, the series suddenly switched right back on track with the fifth episode, 'May the Force Be With You', which featured the first appearance of Jim Broadbent as Del's (and seemingly everyone else's) childhood *bête noire*, Roy Slater. It was ironic that Broadbent, having been forced due to other commitments to turn down the offer to play Del, was now in the show as that character's most hated foe, but he was very content with how things had worked out and was simply delighted to act with, rather than instead of, David Jason. 'I don't know that I would have been as successful as David in the part,' he would later say.'David and Del Boy were a marriage made in heaven.'[8]

The episode was once again driven by a fairly elaborate plot, but, on this occasion, it also found room for plenty of fine comic dialogue and some excellent interplay between the talented character actors. Broadbent's wonderfully oleaginous brand of menace, grinning like an alligator just before it snaps at its vulnerable prey, brought out some fascinating reactions from the regular figures, and also helped to highlight those qualities that made Del, in spite of his own failings, such a likeable kind of rascal.

The reason for Roy Slater's unexpected and most unwelcome appearance in The Nag's Head concerns, ostensibly, the reported theft of a microwave oven. Slater, it transpires, is now not only a policeman, but has also been recently promoted to the rank of Detective Inspector. As soon as he spots Trigger and Boycie at the bar, he orders a large scotch and starts to make them squirm immediately with his sharp little eyes and sinister smile.

He toys with Trigger like a cat with a mouse, confusing him with his questions, and then he causes the normally brash and bossy Boycie to stumble over his words as he glances anxiously from side to side. The pair of them at least manage to protect the absent Del by claiming that he will soon be emigrating ('Emigrating?' says Slater sarcastically. 'Yes, I bet these developing nations are crying out for fly-pitchers!'), but then the nosy DI comes into contact with Rodney, who is too young to know of his notoriety and is therefore quite happy to chat to this old 'schoolfriend' of his big brother, telling him about Del's sudden interest in microwave ovens and inviting him to pop up to the flat at Nelson Mandela House for a nice surprise 'reunion' dinner (RODNEY: 'I can't wait to see his face when you come through the door, eh?' SLATER: 'It'll be a picture, Rodney, it'll be a picture!').

It is only when Slater arrives and he sees the terror in Del Boy's eyes that Rodney realises what a naive mistake he has made. While the unwanted guest makes himself at home in the lounge, Del takes Rodney off to the kitchen to quickly disabuse him: 'He's not an old mate – he's an Old Bill! And when I say an Old Bill – I *mean* an *Old Bill!* That geezer out there'd nick you for anything you did! In fact, he'd nick you for anything you *didn't* do and he wouldn't let a silly thing like innocence get in the way!' Rodney is apologetic but Del warns him to watch what he says because Slater specialises in turning small-time crooks into big-mouthed informers (RODNEY: 'He's got a few grasses, has he?' DEL: 'He ain't got a *few* grasses, Rodney – he got an entire *lawn!*'). Once they are back in the lounge, however, it is already too late: Grandad has just shown Slater Del's new microwave oven, so all three Trotters are duly arrested for handling stolen goods.

Down at the police station, Slater gets nowhere with his questioning until he starts interrogating Del on his own and scares him by threatening to plant some drugs on Rodney and arranging for Grandad to be left on his own. Still horrified by the prospect of becoming a 'copper's nark', but desperate to protect his nearest and dearest, a downbeat Del agrees eventually to make a deal with the devil: in return for immunity for the entire Trotter family, he will reveal the identity of the man who stole the microwave oven and thus become another grass. Slater is thrilled: 'Oh Del! Del Boy, that is *beautiful!* You would be one of my merry men! I'd have you in my pocket. I could bounce you about and make you dance whenever I felt bored! And if you ever stepped out of line, I'd let it be known on the streets that you're an informer!' The gloating DI gets the immunity granted in writing, invites Grandad and Rodney back in to watch the humiliation of his old foe, and then asks Del to surrender his secret:

SLATER: Righto, Del: who nicked it?

DEL: *[Indicating Rodney and Grandad]* They *are* free to go, ain't they?

SLATER: Yeah, they're free to go – no charges, they can leave whenever they like. OK – give me his name.

DEL: You've got nothing on me either?

SLATER: *[Losing his temper]* No! You've got an *immunity from prosecution!* You've got less chance of a pull than the Queen!

[Del signs the paper.]

DEL: Long as I know.

SLATER: Right, for the third and last time of asking: who nicked the microwave off the back of the lorry?

[Del, seemingly broken, looks round anxiously at Rodney and Grandad, then turns back to face Slater.]
DEL: I did!
[Smiling smugly, Del then hands the pen back to the horrified Slater and points at the signed guarantee of immunity.]

The loud cheers that could be heard from the studio audience as the closing credits rolled on was a sign of how successful the episode had been. John Sullivan's clever script, combined with the brilliant rapport between Broadbent and Jason, saw the kind of smooth shifts back and forth between the comic and the dramatic to which the show had always aspired. In the middle of an unusually rushed and uneven third series, it reminded people of just how rich, witty and engaging *Only Fools and Horses*, at its best, could be.

Why did it provide such a lift? Jim Broadbent's contribution certainly helped. Whereas some 'outsiders' can intrude into a sitcom and suddenly break the believability of the familiar fiction, shining a light on the limitations of the central figures, others, like Broadbent, can engage with the other personalities and make the regular characters seem more plausible than ever before.

There was already something of a tradition of great guest appearances adding something different, something fresh, energetic and intriguing, to already established and popular sitcoms. Peter Sellers had done so in an episode of *Sykes* ('Stranger') when he appeared as a deluded but dangerous ex-prisoner who was smitten with the character played by Hattie Jacques; Leonard Rossiter had done much the same in *Steptoe and Son* when he portrayed a psychotic but vulnerable escaped prisoner in an episode entitled 'The Desperate Hours'; Philip Madoc

John Sullivan, pictured in 1997 with Jim Trowers – the teacher who had sparked his interest in literature forty years earlier.
© Alex Lentati/Evening Standard/Rex Features

A working-class writer is something to be: 'I used to drive past the BBC's TV Centre in West London and look at it like a castle that I had to somehow or other breach.'
© Rex Features

Dennis Main Wilson:
the maverick BBC man
who acted as John
Sullivan's mentor.
© BBC Photo Library

'Power to the people!' Robert
Lindsay as Wolfie Smith,
Tooting's answer to
Che Guevara.
© BBC Photo Library

Nicholas Lyndhurst on the set of his first sitcom, *Butterflies*.
© BBC Photo Library

Jason with Ronnie Barker
and Lynda Baron in
Open All Hours, the sitcom
that underlined his comic
potential. © Daily Mail/
Rex Features

David Jason had to wait
patiently for the good roles
to arrive. Here he is, looking
distinctly unfulfilled, in the
ITV soap *Crossroads*.
© ITV/Rex Features

James Gilbert: although unconvinced by the title, he still ensured that *Only Fools and Horses* reached the screen. © BBC Photo Library

The *Only Fools and Horses* milieu: a world away from *Terry and June*. © BBC Photo Library

'It's very Laurel and Hardy in my mind,' David Jason said of the Del Boy–Rodney relationship.
'Because it's about an unknowing fool and a knowing fool.' © Mirrorpix

'Strained Relations': the
moment that a sense of
mortality intruded into
the British sitcom.
© BBC Motion
Gallery

'We're so sorry, Uncle
Albert': the passing of
another character is
marked on the screen.
© Rex Features

Meet Boomerang Trotter:
Buster Merryfield arrives as
the new old fool.

Michael Grade: the man who helped
Only Fools reach a broader audience.

TV

WHO'LL WIN THE HEAD-ON CLASH BETWEEN LONDON'S SHARPEST CHARACTERS?

It's Arfur v Del Boy

How poor Granville became a lovable street-wise trader

By GARTH PEARCE

DAVID Jason nearly lost his job of swaggering Del Boy in ONLY FOOLS AND HORSES (Christmas Day, BBC1, 7.30 p.m.).

Writer John Sullivan could not envisage Jason playing the fast-talking market trader with gold rings and bracelets, camel haired coat and more front than Blackpool.

Jason recalls: "He told the director : But he plays this bit of a loser Granville, in Open All Hours, doesn't he ? He was trying to say that in no way would I be good as Del Boy.

"Del is all mouth and trousers and will go up to a girl and say : 'Ello, darlin'.' But Granville would never have the nerve."

But now such is the popularity of Del, the BBC has put a 50-minute film of Only Fools and Horses — with Nicholas Lyndhurst, of course, playing Rodders—as the main Christmas Day programme.

"We have always wanted to do the show on film because it promotes a quality of its own, like Minder," said David.

It meant a month's filming in Hull, Yorkshire during summer. "Del loves being out of London — because there's a different set of people to con.

"He feels that the world is his oyster and all the people in it are mysteries. You are Wallies, so far as he's concerned."

It is all in sharp contrast to the hapless Granville, nephew to Ronnie Barker's disgruntled shopkeeper Arkwright in Open All Hours.

But David insists that he shares only one thing with the personalities of both Del Boy and Granville. He, like them, is unmarried.

Indeed, he has managed to reach TV stardom with few knowing very much about him at all. He lives between a one-bedroom flat in Soho, London, and a small country cottage 50 miles away.

Privacy

And he avoids parties, public appearances and receptions with a quiet dedication to his own privacy.

Instead, he prefers work : "I am a compulsive doer of things," he says. "If I'm not acting, I have to keep myself occupied.

"I have just rebuilt a motorbike—a 1957 BSA Star Twin—which I've brought back to original condition. It has cost me an arm and a leg.

"I have also built an end-of-the-pier machine with a friend of mine. I find it impossible to just watch television and do nothing."

Even his cottage has not given him the country relaxation that the rest of us might seek : "I knocked the place down and rebuilt it," he says, with almost masochistic pride.

He is now occupying his time starting in Look No Hands in London's West End —with just Christmas Day and Boxing Day off.

So will he get a chance to put his feet up and watch himself on TV ?

"I don't honestly know " he says with a shrug. "I shall probably be decorating a room . . ."

Cheers, you plonker! Rodders and Del

By SARAH BOND

COR, strike a light —or rather "Dieu, frappez une allumette !" as the flabbergasted French might say—Terry and Arfur are going foreign aboard the Orient Express in MINDER the movie.

And little do they guess but their police chum Mr Chisholm is coming too—on a secret pork-pie-hat-and-looking-daggers mission with "Interpol" (Christmas Day, ITV, 7.30 p.m.).

"They're the ones who send the flowers, ain't they ? puzzles Arfur, who is already nervous about going "abroad" with its "Pnd with guns, iffy water, and awn-off toilets."

Luxury

In the long-awaited Minder film, Terry and his latest sexy sort win two berths on the luxury train after he rescues a gangland boss's daughter-turned-floozie Ranger (Amanda Pays) from a mugging which could have cost millions.

And once Arfur clocks the fact that the Orient Express is not a Chinese takeaway, he jumps on the Pullman for a bit of posh too. Especially as it nearly saves him from the "horns of a debacle."

The pair set off not quite blissfully, but unaware that they are about to become involved in a cross-Europe chase for naughty money.

As far as cross-Channel entrepreneur Arfur is concerned the Orient is obviously his lobster, once he sorts out his "pottige " on the French menu from his loup de loup.

"It's the international travel scene for you, isn't it ?" he wisely nods to Terry, after a water closet encounter with Amanda Pays.

"A strange bird accosts you in the khazi and we've not even out of Brixton yet ! "

Joining George Cole, Dennis Waterman and Patrick Malahide on this murderously funny adventure, which leaves piles of brown bread bodies everywhere, are Honor Blackman as a sexy widow hell on seducing Arfur under the old lamp for mysterious ends; Adam Faith almost unrecognisable as a shoot-back-and-sides heavy befriending Terry, with flashing gold hampsteads, and Ralph Bates as

---

Les adventures de two Cockneys sur le premier chuffer de Europe

scualed Interpool agent Sergeant Le Blanc—constantly trying to tempt a very cheesed- off "Chorsum " to be bar.

These two sniff down their noses at each other beautifully, while Maurice Denham and Debbie Arnold help cram the crazy corridors.

Dennis Waterman says the shoot was especially high spirited as it was the last Minder to be made, although he admits he did George Cole a bit of genuine damage when pulling him through a train window Bond-style.

"I didn't realise at the time, but it was a bit nasty because his stomach got caught on the window hatch. I don't think Arfur's ever got involved in so much physical before ! "

The crew had two days on the British Orient Express in the summer steaming down to the coast and back—" Which was smashing," says Dennis—but when it came to the other side of the Channel the train was put on a Twickenham film set on electric rockers.

"We hadn't seen the script, but we heard we'd got one one lot coming up on the Orient Express so we all got excited and thought great, we'd get down to Venice for a nice romantic week's holiday —then we ended up with a week in Boulogne ! "

Patrick Malahide, as Albert Chisholm, had to keep a much straighter face than usual as he played the English copper abroad bravely attempting pidgin French : " Je suis une gendarme Anglais," he mutters doubtfully with a worried frown as he packs.

For Patrick, like Ralph Bates, speaks fluent French. "It was funny pretending not to understand what the French train attendants were saying—and off the set Ralph and I clicked immediately, and had a lot of laughs dressing up a whole new language — Cockney French."

The unlikely duo spoke French to each other all the time off duty and kept throwing in literal translations of Minder-type phrases like "Melies une dissipation de dans" (Put a sock in it), or "Tci. Therlogea-vous oiseau ? " (Here, did you clock that bird ?) — which left both Boulogne and Twickenham locals agape.

Now Patrick is cheerfully "kissing goodbye" to the caustic Chisholm—but will reappear next year as an "evil genius " in several different guises in a Dennis Potter series which promises "real blood."

Alone the crows—or " Pierre les cornelies," as the intercontinental Arfur might say !

Living the high life

● IT WILL be a sky-high Christmas for 250 deprived children having a party in a Jumbo Jet this morning flying around Britain. The party will be seen on the NOEL EDMONDS LIVE, LIVE BREAKFAST SHOW (BBC1, 11.55 a.m.).

The elbow will also enjoy live pictures from a refugee camp in the Sudan with Edmonds talking to British workers from the Save the Children Fund and following them up with their families back home. Charity is the theme of the show and air stalwarts will race up the steps of Broadcasting Tower in London to raise money. At Kingston parents will swim the Thames for a rare disease fund. And there will be a Christmas pudding throwing contest on Richmond Green.

LIFE AFTER ERIC, BY ERNIE—PAGE 23

New hype: Michael Grade boosted the show's profile by scheduling the 1985 Christmas special directly against its ITV rival, *Minder*. © Daily Express

had achieved something comparable in quality in the episode of *Dad's Army* ('The Deadly Attachment') in which he had played the menacingly arrogant German U-boat captain; and Bernard Cribbins was similarly memorable when he turned up as the spectacularly fastidious little man suspected of being an hotel inspector in *Fawlty Towers*. Jim Broadbent's performance deserved to be included among such admirably effective guest appearances, as it not only provided the show with an immediately strong and intriguing new character but also pushed David Jason and other regulars to match its power and guile.

The episode was also impressive because it was so consistently engrossing. Thanks in large part to John Sullivan's growing skills as a writer, the story was one of the best, and most convincing, so far in the show's existence, finding the logic for each phase in the plot's progression within the strengths and weaknesses of the key characters. It drew, most importantly of all, on what the audience already knew of Del's familial focus to set up the tensely dramatic finale, and invited them to share in his triumph as he found an unconventional but very satisfying means of defending the Trotters' honour. There was, in short, an encouraging sense of maturity about this instalment, which encouraged viewers to preserve their passion for the project.

The remainder of the run, alas, returned to the previous patchier form, but there were still enough bright moments to keep the viewers entertained. 'Wanted', for example, was a rather odd episode in which Rodney, after a distressing encounter with a drunken woman (who, unbeknown to him, is notoriously unhinged and prone to shouting 'rape' whenever young men offer her help), is driven into hiding after an unusually mischievous Del deceives him into thinking that the police are hunting for a sex pest called 'The Peckham Pouncer'. Although the storyline failed to convince, there was an effective scene set in The Nag's Head that showcased the increasingly impressive comic chemistry between Del, Trigger and Boycie, and, as Del's mood changed dramatically from cruel and cackling to shamefaced and sorry, and Rodney went from pink-cheeked naivety to dark-eyed depression, both David Jason and Nicholas Lyndhurst were given a good opportunity to demonstrate their considerable, and admirably subtle, acting skills.

The final episode, 'Who's a Pretty Boy?', gravitated away sharply in the direction of farce, as all three Trotters set about decorating a flat belonging to Del's henpecked mate Denzil and his frightening wife Corrine, but then have to find a replacement for Corrine's suddenly deceased pet canary before she can explode with anger at what they have done. Once again, the script was a little scrappy, but the show did intro- duce a promising new character in Del's soft-hearted Scouse 'gopher', Denzil (nicely played by Paul Barber), and the memorably fierce and intimidating Corrine – arguably John Sullivan's first notable female character as far as this sitcom was concerned – would also have had a future but for the sadly premature death of the actor who portrayed her, Eva Mottley.[9] The Nag's Head was also given a landlord in the form of the avuncular Mike Fisher, played by Kenneth MacDonald; Ray Butt had worked with the actor before on the Croft and Perry sitcom *It Ain't Half Hot, Mum* (in which he appeared as Gunner Nobby Clark), and trusted him to make the part of the publican an effective comic foil for Del Boy. As the series closed, therefore, the repertory of characters had expanded, and there were positive signs of the potential for further improvement.

A Christmas special, entitled 'Thicker than Water', followed three days later, and provided another good reason for optimism. In a storyline that, once again, mixed comedy and pathos with great assurance, the Trotter boys' errant father, Reg, made his one and only appearance.

It was, in essence, a remarkably dark context for a festive sitcom feature: after abandoning his family for eighteen years, a father returns with a cruel and callous scam that aims to split up his sons and exploit the consequences. The rest of the action would see both boys traumatised and one of them ostracised and humiliated in public until the father finally gets his come-uppance. It was a testament to John Sullivan's writing, however, that, in spite of all of this, the show still elicited plenty of laughs, and the drama helped to deepen the appeal of the regular characters.

The plot revolved around Reg Trotter's unexpected return to Peckham to inform his two sons that he has recently been diagnosed with a serious blood disorder that is probably hered-itary. When a subsequent pair of blood tests, secretly altered by Reg, seem to suggest that Rodney and Del have different blood types, the first rash response to the news is Grandad's speculation that Rodney must have been sired by a trumpeter, or possibly a saxophonist, whom his mother met during one of her many bitter rows with Reg. 'Great!' Rodney exclaims. 'I can't wait to fill in my next passport application form. Mother's name: Joan Mavis Trotter. Father's name: Herb Alpert and the Tijuana Brass!' Reg then returns to turn the crisis on its head by declaring that it is actually Del, not Rodney, who is the Trotter family's 'Lone Ranger'.

A dejected Del spends much of what remains of the episode as a Peckham pariah, mocked by Reg ('He kept shouting "Hi ho silver!"') as he is reduced to watching the 'proper' Trotters from a distance. When the family doctor reveals the truth of the matter, and Reg's ruse is rumbled, the father makes a sharp exit, Del is restored as the head of the household, and the sitcom's status quo is reaffirmed. The brutal treatment of Del, however, revealed much of why he has turned out as he has, toughened up while being forced into premature service as both bread-winner and surrogate father, and, as the episode ended, the viewer was left with a much better appreciation of his attitude.

Reg, on the other hand, was so unsympathetic as a character that his role now seemed exhausted. David Jason, indeed, was sure at the time that Reg would always be a one-off character, because the storyline had depicted him in such a deeply unfavourable light. John Sullivan was similarly convinced that the character would never return, having blown his chances of being accepted back by the Trotter boys.

The reaction to this audacious seasonal special, and the third series as a whole, was certainly very encouraging. The viewing figures – which averaged 10.5 million[10] – were now heading steadily enough in the right direction, there had been an isolated but nonetheless welcome 'in-house' plug when the cast appeared on an edition of Russell Harty's weekly BBC1 chat show,[11] and the critics were, at long last, starting to sit up and take notice of the show. *The Times*, for example, had praised it not only for its general entertainment value but also for transforming David Jason 'into a comic player of previously unexploited substance,' while the *Radio Times* had judged it 'one of the biggest comedy hits on television' and the *Daily*

Express went so far as to hail the programme as the BBC's latest comedy 'classic'.[12] A few months later, in March 1984, the show was nominated for a 'Best Comedy Series' BAFTA, and then, on 17 April, the show was honoured by the Television and Radio Industries Club with its award for the 'Top Situation Comedy' of the past year.[13]

John Sullivan, Ray Butt and all of their team were thus fully entitled to feel vindicated for having invested so much faith in the sitcom. Although there was so much still to be achieved, the important thing was that, after three years of setbacks and struggles, they were finally free to push on with the project. *Only Fools and Horses* now had a proper chance not merely to survive, but also to flourish.

CHAPTER SEVEN

Hello, Goodbye

It's like the changing of the seasons
And the tides of the sea.

Just when *Only Fools and Horses* seemed to have secured its future and was set to progress, it was hit by yet another setback. It lost Lennard Pearce.

Pearce had started filming the fourth series on location in London with his fellow actors early in December 1984, shooting scenes for the episode entitled 'Hole in One'. Ten days into filming, after completing scenes shot outside Kingston Crown Court on a cold and snowy Sunday morning, he suffered a heart attack and was rushed to Whittington Hospital in Highgate, north London, where, after being struck with another heart attack a few days later, he died, late on Saturday, 15 December, eight weeks before his seventieth birthday.

John Sullivan heard the news at his home the following morning, when his wife, Sharon, took the telephone message and passed it on. Pearce, by this stage, was not just a colleague but was also a family friend, and everyone in the Sullivan household was devastated to learn of the loss. Ray Butt, who was out on location, also received a call and had the sad duty to break the news to all of the cast and crew. When it came to informing David Jason and Nicholas Lyndhurst, who were already in the make-up booth at the time, Butt simply looked in at them, shook his head, and went away. It was obvious what he had meant to convey. As the two actors got up and headed outside, it began to snow again. Jason, his eyes squinting as the white flecks flew into his face, muttered under his breath, and Lyndhurst stopped and stared blankly at a shop window, and then burst into tears.

It was still early in the morning, but the day was already done. 'To most people – cast and crew – Lennard was Grandad,' Ray Butt later said. 'They all called him Grandad and he loved that. So we cancelled filming. No one was in a mood to work that day. It was a very sad time.'[1]

The one source of comfort that everyone took from the news of his death was the knowledge that, after spending so many years as a relatively unknown jobbing actor, the sudden fame that came with *Only Fools and Horses* had given Pearce so much pleasure. He always loved being recognised as Grandad, and was flattered whenever asked for autographs by devoted fans. The role, in his eyes, had been such a delightful kind of redemption.

Pearce would be missed particularly keenly by Jason and Lyndhurst, because, as Lyndhurst acknowledged, the actor was so good at delivering a dry comic line and complementing their performances: 'We used to say, "You sod. We're giving you a twenty-minute lead-in to what you are going to say", and he just used to sit there with a fag in his mouth and say, "I know – but I'm old. I'm allowed." He was great.'[2]

As sad as the news was, however, urgent decisions now had to be made as to the future of the series. It seemed cruelly ironic that the current production, which had been planned to unfold at a far more leisurely pace than the previous one, was now plunged into a crisis at the eleventh hour: the series was already committed to its transmission dates and some serious decisions had to be made within the next few days. On Monday, Ray Butt held meetings at Television Centre with John Sullivan, David Jason and the BBC's new Head of Comedy, Gareth Gwenlan, regarding the best (or least worst) way forward. The most obvious option would have been to have found another actor to play Grandad, but, on this particular occasion, that idea was quickly dismissed. 'We were all too close, too much of a family, simply to change the actor,' John Sullivan later explained.[3]

Sullivan was adamant that, as Lennard Pearce had died, so, too, should Grandad. This was, in fact, an extremely bold decision by the writer, because, up until this moment, British sitcom characters simply never died – they either disappeared with little or no explanation as to their absence or they mysteriously reappeared in the physical form of another actor.[4] Examples of both cases had occurred in Sullivan's own *Citizen Smith*, when Cheryl Hall, who played Wolfie's girlfriend, and Peter Vaughan, who played her father, left after two series: whereas Hall's character was written out of the show, Vaughan's character returned for the next series with Tony Steedman in the role. The decision to actually acknowledge within the sitcom that a character had died was, as far as that genre was concerned, revolutionary, and would lead the way for several other British sitcoms (including *Blackadder Goes Forth* in 1989, with several figures charging over the top into No-Man's-Land; *Last Of the Summer Wine* in 2000, with Compo's demise from a terminal illness; *One Foot in the Grave,* also in 2000, with Victor Meldrew being killed by a hit-and-run driver; and *The Royle Family* in 2006, with Nana's passing) to accommodate the reality of mortality.

What Sullivan decided to do for *Only Fools* was to mark and mourn Grandad's death, and then introduce another character, of a similar age, in order to preserve the comic triangle that had served the sitcom so well. Ray Butt respected his friend's decision and did what he could to help by postponing location filming until after the forthcoming Christmas break and then restart the process on Wednesday, 2 January 1985. That, he hoped, would at least allow his friend a few weeks in which to come up with a suitable solution and then work on a set of new and revised scripts.

Sullivan was grateful for what little time and space he was given, and, thinking hard under intense pressure, he considered a number of options. One possibility was to switch gender and give the Trotter brothers an elderly aunt, but David Jason, among others, soon rejected this notion. Jason explained: 'If you think we're going to have a success with me telling a little old lady to "Shut up, you stupid old cow," and bundling and pushing her into the back of a van, you're mistaken – we'd be off the air in a fortnight.'[5] Sullivan agreed, and, instead, he eventually settled upon the idea of introducing Grandad's long-lost brother, Albert, to the Trotter household (which at least would have a faint ring of authenticity about it as previous series had contained the odd reference to Grandad's peripatetic male relations). The next stage, however, was the even more daunting and exhausting one of altering all of the existing scripts. The cast wanted the Trotter family to acknowledge Grandad's passing, so Sullivan wrote 'Strained Relations', the new funeral episode, preceded by the hurriedly revised 'Happy Returns', as it felt wrong to start the series on such a low, and unconventional, note.

Once the decision had been made to retain the three-man family dynamic, and the basic idea of 'Uncle Albert' was being developed, the search began for a new member of the cast. Ray Butt, as producer, had to deal with the task, which proved a struggle not only because he was working against the clock but also because he was still grieving for the loss of one of his friends and colleagues.

When he first sat down in his office at Television Centre and started reading through the piles of applications that had already come in, he grew angry – the cold opportunism of some of them struck him as deeply offensive – and he threw them all across the room. Later, as he regained his composure, he resumed reading a few of them, and was soon intrigued by one letter in particular. It was handwritten and very brisk and businesslike in tone, and the author did not appear to have any first-hand knowledge of the show, but he sounded keen to be considered for any role that might be available. Butt then looked at the head and shoulders portrait that was attached: it showed a round-faced, bald, snow-white-bearded man who seemed like a cross between Father Christmas and Captain Birdseye. The actor's name was Buster Merryfield, and Butt was sufficiently interested to find out more about him.

Born in 1920 in Battersea, south London, Merryfield (whose real first name, although he preferred to keep it a secret in later life, was Harry) had grown up in a working-class family and won boxing championships while still a schoolboy, but, after being encouraged by his parents to 'better' himself, had gone on to work as a junior clerk with the Westminster (later known as the National Westminster) Bank. His training was soon disrupted by the outbreak of World War Two – during which he served in the Royal Artillery, working at certain times as a PT teacher, a jungle warfare instructor and an entertainments officer, eventually rising up the ranks to become a

Lieutenant – but, once he was demobbed, he resumed his career at the bank. Acting, however, became a passionate hobby of his, beginning during the war with a mime act in Army variety shows, continuing in peacetime with an involvement in local amateur dramatic societies, and then developing into something more serious as he formed his own company, 'The Characters'.

His professional life as a banker continued to improve steadily, and, following a succession of fairly rapid promotions, he became manager of the Thames Ditton branch of the NatWest at the start of the 1970s. By day, he sat in his office, sporting a sober pinstriped suit, a smart bowtie and a neatly trimmed beard, and behaved like any other respectable bank manager. By night, he put on another costume and acted in another play, still excited to be a part-time actor and director. By the age of fifty-seven, however, he decided to take early retirement from the bank and try to go full-time in the theatre.

After writing to countless repertory companies without eliciting a positive reply, he finally talked his way into a job – paying a modest £40 per week – as an assistant stage manager at the Connaught Theatre in Worthing. He then proceeded to sweep the floor, make the tea and, every now and again, appear in minor parts in plays. Eventually, after earning his Equity card and appearing in a few commercials, he managed to start winning the odd role in some interesting television productions, starting in 1980 with a role as an old Navy captain called 'Uncle Jim' in a four-part BBC love story called *Hannah*, and then another BBC drama series in 1983 called *The Citadel* and an Anglia TV P. D. James adaptation in 1984 entitled *Shroud for a Nightingale*.

An abstemious and health-conscious man (he had never

smoked, nor drunk alcohol), he lived quietly with his wife, Iris, in a pretty little bungalow called 'Two Oaks' at Byfleet in Surrey, and concentrated on making the most of his second career. He did not even have an agent in those days, reasoning that he was not yet significant enough a figure to deserve one, and relied on studying the notices in *The Stage* for possible new acting opportunities.

The more that Ray Butt heard about this unusual actor, the more eager he was to see what he could do. After consulting John Sullivan, who was similarly intrigued, Butt went ahead and made contact.

When the call came for Merryfield to audition to join *Only Fools and Horses*, he was appearing in pantomime – playing Baron Stoneybroke in *Cinderella* – at the Theatre Royal in Windsor and therefore explained politely that, as he was already committed to acting in two shows every day, he was unavailable for any other engagements. Ray Butt, however, proved insistent, and arranged for a BBC car to take him across London early in the morning so that he could attend a meeting at Television Centre.

There, in the office of the Head of Light Entertainment (who by this time was John Howard Davies), the politely spoken Merryfield was asked by Butt if he could 'do' a Cockney accent – he assured the producer that, being Battersea-born, he most certainly could – and was then invited to read a few pages of dialogue from an old script featuring Grandad. Merryfield was uneasy about doing so until it was explained that John Sullivan planned to create a completely new character – probably an uncle – rather than make him 'step into a dead man's shoes'.[6] The reading then went well, and Merryfield was returned to Windsor in time for his next theatre appearance at 2.30 p.m. The following morning, he was summoned once again to Television Centre, where he met John Sullivan and then read a passage from another old script alongside David Jason and Nicholas Lyndhurst. He was then sent back to his theatre, still unsure as to what, if anything, would now happen.

He had only just completed that afternoon's matinée when the offer arrived: would he like the part? Merryfield, too excited to resist, said yes. 'Good,' he was told. 'We want you on the set for filming at seven-thirty tomorrow morning. We will send a car for you. Will six a.m. be all right?'[7] An old cap and a duffle coat were picked out from stock to dress him up as the kind of salty old sea dog that John Sullivan had envisaged, and the new shooting schedule was set. For the next two weeks he was working from six in the morning until ten at night, combining location work with pantomime.

Now that the scripts had been revised and the role of Uncle Albert had been cast, the production of the fourth series could at last progress. A new young director, the Scottish-born Susie Belbin, was brought in by Ray Butt to film the episodes because he had only recently finished working on his and John Sullivan's other current sitcom, *Just Good Friends*. Although Belbin's involvement had been planned prior to the disruption caused by Lennard Pearce's death, her calm and cool-headed presence at the heart of what was now a very raw and emotional set turned out to be invaluable. With some members of both the cast and crew still red-eyed with grief (especially when filming Grandad's funeral so soon after attending the funeral of the actor who played him), and John Sullivan writing against the clock to deliver revised pages of dialogue, her ability to maintain her focus and keep on schedule was precisely what the situation required. 'In many respects it was probably fortunate that I was new to the programme,' she would agree, 'because when the news of Lennard's death broke, it really hit everyone hard, including Ray Butt and John Sullivan, whereas I could remain objective because I wasn't so emotionally involved.'[8]

It was a difficult process, but Belbin saw the location shoot through to its completion and then, on Sunday, 20 January, the studio recordings began with the 'new' opening episode, 'Happy Returns'. So much of the procedure – from the presence of the regular warm-up man Felix Bowness to the reconstructed sets – seemed so familiar, but it still proved a painfully difficult night for David Jason and Nicholas Lyndhurst as they were obliged to try not to notice the poignant absence of their friend and colleague Lennard Pearce.

'Happy Returns' begins by making it clear that Grandad is unwell and in hospital. A woman in the local newsagents asks after him, and Del, looking worried but straining to seem light-hearted, replies: 'The doctors 'ave been trying to take his hat off, but he wouldn't have none of it! They gave him an X-ray yesterday, and they found out he got a pulled ligament in the wallet, and severe fraying of the trilby!'

The remainder of the episode sees Del befriend a mischievous young boy called Jason, who, it transpires, is the son of an old flame named June whom he last saw about nineteen years ago. While Del rekindles his romance with June, Rodney, quite independently, starts dating a girl from the newsagents called Debby. Much to each brother's surprise, however, June and Debby turn out to be mother and daughter. It is only when Del ponders why June left Peckham so abruptly, and then discovers that Debby is nineteen years old, that he starts adding two and two together and making five ('Incense!'

exclaims Del, looking accusingly at the randy Rodney). June, eventually, explains what really happened – she was cheating on young Del with his best friend – and then history repeats itself for the poor Trotter boys when Debby cheats on Rodney with Mickey Pearce.

Watched by an impressive 15.2 million viewers[9] – even though the *Radio Times* had more or less ignored it in favour of publicising the arrival of the valedictory series of *Are You Being Served?*[10] – 'Happy Returns' was, in the circumstances, a very effective episode, even though there were a few awkward moments when, probably due to the last-minute revisions, the pace or the plot seemed to falter. It helped that the storyline was sufficiently detailed and driven as to distract anyone from reflecting on Grandad's absence, and, as an opening edition, the show could be considered a success. It would, however, be the second episode, 'Strained Relations', that would shake up all expectations by summoning up such strong and mixed emotions – and the sitcom, any sitcom, would never be quite the same again.

It begins with death. Grandad has died.

The scene is a cold, snowy, crow-cawing cemetery. There is a funeral director, and a couple of his assistants, lounging around, smoking and talking to each other quietly. Resting against the wall of the chapel are several wreaths, and there is one very large, very gaudy, wreath with a floral tribute that reads: 'Grandad'. On a card pinned to the wreath is the dictated, handwritten, message: *'Always in our foughts, love, Del-Boy & Rodney.'* In the distance, a grey group of mourners stand like statues by the graveside. They include Del, Rodney, Trigger, Boycie and Mike, along with the vicar, two old ladies, and, representing the north London branch of the Trotter family, cousin Stan, his wife Jean and Uncle Albert, who is in his mid-sixties and is Grandad's brother. The ceremony cannot be heard clearly, the vicar's voice is nothing more than a shallow drone. Then the ceremony ends and the mourners move slowly away from the graveside, breaking off into small groups as they do so. As Del walks past the vicar, he says nothing, but shoves a few notes into his hand.

Grandad's old trilby hat, it seems, is draped over the Daimler symbol on one of the waiting cars. Del smiles at it lovingly, picks it up and strokes it, thinks for a moment, and then turns and heads back with it towards the grave. Rodney, pale and hollow-cheeked, is still at the graveside, staring blankly down as the gravediggers prepare to shovel the dirt back into the hole. Del appears at Rodney's side with the hat, which the two brothers smile at affectionately, and then Del gestures that it is Rodney's privilege to drop the hat into the grave. As he does so, very gently, Del squeezes his shoulder.

'We'll leave the car, shall we?' Del asks. 'Yeah,' Rodney replies, struggling not to choke, 'we'll have a nice little walk, eh?' As they move off, two gravediggers rush in and start shovelling. 'Oi!' says Del, turning back and pointing at them accusingly. 'Gently!' As the other mourners disperse, the vicar looks over at one of the Daimlers, appears puzzled, and asks: 'Has anyone seen my hat?'

Back at the flat, Del busies himself by darting about offering his guests trays of sandwiches, while Rodney stands still, scowling at the likes of Boycie, Trigger and Mike as they drink, smoke, tell jokes and generally have themselves a laugh. It is at this point that Rodney has his first encounter with the irritatingly chatty little old man who turns out to be his Grandad's brother, Albert:

ALBERT:	Shame really, me and him lost touch with each other years ago. I spent most of my life at sea, you know, Royal Navy, Merchant. D'you know, I was torpedoed five times!
RODNEY:	*[Looking blank-faced and bored]* Yeah?
ALBERT:	Yeah! D'you know what the crews nicknamed me?
RODNEY:	Jonah?
ALBERT:	No! No, they didn't call me Jonah – not many of them! They used to call me Boomerang Trotter, 'cos I always come back!
RODNEY:	Triffic!

Del then meets his snobbish north London relations Stan and Jean, who proceed to niggle him with their pompous remarks about their 'posh' mobile home and apparent contempt for their unwanted lodger, Uncle Albert: 'He's been living with us for eighteen months now,' moans Stan. 'He only popped round to borrow a screwdriver!' When Del hears the couple mention the idea of putting Albert in an old folks' home, he is clearly horrified. 'You can't do that,' he exclaims. 'He's *family!*'

Once all the guests have gone, Rodney sits at the table, staring gloomily at all the piles of dirty plates, half-empty glasses and over-full ashtrays. Del bursts in brightly from the kitchen carrying two large servings of sausage and mash. Rodney sticks a fork in, tastes a tiny piece of potato, and then puts the fork back down again. 'I can't eat that,' he says sadly. 'What's wrong with it?' asks Del. 'Well, it's nothing like Grandad's, is it?' Rodney replies. 'It tastes *nice.*' After trying a few jokes to cheer his brother up, Del gives in and starts pouring out some whisky for them both. As he does so, Rodney – noticing a noise –

points out that someone is pulling their lavatory chain. Alarmed, Del grabs a bottle of Warninks Advocaat and goes over to the door, ready to hit the intruder on the head, only for Uncle Albert to emerge, moaning, from inside the bathroom.

It transpires that he drank too much cognac and dozed off. As it is now 11.30 at night, Del decides, reluctantly, to let the old windbag stay the night. The following morning, however, Del takes him back to north London only to discover that Stan and Jean have moved. Del's distress deepens when Albert, quite casually, remarks that this is by no means the first time that he has been abandoned by his own flesh and blood: his year-long stay with cousin Audrey and Kevin ended when he was sent down to Sainsburys to buy some groceries and, when he returned, they had emigrated; then there was a six-month period 'comforting' young Gillian – Patsy's girl – because her husband was on nights, which came to an abrupt halt when she set fire to her own house ('I can remember thinking as I stood on the ledge and jumped into the fireman's net: "That's gratitude for you!"'). As he shakes his head at the bad behaviour of some family members, a wide-eyed Del moans that he feels 'like a turkey who's just caught Bernard Matthews grinning at him'.

Leaping up with panic, Del orders Albert to 'sling his hook' and find a room down at the local Seaman's Mission. Rodney, in his current emotional state, is appalled to witness such a brutal and unsentimental reaction, but Del is quick to remind him that Albert comes from their father's side of the family: 'You know what *they're* like – you offer 'em a cup of tea and they think you've adopted 'em!' Rodney, however, remains disgusted, and all of the sadness, frustration and anger from the previous day's events crash out in one great tidal wave of pain as he argues about attitudes with Del:

RODNEY: I've seen a side of you I never knew existed.

DEL: You don't understand, Rodney!

RODNEY: You're right about that, Del! I mean, look at
           you last night – you was *laughing,* you was
           drinking, I mean, why didn't you just put yer
           Boney M record on, Del, we could have had
           a good old knees up! It was Grandad's . . .
           [chokes] How could you get over it so easily?

DEL: 'Get over it'? What a *plonker* you really are,
           Rodney! *'Get over it'*? I ain't even *started* yet!!!
           Ain't even *started,* bruv! And d'you know why?
           Because I don't know *how* to!!! That's why!
           I've survived all my life with a smile and a
           prayer! I'm *Del Boy*, ain't I! 'Good old Del
           Boy' – he's got more bounce than Zebedee!
           ''Ere you are pal, what you drinking? Go on!'
           'Hello, darling, you have one for luck!!' That's
           me, that's Del Boy. Innit? Nothing ever upsets
           Del Boy. I've always played the tough guy! I
           didn't *want* to, but I *had* to, and I've played it
           for so long now, I don't know how to *be*
           anything else! I don't even know how to . . .
           Oh, it don't matter! Bloody families! I've
           finished with 'em! What do they *do* to you,
           eh? They hold you back, drag you down, and
           then they break yer bloody heart!

RODNEY: *[Whispers]* I'm sorry.

While an embarrassed Rodney slips away, Del sits down next
to Grandad's old chair, stroking it softly as he fights back the
tears.

The following night, at The Nag's Head, Del is back in full 'Del Boy' mode, pulling wads of cash from his sheepskin coat, joking and flirting with the bar staff and dodging Mike's request for him to pay the bill for all the booze they consumed after the funeral. Sitting down to drink with Rodney, he tries not to notice when Uncle Albert comes in, coughing in a self-consciously loud and dramatic manner. Rodney goes over to see how he is, and discovers that the old man has been roaming the cold streets because the Seaman's Mission 'ain't there no more'. Impressed by his apparent desire to face up to hardship alone, Rodney returns to Del's table and tries to persuade him to take their uncle back: RODNEY: 'I just offered him a couple of quid and he wouldn't take a penny!' DEL: 'No, well, he wouldn't would he, he's still got the hundred quid I gave him this afternoon!' Once again, Rodney realises that his brother has a softer heart than he thought.

Realising that he has said too much, Del smiles resignedly and goes over with Rodney to where Albert is sitting alone:

DEL: All right?
ALBERT: Yeah, all right, son. Just having a drop of rum,
            warm the old cockles.
DEL: You eaten?
ALBERT: Nah, not yet.
DEL: Then why didn't you have something to eat
            when you was in here at lunchtime?
ALBERT: Well, all they had left was sausage and mash
            and I've gone right off that!
DEL: Fancy an Indian?
ALBERT: Wouldn't mind, son!
RODNEY: We'd never get a table this time of night, Del.

DEL: No. We'll have to get a takeaway . . . and eat
           it at home.

RODNEY: *[Realising Del's true intention]* Yeah! Yeah, that's
           what we'll do! We'll get a takeaway and eat it
           at home . . . Eh?

ALBERT: If it's all right with you two, Del. Thanks!

DEL: Don't know what you're thanking me for –
           you're paying! Come on, Sinbad, let's get down
           there before the Health Inspector!

*[Del heads out through the door followed by Rodney, who carries
Albert's hold-all. Albert downs the last drop of his rum and is
about to leave when Mike calls him over.]*

MIKE: Oi, I'm glad I caught you. I've just phoned
           the Mission and they said they've got a bed
           for you.

ALBERT: *Ssshh!*

It was, by any standards, an extraordinary sitcom episode, worthy in terms both of dialogue and acting to be rated alongside the likes of Galton and Simpson at their best. When one also takes into consideration the unusual circumstances in which it was written, the achievement seems even greater. John Sullivan would have been applauded had he simply saved the show by finding a way to overcome a crisis and guide the characters through an exceptionally difficult scenario, but he went so far beyond that brief and produced a brave, funny, touching, true and honest script that deserved to be regarded as a genuine masterpiece of sitcom writing.

Saul Bellow once wrote that 'Death is the dark backing that a mirror needs if we are to see anything,'[11] and John Sullivan, with this one remarkable episode, taught the British sitcom the same lesson. Another level, another dimension, was added to the genre, and it would never be quite the same again.

At the time, in the studio, the reaction was suitably awed. 'There was the up and down, the light and dark, and the audience just went with it,' Susie Belbin would recall. 'At appropriate moments you could hear a pin drop; for example, the argument between Del Boy and Rodney back at the flat was really moving and the audience reacted to that.'[12] John Sullivan, who attended the recording, was both relieved and thrilled at the response. It had been such a strain to do, for so many reasons, but he had stayed true to his principles, done what David Jason had always urged him to do – 'Go where you want to go' – and the actors, as promised, had supported him brilliantly.

David Jason and Nicholas Lyndhurst, in particular, underlined what versatile performers they were, slipping back and forth so swiftly and smoothly between comedy and pathos, never once appearing anything less than completely believable. Jason, with his round soulful eyes and edgy actions, captured Del's internal turmoil quite brilliantly, and Lyndhurst, who often looked like Stan Laurel possessed by Buster Keaton, conveyed Rodney's callow melancholy with exceptional finesse. Susie Belbin was certainly greatly impressed, describing Jason as a 'master' of timing and praising Lyndhurst for his intelligent and understated responses to emotional, as well as comical, moments: 'I have never seen anybody do stillness the way he does; where another actor would feel it necessary to pull a face, Nick doesn't move. His reactions are superb.'[13]

Those viewers who wrote in to the BBC were similarly impressed. One of the many positive responses included the remarks: 'This episode treated the death [of Grandad] in a very moving, touching and realistic way. My admiration goes to both David Jason and Nicholas Lyndhurst whose performances were so rich in genuine feeling that I was moved to tears. A fitting and moving tribute to a man who has made so many laugh.'[14]

The show was also quite a triumph for Buster Merryfield, who made his debut with remarkable ease, overcoming his inevitable nerves to interact very effectively with the regular members of the cast. David Jason, in fact, had helped him settle with a very generous and thoughtful gesture: when, early on during the recording, Merryfield forgot one of his lines and 'dried', Jason proceeded to deliberately stumble over one of his own lines and then jokingly berated the audience for noticing ('What are you lot laughin' at then? You got in for nuffink dint ya?'). 'David had seen how tense I was,' Merryfield would later acknowledge, 'and had deliberately messed things up to put me at ease. He was that kind of chap.'[15]

The episode that followed the superb 'Strained Relations' was, probably very sensibly, a much more conventional affair. 'Hole in One' saw Albert appear to accidentally fall through an open door in The Nag's Head, tumbling down some steps and ending up in the cellar; Del, feeling the pinch after Rodney's rash decision to invest £500 on sun-tan lotion during one of the worst winters in living memory, spots the chance to recoup some money by suing the brewery for damages. Once in court, however, Albert's dubious past comes back to haunt him and the case collapses, but he redeems himself in the eyes of the boys when he confesses that he was only trying to help them pay for Grandad's fibreglass headstone.

It was an awkward episode for Buster Merryfield, as the script had been rewritten to replace Grandad's role with that of Uncle Albert, but, once again, he fared very well, with some nicely observed little moments – such as the opening sequence in which he hangs up his hat and coat, hears some post land on the doormat, picks it up, realises that both of the letters are bills, so he posts them back through the letterbox. The closing scene – strongly reminiscent of the Laurel and Hardy movie *Block-Heads*, in which Ollie visits Stan in an Old Soldiers' Home and, finding him in a wheelchair, assumes that he is unable to walk and so carries his friend home in his arms – was also very effective, with an emotional Del and Rodney pushing Albert home in his wheelchair until it finally dawns on them that he still has full use of his legs ('You lazy old sod!').

Merryfield had actually assumed, after completing the location work for these episodes, that his work on the programme was more or less done. The TV job, as far as he was concerned, was only ever likely to be for two episodes. 'I was given no indication of being wanted for more,' he would later recall.[16] It had been an enjoyable experience, and had certainly whetted his appetite for trying more small-screen comedy, so he made plans to find himself an agent and started pondering his next move. It would only be after he had also been used in several more episodes of *Only Fools* that he started to feel as though his involvement would probably be made permanent.

Sullivan, Belbin and Butt, however, had already seen enough. The character of Uncle Albert, as played by Merryfield, had changed the comic dynamic – probably without either improving it or harming it, but certainly revising it in an interesting and sustainable way – by injecting much more energy into the sitcom, with Albert's lively and loquacious presence suggesting a new set of options for future storylines.

One alteration in particular was very evident more or less right from the start. Whereas Grandad's preternatural passivity had meant that, on most occasions, he was there merely to listen at length to Del and Rodney before delivering one of his 'Wendy House'-style one-liners (making, in effect, the boys a pair of straight men), Uncle Albert's chronic garrulousness meant that these roles would now be reversed, with him often dominating the dialogue, and Del and Rodney waiting impatiently to deliver the pithy comic put-downs.

Although no one involved had wanted the change to have come about through such tragic circumstances, once some of the sadness began to fade a sense of renewed enthusiasm returned as some of these new options became clear. As soon as John Sullivan had the chance, therefore, he would start writing Albert some of his seemingly interminable 'during the war' anecdotes, and a whole new way of generating laughs would be in place.

The remaining episodes, however, were revised in too much of a hurry for any further development, and so, for the rest of the fourth series, Uncle Albert would often seem a fairly peripheral figure. 'It's Only Rock and Roll', for example, revolved mainly around Del and Rodney, as the former promotes, in a knowingly perfunctory manner, the latter's amateur rock band. Albert's contribution was curtailed, rather neatly, via a brief and brusque exchange with Del: ALBERT: 'Still, it's got nothing to do with me.' DEL: 'No, that's right!' ALBERT: 'I'll keep my opinions to myself!'

A rather better instalment, 'Sleeping Dogs Lie', made up for Albert's relative inactivity by introducing the most interesting female character – as far as this particular show was concerned – that John Sullivan had created so far. Having been teased about his under-written women ever since the days of *Citizen Smith,* when Robert Lindsay's co-star Cheryl Hall had accused him of only producing decent roles for men, Sullivan had been trying hard to come up with a memorable female figure, but, by his own admission, had failed time and again to do so. 'When I've tried,' he would admit, 'they've come over as men in dresses.'[17] He had, in fact, already made the breakthrough with his other current sitcom, *Just Good Friends*, where the character of the advertising executive Penny Warrender, played so well by Jan Francis, was attracting an avid soap-like following as she struggled to balance her romantic impulses with her professional ambitions. In the case of *Only Fools*, however, Sullivan had signally failed to introduce a similarly interesting female character until he decided, for this episode, to make the previously unseen wife of Boycie, Marlene, visible.

The character had already acquired a somewhat notorious reputation (to which only Boycie appeared oblivious) simply via the various comments about her in past episodes. During the previous series, for example, in 'May the Force Be With You', even the deeply unpopular misfit Roy Slater grins lasciviously just at the thought of her, commenting sarcastically, 'Give my love to Marlene – everyone else used to!' By the time that John Sullivan was ready to put her on the screen, therefore, he had developed a much more detailed view of what she should look like, how she should behave and what kind of personality she should have. He also realised, however, that much of how she would develop, or fail to develop, would depend on the person who played her.

Ray Butt cast Sue Holderness in the role. Born in Hampstead in 1949, Holderness began her acting career with Manchester's 69 Theatre Company, appearing in productions of *A Midsummer Night's Dream, Peer Gynt* and Jack Good's Othello-inspired rock musical *Catch My Soul*, and then started working regularly on television in programmes ranging from children's series to sitcoms and period dramas. Among her more notable perform-ances were her roles as personal assistant Marianne Straker in the popular ITV Cold War drama series *The Sandbaggers* (1980), the love interest Liz in the last two series of the sitcom *It Takes a Worried Man* (the first broadcast by ITV and the second by Channel 4, both in 1983) and Cleopatra IV in the controversial 1983 BBC drama series *The Cleopatras*. Ray Butt first spotted her in an under-valued ITV sketch show called *End of Part One* (1979–80), in which she appeared in a wide variety of roles and impersonations, including a *femme fatale*, a male civil servant, Leela from *Doctor Who*, a cheesy quiz-show assistant, *The Rag Trade*'s Miriam Karlin, a stern television executive, news presenter Sue Lawley, *That's Life* host Esther Rantzen and, most auda-ciously of all, the union leader Clive Jenkins. Impressed by her versatility, Butt hired her without bothering with an audition.

Although brought in initially only for one day's filming, Holderness was delighted to get the part and intrigued by how much care had already been invested in preparing for Marlene's appearance:

> In the script, John Sullivan had given a clear description of how the character should look, and I liked the idea of this big, fuzzy mane of hair, long, painted nails and far too much make-up; she has more time on her hands than she knows what to do with to make herself look gorgeous, as well as lots of money, but not a lot of taste. [. . .] She's got a heart of gold, and although she's not the brightest girl in the world, she's streetwise and pretty manwise, and Del and Marlene, who fancied each other rotten, are now mates – there's certainly a lot of history between them.[18]

'Sleeping Dogs Lie' opened with Boycie and Marlene getting ready to go on holiday, and Del has persuaded them to pay him £60 per week to look after Marlene's beloved Great Dane puppy, Duke (which Boycie has bought for his permanently broody wife in lieu of the baby that she craves). Even in the first brief scene, it was clear that Del's flirtatious relationship with Marlene, and the discomfort that this causes the normally self-assured Boycie, had plenty of comic potential:

DEL: Hello, Marlene, my love!

MARLENE: Hello, sweetheart!

[Del touches her up as they kiss each other.]

DEL: Wo-*hoo!*

MARLENE: Did you have a nice Christmas?

DEL: Oh, triffic, yeah.

MARLENE: I had a dog!

RODNEY: Yeah? We had a turkey, same as every other year!

MARLENE: Oh, yeah! Honestly, you two are as bad as each other! Wo-ho!

[Del touches her up again.]

MARLENE: Ooh, *Derek!!*

BOYCIE: *[Testily]* Marlene, why don't you go an' get the dog and then perhaps we can get going!

MARLENE: Yeah, all right, I'll fetch his food as well.

[Marlene exits into the house. Boycie glares at the kiss mark she has left on Del's face]

BOYCIE: I don't like your lipstick, Del.

Although Holderness had treated the appearance as a one-off engagement – 'I was three months pregnant with my first child and very happy to pop along for just one very nice scene on film'[19] – she did more than enough to make the team eager to bring her back as soon as possible. 'It's very daunting for actors coming into a successful series, but Sue did well from the start,' Susie Belbin would say. 'I liked her as an actress and she had the full measure of the character from day one. It would have been easy for Sue to have turned the part into an over-the-top caricature, but she remained on the side of believability.'[20]

'Sleeping Dogs Lie' – which also featured another very encouraging performance from Buster Merryfield – attracted a huge audience of 18.7 million,[21] highlighting how popular the show had now become. The final two episodes in the series, 'Watching the Girls Go By' and 'As One Door Closes', were relatively run-of-the-mill affairs, but, by this stage, the sitcom could do no wrong in the eyes of its fans.

John Sullivan was certainly still doing his best, and the brief dip in quality was understandable in the circumstances. Always the kind of writer who continued typing right up to, and sometimes beyond, his deadlines, the exceptional strain he had endured while revising this current series had taken its toll. Most other writers of sitcoms had been able to draw strength and support from a creative collaborator: Muir had Norden, Galton had Simpson, Croft had Perry, Clement had La Frenais and John Cleese had Connie Booth. True, Johnny Speight had remained solo, but only somewhat chaotically and at considerable cost to his health.[22] John Sullivan, therefore, was unusual in the doggedly determined way that he continued writing his sitcom alone. Whenever he was faced by a problem, a puzzle or, worst of all, a mental blank, all he had for company was a depressingly white piece of paper and a nigglingly noisy clock.

This set of scripts had been his toughest challenge so far, and the fatigue that he was feeling became evident at times during the fag-end of the series.

'Watching the Girls Go By' began with a good example of how hard Sullivan was working, in spite of all his many other pressing concerns, to build up Uncle Albert's screen time. David Jason had arrived at rehearsals one morning to find Buster Merryfield amusing himself by playing the piano. 'I didn't know you were a pianist,' said Jason. 'I'm not,' Merryfield explained. 'I'm just killing time.' Jason could not resist replying: 'Sounds like you're killing the tune at the same time.'[23] When John Sullivan was told about the incident, he quickly altered his script so that Albert would be seen playing the piano, enthusiastically but rather clumsily, in The Nag's Head. 'He's good, ain't he? I like that,' says Trigger, before adding hurriedly, 'Hope he don't do no more, though!'

The rest of the episode revolved around Rodney's non-existent love life, when the amount of teasing he receives for his 'imaginary' girlfriend drives him to bet Mickey Pearce that he can find a woman to accompany him to the next Saturday night 'do'. Del, sniffing a share of the winnings, bribes an old flame of his, an 'exotic' dancer called Yvonne, to act as Rodney's date, but the effect is spoilt when she gets up and performs a striptease in front of all of his mates.

Structurally, the show was uncharacteristically loose and poorly paced, setting the plot slowly in motion with a fairly messy seven-minute scene in the pub, followed by twelve minutes of rambling dialogue inside the flat, then six minutes searching for a suitable date in a club, and then ending with a clumsily expository three-minute scene back in the flat where Rodney has to describe all of the action that the audience never got to see. With so little action and so much talk it was more like a radio, rather than a television, sitcom episode. Some of the dialogue – particularly that featuring Rodney – was also unusually laboured, and – the most obvious sign of the script-writer's tiredness – there was even room for the odd prehistoric gag (YVONNE: 'I've been hitting the bottle a bit too much. Doctor says I've got a drink problem. I says to him, "I ain't got no problem – I like it!"'). There were still enough laughs to keep most fans relatively contented, but the episode was certainly sluggish by the highest standards already set by the show.

The similarly patchy but slightly more effective series finale, 'As One Door Closes', was particularly memorable for the return of Denzil as Del's dangerously impressionable friend, sowing the seeds of an ongoing relationship that would echo the one between the crafty Sgt Bilko and the easily duped Rupert Ritzik in *The Phil Silvers Show*, as both Ritzik and Denzil are just bright enough to realise that they are far too weak to resist their respective tormentor:

BILKO: Rupert, listen to me—

RITZIK: Look, you've cleaned me out! All I got left is my wife – I don't wanna bet her!

BILKO: Look, about the bet . . .

RITZIK: The bet? I wouldn't bet *you* that my name is Rupert Ritzik!

BILKO: *IT'S A BET!*[24]

DEL: What did Denzil get the sack for?

RODNEY: Oh, he didn't, he was made redundant.

DEL: Hold on: if he was made redundant, that means he's got redundancy money?

RODNEY: Yeah, I suppose so.

DEL: *[Calls]* Denzil! *Denzil!*

DENZIL: *[Alarmed]* You're not having any!

DEL: I'm your friend, Denzil. Denzil! *DENZIL!!*

DENZIL: *[Running away]* You're still not having any!!!

DEL: *[Rodney lifts Del up so he can shout above the crowd]* Oi, Denzil, I'm gonna make you *rich,* Denzil! *[To Rodney]* Put me down! *[Pushes through the crowd]* I'm a policeman . . .

DENZIL: Please don't make me rich!

DEL: Denzil, don't be a plonker all your life!!

The episode was also notable for one of Del's surprisingly rare scenes actually being a fly-pitcher on the local market:

Ask yourselves this, ask yourselves this: how much do you spend on hairdressing, eh? Now it's gotta be six or seven quid a hit these days, innit? You work that out over a year and it comes to a national debt! Right? But, for just one pound fifty, you could invest in one of these super de-luxe trimming combs! I mean, you can save yourself a fortune in the comfort of yer own front room! Could you just – just come round a bit closer, come closer, 'cos at these prices I can't afford to deliver!

David Jason performed these street routines so brilliantly, capturing all of the bravado, quick-wittedness and breathless persistence of the stand-up seller, that it was a pity that this integral aspect of Del's daily activity would, in future, all but fade away from the on-screen fiction.

Such eye-catching excellence was by this stage more or less

the norm for a show that had now well and truly established itself as one of the most popular, and critically admired, entertainment programmes on British television. Ending on 4 April 1985, the fourth series, distinguished most profoundly by the dramatic audacity of 'Strained Relations', had averaged 14.9 million viewers each week,[25] and received many glowing encomia from the reviewers. David Jason was named 'BBC Personality of the Year' by the Variety Club of Great Britain and was also nominated for a 'Best Light Entertainment Performance' award by BAFTA, and the show itself triumphed by winning the BAFTA for 'Best Comedy Series'.

Only Fools and Horses was thus already an undeniable success. As far as the still-ambitious John Sullivan and the rest of the team were concerned, however, the show had only just begun.

CHAPTER EIGHT

New Depth, New Hype

This is my golden opportunity to fulfil my potential.

Following the great success of the fourth series of *Only Fools and Horses*, when the team responded to the sad loss of Lennard Pearce with a set of episodes that elevated the show to an entirely new level in terms both of art and audience figures, there was a renewed sense of optimism within the camp. Points had been proven, reputations enhanced, and now the appetite was there to build on the burgeoning success. John Sullivan wanted to write longer, more elaborate and multi-faceted fictions, and he wanted them promoted far more assiduously and imaginatively than any previous efforts had been.

The first promising sign that progress would really happen, on both of these fronts, arrived in the spring of 1985, when the show's first feature-length festive special was commissioned, and then Michael Grade, the new Controller of BBC1, pledged his full support to the project. While the commission itself was encouraging, Grade's own involvement would turn out to be crucial.

Bill Cotton had been responsible for bringing Michael Grade to the BBC a few months earlier. Shortly after becoming Managing Director of BBC Television early in 1984, he began talking to Grade, who was currently based in Los Angeles as

the president of Embassy Television (a well-respected production house for situation comedies), about joining him at the
Corporation. The two men had been extremely good friends
for many years, and Cotton saw him as the ideal ally to have
as he sought to freshen up the output of BBC TV and make
it more broadly appealing, critically admirable and far more
competitive. After discussing a number of possible positions,
Grade agreed, in the autumn of 1984, to return to the UK as
the new Controller of BBC1.

As Cotton later reflected, Grade made an immediate, and
very favourable, impact on the channel:

> Although, in some quarters, Michael had already been
> dismissed as merely a commercial operator who would reduce
> BBC1 to some sort of vaudeville operation, he actually under-
> stood the meaning of public service broadcasting very well
> indeed, and I was in no doubt that he was well-equipped to
> make it function better. For one thing, he was a great man
> manager: he took the time and trouble to watch his producers'
> programmes, he called them to offer encouragement, congrat-
> ulations and helpful advice, and the door to his office was
> always open. So you suddenly had a much happier and tighter
> team. Another strength was that he was a brilliant scheduler:
> he knew and enjoyed the process of moving programmes
> around, taking things out, putting things in, and generally
> creating a tremendous air of confidence. And there was one
> other invaluable thing: he'd worked in newspapers earlier on
> in his career, as a sports journalist at the *Daily Mirror*, and had
> kept up his contacts, so Michael knew, very, very, well, how
> to handle the press. That would also help significantly in
> improving the performance of BBC1.[1]

Grade's early actions included commissioning a special audience survey to assess every aspect of the current schedules, modernising the means whereby ratings were analysed and acted upon; organising regular weekly meetings with senior members of the BBC's Promotions Department to plan new strategies; ordering a major revamp of the way that programme trailers were made and displayed; revitalising the ailing flagship current affairs programme *Panorama*; introducing the new sitcoms *Bread* and *Blackadder*; dropping coverage of the 'close to offensive' *Miss Great Britain* beauty contest and several other 'anachronistic' sporting game shows; overseeing ongoing plans to introduce the major new twice-weekly soap *EastEnders* and Terry Wogan's new thrice-weekly, prime-time chat show; championing the coverage of Live Aid; and rescheduling a number of existing programmes to instantly boost their ratings.[2] It represented a clear and powerful statement of intent, and certainly encouraged many of the BBC's production teams to believe that they now had an imaginative, energetic and ambitious Controller who would listen, provide support and, if he liked what they delivered, promote the programmes with great confidence, urgency and flair.

As far as the people responsible for *Only Fools and Horses* were concerned, Michael Grade must have seemed like the television executive of their dreams. After enduring four years feeling as though they were never really trusted or taken seriously by some VIPs within the BBC, the team suddenly found themselves overseen by one of the most dynamic and populist figures in British television. If *he* believed in them, they reasoned, he would surely back them to the hilt.

The first sign that he was indeed going to be a great supporter of the show came in May 1985, during a dinner at the Montreux

Television Festival in Switzerland, when Ray Butt found himself seated next to the new Controller of BBC1. The two men had not met before, but Grade was quick to congratulate Butt on his recent programmes and asked him how his current projects were developing. Butt proceeded to explain that *Only Fools and Horses* certainly had an urgent problem: although a ninety-minute Christmas special had recently been commissioned, the idea that John Sullivan now had for the script – which involved the Trotters hiring a boat and travelling abroad on a dubious money-making mission – was going to be too expensive to film on the £600,000 budget they had been allotted. Grade responded by asking Butt how much more money was going to be needed. Butt estimated that it would take around an additional £250,000. Grade simply said: 'You've got it.'[3]

Grade wasted little time in further demonstrating his eagerness to see the show succeed. In August, when it became known that ITV was planning to screen a feature-length edition of the still very popular *Minder* – entitled *Minder on the Orient Express* – as its main prime-time attraction on Christmas Day, Grade knew exactly what to do: he announced that BBC1 would be scheduling the *Only Fools and Horses* special in direct competition.

It was an inspired move by Grade. *Minder* was not only one of ITV's major audience attractions (although now past its peak in terms of ratings, it was still one of the few programmes of the time, other than soaps, that made it consistently into the channel's weekly top ten, averaging just over 13 million viewers[4]), it was also linked unusually closely to *Only Fools* because of their shared focus on the figures and themes associated with London's contemporary black market. No other two shows had tapped into the Thatcherite ethos so brightly and then teased it in such a smartly comical fashion; both featured a strongly characterful double act, dodging and diving while always hoping to get on a nice little earner; and both had spawned several popular catchphrases (such as, in *Minder*'s case, 'The world is your lobster') and been alluded to in real-life reports on a wide range of low-life incidents and adventures. There was, in particular, an obvious elective affinity between Del and Rodney Trotter, and Arthur Daley and Terry McCann, and a sign of how keenly the latter pair continued to compete with the former to command the affection of the British public had come the previous Christmas, when George Cole and Dennis Waterman managed to drag a cheerfully awful novelty song, 'What Are We Gonna Get 'Er Indoors', into the top five of the singles charts. Grade's thorough knowledge of how the tabloids worked thus ensured that every possible angle relating to the imminent clash of the Cockney comedy–dramas would be duly explored and exposed, prompting four months of priceless publicity in the form of newspaper debates and discussions.

As the festive season drew closer, several of the papers went even further, berating the rival broadcasters for the 'agonising choice' (in an era long before the advent of set-top boxes with built-in digital video recorders) they were forcing viewers to make, interviewing all of the key participants for provocative comments (David Jason: 'We will be funnier and better') and cranking up the pressure with such headlines as 'It's Arfur v. Del Boy' and 'Who'll Win the Head-On Clash Between London's Sharpest Characters?'[5] Grade was not finished yet: apart from numerous other press and radio promotional spots, he also arranged for Del Boy to be interviewed at the market for a spoof consumer report on BBC1's high-profile *Breakfast Time* programme, regarding allegations that he had sold six white mice to a customer called 'Mr Buttons' with the promise that they would turn into horses at midnight on the day of purchase. After complaining for so long about the 'mythical' BBC Publicity Department, John Sullivan and his colleagues now saw the real thing very much in action.

The show itself did not quite live up to expectations – in part, perhaps, because they had been hyped up so high – but it still proved very entertaining. Entitled 'To Hull and Back', the plot – the kind of tightly constructed and self-contained tale that had been one aspect of John Sullivan's writing range ever since the third episode of series one, 'Cash and Curry' – concerned a plan by Boycie and his shady associate Abdul to buy some diamonds from a 'Mr Van Kleefe' in Amsterdam and then sell them on for a handsome profit. Del, on the promise of a £15,000 payment, is drawn in to act as a courier, taking the money across the North Sea, delivering it in person to Mr Van Kleefe and then returning to the UK with the stones. The story becomes more complicated once Del discovers that his old nemesis, Chief Inspector Roy Slater, is on the trail of Boycie and Abdul, and, as the devious policeman is about to retire and is keen to end his career on a high note, the tension grows.

After avoiding Slater's men by hiding in Denzil's lorry, and then being navigated, very unreliably, by Uncle Albert across the sea, Del arrives in Amsterdam, does the deal, and then makes his way back to England. What follows involves a couple of double-crosses, the ignominious arrest of the crooked Slater (who has tried to pocket the diamonds for himself), and an unexpected triumph for Del.

The reviews were at best lukewarm, with some critics keen to suggest that the show had seemed far too stretched by the unfamiliar feature-length time slot. Herbert Kretzmer, the *Daily Mail*'s reviewer, dismissed the special (along with its *Minder* rival) as a 'rather dullish affair',[6] while Maureen Paton, writing in the *Daily Express*, provided the most swingeing criticism of all, complaining that the 'preposterous' plot 'would have insulted the intellectual capacity of an amoeba' and, although acknowledging the 'good jokes' and 'superlative acting', she concluded that the need to keep the episode going for ninety minutes had turned the show into a 'parody' of its normal self.[7]

As far as the viewing figures were concerned, however, Michael Grade's gamble had paid off handsomely for both the show and the channel as a whole. The headlines that followed included such eye-catching lines as 'Grade's Christmas Cracker – ITV massacred as BBC hit high spots'.[8] While ITV slumped to what was then an all-time low for a Christmas Day audience, BBC shows dominated the list of the twenty most-watched programmes, with *Only Fools and Horses* (which easily won its own battle with *Minder*) attracting a very impressive 16.9 million viewers.[9] 'It is,' said a delighted Michael Grade, 'an extraordinary success story.'[10]

With the demand for more shows now greater than ever, work on a fifth series began early on in the following year, with Grade – who made sure the press knew that he was planning a 'spectacular' £60m autumn package of programmes[11] – once again promising the team his full support ('*Only Fools,*' he would later explain, rather too modestly, 'was one of those shows I inherited as Controller of BBC1 that were clearly brilliant, but clearly unloved and just thrown into a schedule that was a total muddle. All I did really was to find it the best slots I could and build evening viewing around it'[12]). With John Sullivan already very busy at the time with his other projects – which included not only the third and final series of the keenly anticipated *Just Good Friends* (which was scheduled for the autumn) but also a new sitcom, about a lonely divorcée, called *Dear John* (which began in February) – it was decided to keep the new *Only Fools* episodes at thirty minutes in length, although the option of extending the show at some point in the future would remain very much on the agenda.

Ray Butt, once again, oversaw the production, but – as he, too, currently had other obligations – enlisted a suitably experienced colleague, Mandie Fletcher, to direct the first four of the six episodes. John Sullivan (once again, alas, rather too rushed to develop the kind of shows that realised all of his creative goals) concentrated on writing a set of scripts that were more plot-driven than in previous series, but still explored some interesting themes and emotional tones, and also made more use on a regular basis of the full range of characters that he had now established, including Trigger, Boycie and Marlene, Mike the landlord and Mickey Pearce.

The opening episode, for example, concerned the plight of a pregnant young language student from Germany, but also revealed Marlene's sadness about her struggle to conceive due to Boycie's low sperm count. Although it was quite a convoluted storyline, it still managed to find room for the best writing that John Sullivan had produced so far – at least in *Only Fools* – for a female character.

Entitled 'From Prussia With Love', and broadcast at 8.35 p.m. on Sunday, 31 August 1986, the episode began at closing time in The Nag's Head, where Del and Rodney encounter the tearful Anna. After discovering that the family for whom she has been working part-time as an au pair have thrown her out for getting pregnant, they resolve to help her find alternative accommodation but, after Rodney fails to locate a suitable hotel, he ends up taking her back with him to Nelson Mandela House. Del is not at all pleased about this (RODNEY: 'We're in the European Community now, we've gotta stick together.' DEL: 'Pity her knees didn't!'), but once he hears of how the son of the couple who employed her had made her pregnant and then denied it and let her be dismissed, he takes pity on her. He also hatches a plan to profit from the pregnancy: knowing how much Marlene longs to have a child, he proposes that she and Boycie adopt Anna's baby as soon as it is born – and, as he will be arranging it all, claims £3,000 in 'expenses'. The couple cannot resist, and the plan goes ahead.

When Anna goes into labour, Del does his best to comfort her ('*Vorsprung durch Technik!*') while Albert looks confused and Rodney calls for an ambulance. A week later, Del, Boycie and Marlene all gather round in the lounge waiting for Anna, Albert and Rodney to return from hospital. When Rodney finally arrives, he has more than one little bit of bad news to break to the adopting couple: first, the boy that they were expecting is actually a girl; and second, Anna has fallen in love with her baby and does not want to give her away. The broody Marlene is unaffected by such details: she just wants a baby, of either sex, and Del has assured her that Anna's sudden possessiveness is merely a brief bout of the 'baby blues'. As Boycie moves towards the cot, Del – sensing the icy opprobrium aimed at him from Rodney's glaring eyes – finally feels guilty at pushing the deal through, and suddenly announces that it is off. 'Too bleedin' right it's off,' barks Boycie, who has just spotted something else unexpected about the baby: its colour.

Rodney explains belatedly that the family who had employed Anna were, in fact, West Indians. Boycie is apoplectic but Marlene – as the scene turns tragic-comic – cannot bear to think that her dream of a baby has died:

MARLENE: Well, it don't bother me, Boyce.

BOYCIE: Leave off, Marlene. The baby's *brown!*

MARLENE: So is Duke.

BOYCIE: But I ain't claiming to be Duke's father!

ALBERT: There is a likeness, though.

BOYCIE: Just shut it!

MARLENE: We could say it's a throwback.

BOYCIE: For Gawd's sake, Marlene! I might be able to con people into buying cars. I might be able to convince 'em that you conceived and gave birth in seven days flat, but how the hell am I gonna persuade 'em that my grandad was Louis Armstrong!?! You ain't heard the last of this, Del Boy!

[Boycie exits]

MARLENE: I s'pose he's right, eh, Del?

DEL: Yeah, yeah, you know it makes sense, darlin', eh?

MARLENE: Still, it was a nice little dream while it lasted, eh? I'm gonna turn round now, I'm gonna walk out that door . . . and I ain't gonna look back.

It was another clever switch by John Sullivan: ending an episode that, for most of its duration, had been very light-hearted with a moment that mined raw emotions. The normally frivolous and flirty Marlene – very well played by Sue Holderness – suddenly seemed genuinely vulnerable, sympathetic and unexpectedly dignified, as she faced the loss of the thing she wanted most.

Subsequent episodes tried for the same sort of mixture, but with varying degrees of success. A couple, 'The Longest Night' (in which all three Trotters find themselves embroiled, unwittingly for once, in an elaborate scam to embezzle money from a local supermarket) and 'Video Nasty' (in which Del hijacks Rodney's plans to make an earnest film about the local community and aims instead to create something more commercial with 'suspense, lots of killings and a bit of humpty dumpty'), were like throwbacks to much earlier John Sullivan scripts: busy little 'yarns' that, like the proverbial curate's egg, were good in parts but lacked the multi-dimensional coherence of his more mature efforts. 'The Longest Night' did, to its credit, tell a decent story, with some excellent dialogue, one or two twists and turns and a clever denouement, but 'Video Nasty' suffered from the fact that it seemed like a story-driven episode stuck with large chunks of static dialogue scenes, as far too much of the convoluted action actually happened off camera (Mickey Pearce is said to be off filming local weddings, then Del is away making some calls, then Mickey is left to shoot a 'blue' movie inside the Trotters' flat).

A similar, but slightly better balanced, 'shaggy dog'-style episode, called 'The Miracle of Peckham', saw Del suddenly appearing to feel a few pangs of guilt about his unconventional lifestyle. In a move that shocks Rodney and Albert, he sets off for the local Catholic church, and then shocks the priest, Father O'Keith:

DEL: I have come to confess my sins.

O'KEITH: Oh, Derek, please! I've been invited out to dinner this evening!

DEL: Well, it's just one *main* sin, really.

O'KEITH: Oh, thanks be to God for that! Wait a minute: I didn't know you were Catholic. *Are* you a Catholic?

DEL: Eh? Well, I don't know, do I? I don't know *that*. I was only a kid, but me Mum was a Catholic.

O'KEITH: Have you ever been to this church before?

DEL: Well, of course I have, when me Mum and Dad got married.

O'KEITH: You were just a little baby then! I mean have you ever been to this church since then?

DEL: Ooh, um . . . no.

O'KEITH: Del, my boy, you disappoint me.

DEL: I watched *The Ten Commandments* on the telly! Look, Father, I don't wanna get up there on Judgement Day and find out that I'm on the hit list. I mean, God sees everything, doesn't he?

O'KEITH: Look, Derek, this is not the God'll Fix it Show. Forgiveness is only for those who feel shame and remorse.

DEL: I *do* feel shame and remorse. Father, does it matter what religion I am?

O'KEITH: Well . . . I don't know that you're *not* a Catholic, do I?

DEL: No, that's the spirit, you know it makes sense!

Del ends up agreeing, by way of penance, to raise an impressive sum of money for a local hospice, but he does so by publicising the 'fact' that the statue of the Virgin Mary in the church has now – via 'an authentic deluxe miracle' – started 'weeping' holy tears. Once the curious media has been and gone and the cash has been collected, Father O'Keith, glancing up at the rain that is now pouring down from the roof, realises what has really been happening: 'This isn't a miracle – it's a flaming leak!' he shouts. 'Someone has stolen the lead!' Rodney's face lights up at this news: 'No, wait, you're in luck, because we've got a load of lead in our ga . . . rage.[To Del] I don't believe you!' This prompts a compromised Father O'Keefe to contemplate Del's true reason for his confession.

Probably the most successful episode in the series was 'Tea for Three' – which, although again driven on by the storyline, found plenty of time for the key characters to interact, and contained another one of those outstanding set-piece scenes that embedded itself on the memory. The story saw Del and Rodney compete for the affections of Trigger's attractive young niece, Lisa, who is staying with him for a while before heading home to Winchester. After both of them invite her to join them for tea at the flat (with Del providing the Chicken Italienne, fruit salad and Dream Topping, and Rodney supplying the cheese), the battle for supremacy begins.

Del, predictably, is the first to resort to dirty tricks: realising that Rodney has dozed off while using their new 'home solarium', Del cranks up the heat and then saunters off to buy another packet of Smash and a bottle of Brut. By the time he gets back and Lisa arrives, Rodney's face is lobster red, leaving him to watch helplessly as his big brother tries his hardest to impress their guest, boasting about his supposed days as a paratrooper ('I used to freefall from 20,000 foot!') and his completely imaginary expertise as a hang-glider.

Eager for revenge, Rodney takes note of Lisa's own interest in hang-gliding, and so, when the two of them volunteer to drive her back to Winchester, he arranges with Lisa to give Del a surprise 'treat' to mark his forty-sixth birthday: a special session up in the air at the local hang-gliding club. Horrified at the thought of his feet deserting 'terra cotta', but desperate not to disappoint the watching Lisa, Del takes the smug-looking Rodney to one side and begs him to come to the rescue: 'I know that we haven't been seeing eye to eye for the last few days, but, I mean, listen to me, we are *brothers* after all, ain't we? I mean, it's *blood!* It's like Uncle Albert said, he said brothers shouldn't fall out over a woman. Didn't he, *eh?* Come on, what d'you reckon? Eh, Rodney, *eh?*' Rodney appears to agree, hugging Del and agreeing to halt his flight at the very last minute by rushing over with the news that they have had an urgent call on their car phone and must leave for London immediately.

Del is delighted with the plan. He marches back cockily to the hang-glider, gets himself dressed up and strapped in, and then waits for Rodney's arrival. Rodney, however, is still in the distance, leaning against the yellow van, looking thoroughly uninterested in the proceedings. Del begins to panic. After casting several anxious glances in his younger brother's direction, he cups his hand to his ear and shouts:

DEL: Er, is that, is that our *phone* I can hear ringing,
            Rodney?
RODNEY: Eh?
DEL: I said: is that our *phone* I can hear *ringing?*

RODNEY: No!

DEL: Are you *sure?*

RODNEY: Yeah. *[Smiling slyly in triumph]* We ain't got a car phone!

[Del's eyes widen in horror. He is speechless.]

RODNEY: Get up as high as you can, Del. You might get a tan!

The next thing that Del knows is that he is flying high above the countryside, screaming into the breeze as he heads off helplessly to sea.

Rodney's pleasure turns to anxiety when Del disappears for twelve hours. When, much to his relief, Trigger and Mike bring his brother back, bandaged and in a wheelchair – it seems that he crashed into a TV transmitter somewhere in Redhill – Rodney suspects yet another sibling scam: 'Hospitals do not send home paralysed people by bus! What is it you are after, Del – sympathy from Lisa or a disabled sticker for the van, eh?' Del snaps at such an accusation, and leaps up from his wheelchair and grabs Rodney by his lapels: 'You listen to me, you vicious little git! I may never walk again for the rest of . . . *[Suddenly realising that he is standing]* Although, I must admit, I'm getting *some* feeling back.'

Before any further devious tricks can be planned, Trigger mentions, in a matter-of-fact manner, that Lisa is getting married, and she has invited both brothers to attend. Stunned and deflated, the two Trotters slump down into their chairs, while Albert stands and laughs at 'what a couple of wallys' they are.

The episode was another classic edition of *Only Fools and Horses*, with David Jason and Nicholas Lyndhurst combining brilliantly to bring out not only all of the comedy, but also all of the realism, in what could otherwise have so easily been a rather cartoon-like story of sibling rivalry. Although it lacked the more dramatic aspects of some of the other outstanding programmes, it was structured with admirable precision (seven minutes to set up the story, seven minutes for Del's prank, seven minutes for Rodney's, and then just under seven minutes for their mutual comeuppance) and the comic climax was timed to perfection. Once again, the show not only made people laugh – it also, as a 'did you see' television event, got them talking about it during the days ahead.

Ironically, however, it could have been the last of such shows. At the start of the week when John Sullivan was about to write the final episode of the series, David Jason had said that he wanted to finish with *Only Fools*.

The actor broke the news over dinner at Le Caprice restaurant in St James's in the West End of London. Sullivan and his wife had gone there with Jason and his girlfriend for what had seemed, ostensibly, to be just another pleasant social occasion. As the evening went on, however, Jason shook Sullivan by saying that, as proud as he was of what they had achieved, he felt the time had come to pursue other projects.

Sullivan went home, saddened by, but respectful of, his friend's decision. The following morning, he had to start thinking about what should be done. He knew that recasting the role of Del Boy was not a realistic option, but he was not ready to completely abandon the comic world that he had created.

He asked for a meeting with Gareth Gwenlan, the BBC's current Head of Comedy, and they discussed the matter at length. It was decided, eventually, that Sullivan would write a final episode – 'Who Wants to Be a Millionaire?' – in which Del is offered the chance by an old mate of his to emigrate to Australia, and Rodney, because of his minor drugs conviction, is forced to stay behind. The last scene would show Del flying out of the country and Rodney walking back out of the airport looking lost. The plan, after that, was to launch a spin-off sitcom for the younger Trotter, called *Hot Rod*, which would still feature all of the other familiar members of the Peckham posse and would always leave the door open for Del, and David Jason, to reappear.

That last scene, however, would never be written, because, as Sullivan was in the middle of working on the episode, David Jason suddenly changed his mind, the spin-off was scrapped and talks began about making more specials and series. Delighted though Sullivan was to hear about this last-minute *volte-face*, it did leave him with no choice but to complete the episode he had planned, hastily rethinking the ending to ensure that Del declined the move Down Under.

'Who Wants to Be a Millionaire?' was, given the extraordinary circumstances, a very impressive effort by the scriptwriter, with a cleverly choreographed sequence of events, and emotions, bringing the fifth series to a thoroughly entertaining end. It commenced with the arrival back on British shores of Del's old business partner, Jumbo Mills, to close a deal with Boycie. Although his brashness and boorishness irritates most of the regulars in The Nag's Head, Del is pleased to see him again, and is soon seduced by his promise of a new partnership in Australia: 'They'd love you over there – they've got no class!' After ensuring that he can take Rodney and Albert with him, the problems begin to arise: first, Albert declares that he has travelled quite enough and is set on ending his days in Peckham, and then Rodney's past problems with the 'waccy baccy' cause his request for a visa to be rejected.

Del rather stuns Rodney by saying that he is still keen to leave. It is, he explains, his 'golden opportunity' to make himself, this time next year, a millionaire. Rodney, glancing around the flat at the twenty-four boxes of computers that do not compute, a rug with a sell-by date and Del's little black book of ageing dates, declares that he is not at all happy about his own prospects stuck in Peckham. Insisting that, with money so tight during a depression, people cannot afford inflated shop prices and will turn instead to 'people like us', so the 'real opportunity' is actually to be found here in the UK, Rodney urges Del to think again, but when his big brother repeats his determination to leave, an emotional Rodney snaps, 'I'll see you around, "*sport*"!' and heads for the door. After Rodney storms out, Del goes ahead and calls Jumbo, now back in Australia, to let him know when he is coming, but, when he gets through, decides that he must stay where he is ('It's loyalties, innit? Family ties, an' all that'). The telephone is put down. 'What else could I do?', he says glumly to Albert.

Rodney – having thought things through – returns, ready to apologise, but Del surprises him by admitting that he has changed his mind. In a closing exchange that, for the remarkably deft and poignant way that it brought the brothers back together, would have been impressive had Sullivan written it at leisure, let alone frantically against the clock, the old order of things is restored:

RODNEY: Because of what I said?
DEL: Well, yeah, in a way, Rodney, in a way, because you said, 'The real opportunity lies here.' Didn't you? You know, the country's in a bad way, money's tight, people are looking for bargains, and, you know, who do they turn to first, eh?

RODNEY: Blokes like us.

DEL: Yes, blokes like us. See, I was sitting here, and I thought, 'No, Rodney has hit the nail right on the head there.' I thought, this wonderful land of ours is on the *eve* of a *golden* age of the black market. And you and me, you know, we're gonna be in there first! I'm glad I listened to you, Rodney, I really am, because if I'd have taken that 'Chance of a Lifetime' it could have ruined me!

RODNEY: So we're . . . we're still partners?

DEL: Yes, if you'll have me back.

RODNEY: Oh, well, let me sleep on it, eh?

DEL: I'll smack you in the nose, saucy sod!

RODNEY: *[Choking with emotion]* Hey Del: this time next year, eh?

DEL: Yeah, you know: this time next year, eh?

RODNEY: Well, I'll see you in the morning.

DEL: Yeah, see you in the morning.

RODNEY: And Del, you know . . .

DEL: Yeah, I know, bruv. Goodnight . . .

[Rodney exits to the bedroom]

DEL: Yeah . . . this time . . . next year.

[Del downs his drink with a vengeance. He crosses to the door and looks back at the room. He is deeply saddened. A tear is in the corner of his eye. He sings, his voice faltering with emotion and frustration.]

DEL: 'Who wants to be a millionaire . . .?'

Moving, amusing and exceptionally well-observed, it was an inspired end to the series, showing yet again how richly rewarding the show could be when both the scriptwriter and the actors were at their very best. Broadcast on 5 October 1986, an audience of 18.8 million[13] – the biggest so far – saw it, and there was little doubt as to how warmly this, and the other episodes, had been received. The fan mail was pouring in, the actors were being called by their characters' names in public, the teetotal Buster Merryfield was being offered a seemingly endless succession of glasses of cognac and rum, and Del's distinctive lingo – including 'cushty', 'luvvly jubbly', 'wally', 'twonk' and 'plonker' – was now in wide circulation in offices, factory floors, streets and schoolyards. The series as a whole, which averaged 16 million viewers per week,[14] once again impressed the critics (with *The Stage*, for example, applauding it for being 'brilliant in conception, writing and playing'[15]) and also attracted three BAFTA nominations (David Jason and Nicholas Lyndhurst for 'Best Light Entertainment Performance' and the show for 'Best Comedy Series').

The fifth series, in truth, had not been without its faults. Buster Merryfield, for example, had seemed, at times, rather too noticeably like the relatively inexperienced professional actor that he was. The series had seen him start to slide into a few old 'am-dram' bad habits – particularly the head jutting mechanically back and forth like a manic tortoise, the mouth gaping open for too long and a swaying, jerking, rolling gait that resembled a tipsy Norman Wisdom trying to stand up and walk in a rowing boat – that would increasingly undermine some of his later performances, occasionally making Uncle Albert appear a little too cartoon-like to complement such wonderfully subtle character actors as Jason and Lyndhurst. He remained, nonetheless, a very popular figure with most viewers, was clearly having the time of his life, and his dual roles as a comic feed and a source of light relief would continue to serve the show well.

The many strengths of the series far outweighed any weaknesses, and its current high profile as the sitcom *du jour* soon led to a belated invitation for the team to make an appearance at that year's *Royal Variety Performance*. Scheduled to take place on 24 November 1986 at the Theatre Royal, Drury Lane, it was an honour that placed quite a strain on John Sullivan and the crew, as they were already hard at work filming another feature-length Christmas special on location in Salisbury in Wiltshire. Sullivan hurriedly wrote a short (four-minute) sketch, shooting was temporarily halted, and Jason, Lyndhurst and Merryfield travelled back to London to take part in the show.

In an effective little routine, Del, Rodney and Albert arrived on stage at Drury Lane thinking that they were delivering some dodgy goods to someone called 'Chunky Lewis' – a nightclub owner in the West End. Unfortunately, having taken a wrong turn, they realise eventually that they have ended up walking into the middle of the *Royal Variety Performance* – where they mistake the Duchess of York for Chunky Lewis. Their contribution was deemed a great success, and, in the post-show lineup, the Queen Mother (who had smiled and waved at Rodney and Del during the performance) studied Buster Merryfield carefully – 'So the beard is real then!'[16] – and told all of the actors how much she and the rest of the Royal Family enjoyed watching their show.

It was a welcome tribute, but, once location work was resumed back in a very wet and chilly Wiltshire, the cast and crew began to rue the disruption the royal show had caused. An already tight schedule now seemed even more problematic – and then things went from bad to worse. First, three more days were lost when David Jason lost his voice, and then, soon after, shooting was stalled yet again when Nicholas Lyndhurst was felled by a bout of flu. These delays meant that the production was now so far behind schedule that there would be no time for the completed film to be screened in front of a studio audience – hence there would be no laughter track – and there would also be no time available for any music to be added to the soundtrack. The team was now in very serious trouble.

A less important show, being made at a less important time of the TV year, might well have been postponed to ensure that a proper professional job was done as far as preparing the programme for the screen, but this was an *Only Fools and Horses* Christmas special, which had already been heavily promoted for several weeks, and it simply had to appear in its designated slot in the Christmas Day schedules. The pressure on everyone involved, therefore, was immense.

The interior scenes were shot on a set built at Elstree Studios, but, at one stage, time was so pressing that contingency plans were even made for the final scene in the Trotters' flat to be filmed live on the day of transmission. Eventually, following a concerted effort from all of the cast and crew, the recording was completed just in time. Ray Butt – who was back as producer–director – and his assistant Tony Dow took the tapes and finished off the editing in the early hours of Christmas morning. They had, against the odds, delivered.

The result – a seventy-five-minute special entitled 'A Royal Flush' – was broadcast that evening at 7.05 p.m. The fact that it went out at all was regarded as something of a triumph by those who had made it, but, to those 18.8 million people who simply saw it,[17] 'A Royal Flush' was a huge disappointment, and arguably represented the nadir of *Only Fools and Horses*.

It had been a rushed and sometimes incredibly chaotic production, and, alas, it showed on the screen. The programme was a very *Steptoe and Son*-style story of one working-class man's upwardly mobile aspirations being thwarted by the actions of his far more vulgar relation, but, in stark contrast to *Steptoe and Son*, the spectacularly clumsy way in which the tale was told undermined whatever message was originally intended.

Rodney becomes romantically involved with a woman called Vicky, a seemingly impoverished artist who turns out to be the daughter of the Duke of Maylebury. Del, however, ruins his brother's chances of making the relationship work by popping up in all of the posh places the couple frequent. When, for example, they go to the Royal Opera House to see *Carmen*, Del and his peroxide blonde girlfriend turn up, talking non-stop, munching on liquorice allsorts, licking ice-creams and arguing with other members of the audience. Vicky then invites Rodney to a party at her father's elegant country home, but Del, once again, arrives, hits the 'vino-plonko', insults his fellow guests and ruins everything for his younger brother.

The main problem with the show was that, within the context of this particular sitcom, it seemed to lack any logic. After working so hard during the previous five series and festive specials to emphasise the complex but very strong emotional bonds that bound the two brothers so tightly together, this story seemed to depict Del as an utterly insensitive and uncaring individual who was oblivious of Rodney's own needs and feelings. More specifically, his behaviour at the Duke of Maylebury's country home – when, during the painfully long dinner scene, he happily gets drunk, abusive and boorish, upsets everyone around him and seems utterly unaware of how badly he is humiliating his own brother – makes him seem like some kind of simple-minded pantomime villain.

It would later transpire that, in the haste to complete the filming, lines got crossed and errors were overlooked. John Sullivan would definitely have intervened had he been around at the time, but he was in Paris on location with one of his other sitcoms, *Just Good Friends*. 'I wish to God I'd been on [the set of] *Only Fools* instead,' he would later confirm when reflecting on the notorious dinner scene. 'It was written for laughs, not drama, and I wanted David to be Del as a jolly drunk rather than a morose drunk, which is what he ended up looking like.'[18] The director Ray Butt would later claim to feeling similarly contrite, expressing regret that, during the filming of this particular scene, he failed to realise that David Jason, for once, was pushing his performance too far.

Butt was surely being somewhat disingenuous, however, when he said that the dinner scene was the 'only' part of the show that he regretted. That was indeed by far the worst scene, but there was plenty else that really ought to have prompted some blushes. The opera sequence, for example, was another over-long and over-done affair (which, amazingly for a John Sullivan script, seemed to drip with contempt for Del and his girlfriend's working-class attitudes, while completely ignoring the vapid outlook of Rodney's spoilt and one-dimensional companion), and the final scene back in the flat, when Del callously admits to his brother that he arranged a £1,000 pay-off from the Duke for him to stop seeing Vicky, and then squeezes Rodney's injured hand to punish him for turning it down, were two more scenes that should have made Butt and his team uneasy.

A better sign of how dissatisfied they were with the show

would come in 2004 when the special was released on DVD. It was heavily re-edited (with at least eighteen minutes of cuts) and an audience laughter track was also added.

The following year saw various members of the *Only Fools* team disperse to work on other projects – David Jason, for example, appeared in the award-winning four-part Channel 4 adaptation of the Tom Sharpe comic novel *Porterhouse Blue*, Nicholas Lyndhurst continued his involvement in the ITV sitcom he had joined a few months before called *The Two of Us* and John Sullivan was writing the second series of *Dear John* – and Michael Grade left the BBC to become Chief Executive of Channel 4. Interest in *Only Fools*, however, remained intense, and no one involved could resist an opportunity to return. The new Controller of BBC1, Jonathan Powell, made sure that more programmes were commissioned, and the team came back together in autumn 1987 to start location work in Ipswich on another Christmas special (this time lasting an hour) called 'The Frog's Legacy'. It would prove itself to be, thankfully, a much more relaxed and rewarding project than the previous year's shambolic effort, and resulted in a much more effective show.

It began, very wisely, with the Trotters back on familiar territory, trying and failing to shift their dubious wares. Some faulty 'RAJAH' computers, in particular, are failing to attract much of a market, and even the odd one or two that have been sold ('It's got ROM, it's got RAM, it's got them little red and green lights . . .') are doing Del no favours at all by causing havoc. The belated wedding of Trigger's niece, Lisa, provides them with a welcome distraction, and, as they chat to a few old family members, one particular anecdote causes Del to sit up and take notice.

The story goes that Freddie 'The Frog' Robdal was an art-loving gentleman thief from Rotherhithe who had a brief affair with Del's mother back in 1959 (not long before Rodney was born). He was part of the gang that robbed a London bank of £250,000 in gold bullion in 1963. While the rest of the gang were swiftly apprehended, Robdal managed to escape and hide all of the gold. Shortly after this incident, so the rumour goes, Robdal and an explosives expert, known as 'Jelly' Kelly, attempted to break into a post office in Plumstead, but as the robbery seemed to be proceeding according to plan, Robdal inexplicably sat on the detonator, killing both men almost instantly. Robdal's body was found on the roof of a building opposite.

Del's curiosity is roused even more when he hears that Robdal's will bequeathed all of his ill-gotten gains – including the lost gold – to Mrs Trotter, who in turn left everything to Del and Rodney. 'I'm a millionaire,' Del exclaims, although he admits that it is a bit of a 'choker' that no one knows where any of the million is.

A breakthrough is made, quite by accident, when Del gets Rodney a new job working for the local funeral directors as the chief mourner. After expressing his anger at Del for pushing him into yet another humiliating situation, he makes good use of his new position by picking up some information: it appears that, long ago, Robdal had purchased a coffin from Rodney's employers for a so-called 'friend' by the name of 'Alfred Broderick'. Rodney soon deduces not only that 'Alfred Broderick' is actually an anagram of Frederick Robdal, but also that Robdal must have purchased the coffin to hide the gold inside and then bury it via a fake funeral.

Now hot on the scent, an excited Del eventually tracks

down where the burial took place: somewhere at sea. The local vicar informs him that Robdal got the nickname of 'Freddie the Frog' not because he was a cultural Francophile but rather because he was a frogman in the Royal Navy. Del, nonetheless, refuses to acknowledge that he has abandoned the gold, even though he has no idea how to retrieve it. This time next year, he vows, he and Rodney will be millionaires.

Broadcast at 6.25 p.m. on Christmas Day, the show attracted a slightly disappointing audience of 14.5 million,[19] but those who did see it – and had been disappointed by the previous year's effort – probably had their faith more or less fully restored in *Only Fools and Horses*. The episode had a strong storyline that unfolded at a lively pace, and the old balance between sharp comic dialogue and strong character acting was very much back on display. There was the regular range of familiar characters – Uncle Albert, Trigger, Boycie, Marlene and Mike the landlord – and several entertaining exchanges in the flat, and, most reassuringly of all, the complicated, emotional, funny relationship between Del Boy and Rodney was back to normal. It was a decent episode, and a highlight of the night.

It would turn out to be the last time that Ray Butt, the producer–director, was involved with the show, because, at the start of the following year, he left the BBC to become Controller of Situation Comedy at Central TV. As much as he was excited at the prospect of assuming responsibility for Central's sitcom output, he greatly regretted having to cut his ties with a programme that he had helped guide all the way from obscure conception, back in that smoky old pub early in 1981, to high-profile peak-time success on BBC1.

Butt did attempt, however, to maintain his involvement with

the team by proposing, a short while after his departure, a stage show for *Only Fools and Horses*. It made good sense at the time, commercially, because, ever since the cast of *Dad's Army* had appeared in the West End in a very popular stage version of the sitcom in 1976, and, more recently, the team responsible for *'Allo 'Allo* had drawn a similarly enthusiastic television audience into the London theatre scene, such spin-offs were well-received. The three lead actors were keen on the idea, but their and Sullivan's increasing commitments to other projects meant it never came to fruition.

Gareth Gwenlan, one of the show's first supporters and the BBC's current Head of Comedy, was the obvious choice to take over Butt's responsibilities as producer, and he chose Tony Dow, who had previously worked on the show as an assistant floor manager and then production manager, to direct. 'I couldn't take the show on myself,' Gwenlan would explain, 'so we decided to give Tony a chance, while I would babysit him – not that he needed much of that.'[20]

As much as John Sullivan was sad to see his old friend Ray Butt depart, he was pleased to welcome Tony Dow to such a prominent position in the team, not least because, after a few years of being kept at a certain distance from the 'business end' of the production process, Dow was perfectly amenable to the scriptwriter playing a more significant role. 'He came through slowly,' John Sullivan would say of Dow, 'and we'd been mates – I was his best man and all that – so that at the time he took over directing we knew each other very well personally. Once Tony took over I became even more involved.'[21]

The new team's first collaboration came at the end of 1988 with another Christmas special – this one an eighty-minute episode entitled 'Dates'. It was an encouraging start, with an engaging blend of comedy, romance and drama that developed gradually into quite an affecting finale.

The story opened in the flat, with the two Trotter brothers totting up their recent sales. It transpires that Trotters Independent Traders has been doing very well in recent months, so Del and Rodney are in a celebratory mood. Uncle Albert, on the other hand, seems more interested in wallowing in nostalgia. After enduring another one of his Navy-themed monologues, Rodney realises that it will soon be the old boy's birthday, so Del decides to stage a surprise for him at The Nag's Head.

Meanwhile, inside the pub itself, Trigger is causing a stir with his bright blue suit and his announcement that he is about to meet a woman with whom he has been matched by a local dating agency. Del is shaken when, a short while later, he spots Trigger entering an Italian restaurant alongside someone who does indeed resemble a proper woman. Impressed that even Trigger can be set up with a female, Del decides to sign up himself at the same dating agency, styling himself as 'Derek Duvall', managing director of a successful import and export business. Guaranteeing the lucky woman a steak meal, he specifies that she must live locally, have everything in the right place, appreciate the arts and be sufficiently refined to recognise the difference between a Liebfraumilch and a can of Tizer. The candidate suggested is a thirty-year-old actress called Raquel Turner. Del is intrigued – 'Raquel is my most favourite name!' – and so a lunch date is duly arranged.

Rodney has also arranged to meet a young woman: a barmaid from The Nag's Head called Nerys, best-known to every regular except him as 'Nervous Nerys'. Mickey Pearce, sensing another chance to trick his old friend, convinces Rodney that the best way to impress Nerys is to adopt a wild and dangerous 'James Dean' persona.

Del's date goes surprisingly well. Although reeking of cheap cologne, carrying an ostentatious bouquet of carnations and feeling far too confident for his own good ('My old *joie de vivre* will knock her bandy'), he seems to charm Raquel (nicely played by Tessa Peake-Jones) more or less immediately. She is honest enough to confess that her acting career is modest in the extreme, whereas Del continues to imply that he is a successful international businessman, and the couple agree to meet up again as soon as possible. Rodney's date, on the other hand, proves to be an unmitigated disaster: from the moment when he picks her up in the dirty yellow three-wheel van and almost chokes her with his cigarette smoke, to the moment when they speed off to avoid a gang of punks, swerve past two shocked police officers and narrowly avoid knocking over several pedestrians, poor Nerys is terrified and tearful.

Del invites Raquel to join him on Friday for Albert's surprise party, but she has to decline, explaining that she has to attend her regular acting class on that date. Del, therefore, has to make do with Rodney, who is still recovering from his humiliatingly unromantic ordeal. Down at The Nag's Head, as a well-oiled Albert pounds the pub piano and slurs his way through a succession of bawdy music-hall songs, Del tells his younger brother all about his beautiful, refined and supremely talented actress girlfriend. The birthday celebrations reach their climax when Del's most special surprise arrives: a strippergram who proceeds to dance in front of a startled Albert. All goes wonderfully well until the woman spins around and she spots Del, and he spots her. It is Raquel.

Humiliated by all of his friends' mocking laughter, he races out of the pub and goes into the car park to kick the van. As Rodney chases after him, Raquel emerges, begging him to let her explain. She only strips in order to pay for her drama lessons, she says, and, although she has indeed deceived him, so has the so-called Derek Duvall deceived her. Del is too proud to back down, and turns his back on her, leaving her to walk off alone.

Regretting his behaviour, he is secretly pleased when he bumps into her again a few days later. Raquel tells him that she has quit her job as a stripper and plans to move to the Middle East. If he is still interested in her, she says, he should visit her before her flight leaves. Softening, Del intends to do so after one last drink at The Nag's Head, but then encounters the two police officers – one male, one female – still looking for the owner of the Rodney's speeding yellow van. Believing the female police officer to be a 'revenge' stripper hired by Albert, Del promptly tears her blouse open, and is arrested.

Believing she has been jilted, a heartbroken Raquel gets into a taxi and sets off for the Middle East just as Del is taken into custody. 'You don't know the code for Addis Ababa, do you?' Del asks plaintively.

'Dates' once again confirmed the popularity of *Only Fools and Horses*, with 16.6 million people watching it on Christmas Day.[21] It also impressed the critics, attracting plenty of favourable reviews, and would go on to win a BAFTA award for 'Best Comedy'.

Buoyed by this fresh success and optimistic about the idea of taking the show into a new era, the team now wanted to change something before the next series was made. What they wanted was more time.

The reason for this was that John Sullivan had struggled for

The sitcom-soap commences:
Del loves Raquel . . .

. . . and Rodney loves Cassandra.

Tempus fugit: no longer a timeless sitcom, *Only Fools* moves on with the clock ticking. © BBC Photo Library

On the set of 'Miami Twice': a special sitcom starts concentrating on seasonal specials. © Mirrorpix

Time on Our Hands:
a fine finale for the
1996 trilogy.
© BBC Photo Library

So long, farewell, auf wiedersehen, adieu: the 2001 return struck some critics as one goodbye too many.
© Liam Daniel/BBC Photo Library

David Jason refused
to be typecast as Del,
finding fresh fame first as
Pop Larkin . . .
© ITV/Rex Features

. . . and then as
Detective Inspector Frost.
© ITV/Rex Features

Nicholas Lyndhurst also relished appearing in other roles, most notably as the time-travelling Gary Sparrow in *Goodnight Sweetheart*.
© FreemantleMedia Ltd/Rex Features

John Sullivan built on the success of *Only Fools* by writing several more warmly received sitcoms, beginning with *Just Good Friends*.
© BBC Photo Library

At the heart of every great sitcom is a special relationship: in *Only Fools*, David Jason and Nicholas Lyndhurst combined to give a master class in great character acting.
Above: ©Terry O'Neill/ Getty Images;
Below: © Getty Images Entertainment

'It's family, innit!' *Only Fools* came to thrive, more and more, on great ensemble acting. © BBC Photo Library

'TVs, deep freeze and David Bowie LPs': the Trotters' flat, preserved as a museum piece for fans of *Only Fools and Horses*.
© Rob Howarth/Rex Features

The much-missed John Sullivan: a shy, decent, hugely talented man
who proved that good guys sometimes do get to the top.
© Rex Features

a while to cram all of his ideas into the sitcom's conventional thirty-minute format, and, after three years of writing feature-length specials, was in no mood to return to the old constraints for a new series. David Jason was firmly behind his writer's ambitions: 'John was really beginning to get the bit between his teeth – he was amazingly on song. He was producing some of the funniest material I'd ever read, and I said to him one day: "John, I'm really fed up with this." He asked why, and I replied: "Because you're over-writing, we're having to cut, and we're throwing away more funny lines than most situation comedies have in their whole thirty minutes." We'd often had to cut John's work, but it was becoming a hatchet job.'[23]

Sullivan himself had done his best over the years to keep a sense of balance between his artistic principles and his professional pragmatism: 'I always fight and argue like hell about the structure [of a script] when people want to make changes, and I go, "No, it upsets the structure, the balance is gone." Then we finish the show and they say: "God, we're ten minutes too long," and immediately I go: "Oh, we can cut that bit, cut that out . . ."'[24] Now, however, he wanted his principles to be given greater weight.

The campaign to extend the show's running time had actually commenced back in 1984. Ray Butt had first tried to change things shortly after the third series, when he asked the then-Controller of BBC1, Alan Hart, to consider increasing the length of each episode from thirty to forty-five minutes, but Hart had rejected the request on the grounds that it would dilute the comedy content. The argument, however, had continued over the next few years, and, when Gareth Gwenlan assumed control of the show, Sullivan and Jason asked him to address the issue again.

Gwenlan was not opposed to the idea in principle, but his problem in practice was that the studio time had already been booked for the next series, and that meant that each episode (regardless of its length) would have to be rehearsed and recorded within a week. Filming a forty-minute episode, let alone anything longer, was deemed to be close to impossible given that timescale, but Gwenlan still went ahead and arranged a meeting with the then-BBC1 Controller, Jonathan Powell, to explore the possible options. Gwenlan suggested, as a practicable compromise, adding an extra five minutes. Powell, like his predecessor Michael Grade, was very pleased to do what he could to support the show. He said that a thirty-five-minute show would not be too difficult to schedule, and told Gwenlan to go ahead.

Gwenlan then told Sullivan to write his first thirty-five-minute script. Sullivan thanked him, wrote it, and sent it in. The producer was delighted with the result. There was only one problem: it lasted an hour.

An anxious Gwenlan contacted his writer immediately and pointed out that this was simply impractical. Sullivan suggested cutting the script down to fifty minutes. Gwenlan said that he suspected that Jonathan Powell would be happy with a set of episodes of that length, but the fact remained that the production schedule could not now be changed and recording a fifty-minute show in a single day was a dauntingly tall order. Sullivan, however, still had the full support of David Jason, and Nicholas Lyndhurst was also backing the idea of longer episodes, and so the decision was made to attempt the improbable – or impossible – and get the shows made.

A huge 40 per cent increase in the budget had to be sanctioned by Jonathan Powell, and the period allotted for location shooting was promptly extended to enable the team to film enough inserts for each episode and thus reduce the amount of time required for recording in the studio. Although this helped to make the task seem a little more manageable, the realisation that the last three scripts were set almost entirely indoors meant that the team was still facing an almost unbearably punishing schedule.

Jason, however, would be unrepentant about forcing the changes through. 'I'm so glad John and I stuck to our guns,' he said, 'because it broke the mould, and gave John a much better chance to breathe. He could actually flesh out his characters more, and had extra time to develop his storylines.'[25]

Now, the team agreed, the big step forward could finally be taken. They had serious backing from the BBC, and the added breadth and depth to make each episode a major event. The new series, as a result, promised to be something rather different.

CHAPTER NINE

The Sitcom Soap

Marque de fabrique!

British television had already seen a number of successful sitcoms that ran on for many series. Prior to *Only Fools and Horses*, however, such sitcoms had seemed broadly the same at the end as they had done at the start; the content might have matured a little but the form stayed firmly the same. They always seemed like sitcoms. *Only Fools and Horses*, however, was not like that. It changed – not necessarily for the better, or for the worse, but, nonetheless, quite profoundly.

In the traditional sitcom, the essential ingredients are static: people do not meet their soul mates, people do not breed, people do not die and people do not move on. Inside this fenced and gated fictional community, the key characters are constrained by their situation and trapped by their relationships. That is how the centre holds, and why the sitcom never falls apart.

Only Fools and Horses had conformed to this norm completely until the fourth series in 1984, when death – with the passing of Grandad – intruded into the fiction. It would only be with the arrival of the sixth series at the start of 1989, however, that the show suddenly deviated so much further from the norm that it started to seem like a strange kind of hybrid of a sitcom and something else entirely.

It was the romance that did it. Up until the sixth series, any romance in *Only Fools and Horses* had been kept strictly within the rules of the typical sitcom: short, shambolic or bittersweet, and always doomed. In the first series, Del got engaged again to an ex-fiancée, only to break it off at the end of the same episode; in the second series, Rodney dated a policewoman until she discovered what the Trotter family did for a living, then he fell for an older, married woman and had to be extricated from that dangerous relationship by Del; then Del himself had a brief dalliance with a married woman until she returned to her husband; later on, during the fourth series, Del dated a mother and Rodney her daughter, only for both women to leave Peckham just as suddenly as they arrived; then, in 'A Royal Flush', Del sabotaged Rodney's relationship with a posh young woman; and, in 'Dates', Del met and promptly lost Raquel.

All of this transient romance would change, however, with the advent of the sixth series. John Sullivan now believed that it was time for the Trotter brothers to grow up and settle down.

It was part of the writer's ambition to make his longer, and more elaborate, episodes a much richer and regular mix of comedy and drama, full of emotional twists and turns. 'The first series was difficult,' he would say. 'I never really enjoy the beginning because you haven't had a chance to establish the characters in your mind – but now I know everything about Del: I know where he went to school, I even know what desk he sat at.'[1] It thus felt like the right moment, he believed, to make Del and Rodney act more like their actual age, and make them seem more real – and to make those of a similar age who were watching them identify with them more strongly than ever before.

They no longer seemed merely like sitcom characters to their fans; they now seemed like friends, neighbours or work-mates, or like members of the family, and Sullivan therefore wanted to show them experiencing not only the highs but also the lows, in public as well as in private, just like ordinary viewers were doing at home. 'My argument,' he would say, 'always has been that my wife and I can be sitting in here celebrating something wonderful . . . the champagne's going . . . and over there, there could be a death in the family.'[2] He wanted it to be like that on the screen.

Sullivan's boyhood literary hero, Charles Dickens, had coined a phrase for such a fictional blend: 'streaky bacon'. The approach, as Dickens put it, was to 'present the tragic and the comic scenes, in as regular alternation, as the layers of red and white in a side of streaky, well-cured bacon'.[3] The modern television format most suited to such 'streaky bacon' was the soap, not the sitcom, and so, although Sullivan did not plan it consciously at the time, his show was about to synthesise aspects of both of these genres and evolve into what one might term a 'sitcom soap'.

The familiar one-off comic plots would still be featured, but certain other storylines – dealing with Del and Rodney's respective romantic entanglements – would start running from one episode, and series, to the next. New characters would come in, the old ones would be affected, and time – real, remorseless, ticking time – would go from seeming all but irrelevant to progressively more pertinent. From now on, Del and Rodney, in particular, would not only act – they would also live.

One broad and immediate sign of this change, as work on the sixth series began, was the updating of the Peckham environment.

The year was now 1988: Margaret Thatcher's Conservatives had recently won their third successive General Election; the financial markets had been deregulated in the so-called 'Big Bang' of October 1986, which saw traditional trading floors supplanted by keyboards and computer screens and the City of London's cosily parochial business practices over-ridden by the actions of international investment banks; and, although there were still high levels of unemployment, an economic boom had created a new class of *nouveau riche*. There were real-life entrepreneurs such as Clive Sinclair and Alan Sugar eagerly preaching the Thatcherite gospel of meritocratic individual enrichment, and satirical fictional figures such as the movie *Wall Street*'s Gordon Gekko and Harry Enfield's TV plasterer Loadsamoney brashly boasting that 'greed is good'. In place of the humble old dodging and diving fly-pitchers, the contemporary commercial marketplace seemed to be dominated by a brash new breed of so-called 'yuppies': young upwardly mobile professionals all too ready and willing to flaunt their newly accumulated financial clout. As Mark Lawson observed in another satirical fiction of the time, there was a new and peculiarly crass take on the concept of classlessness now in circulation: 'It is no longer true that only the very very stupid, vulgar people who went to public school can make money. Now, very very stupid, vulgar people who left state school at sixteen can do too.'[4] The world of *Only Fools and Horses* would thus have to reflect these kinds of developments in its own little comic world.

One consequence was that Del Boy, in particular, needed to be 'remodelled' for the new era. John Sullivan saw him now, at the age of forty-three,[5] trying desperately hard to pass himself off as part of the younger yuppie generation and start riding their wave of success. Reasoning that Del would have been hugely impressed – for all the wrong reasons – by watching *Wall Street*, Sullivan imagined him rushing out of the cinema in Leicester Square to restock his wardrobe with the trendy yuppie uniform of the striped shirt, brightly coloured braces and shiny suit, along with such essential accoutrements as the chunky mobile phone, fat Filofax and sleek aluminium brief-case, and then forsaking the traditional working-class pub for the more fashionably bourgeois wine bars and bistros. Robin Stubbs, the show's current costume designer, thus followed Sullivan's brief carefully and bought Del some new suits from a local branch of Austin Reed, some shirts from Marks & Spencer, a few shiny ties from Tie-Rack and, in place of the common old camelhair coat, a much smarter banknote-green mackintosh from Dickins & Jones.

Rodney, John Sullivan felt, would now – at the age of twenty-eight – have reached a stage in his life when, rather more earnestly and methodically than his big brother, he was looking to prove, and better, himself. Unnerved by the thought of remaining 'self-unemployed', he would be looking to build belatedly on his earlier academic promise by struggling to catch up at evening classes, and so he, too, was given a makeover to reflect the fact that, while his brother was trying to look a little younger, he was eager to look a little more mature. He was thus given a more 'grown-up' wardrobe, with several cheap, bland, slightly ill-fitting but sober-looking suits, shirts and ties designed to make him – he hoped – blend into a 'proper' professional environment.

Uncle Albert simply needed to remain just as he was in order to appear more 'traditional' than ever. The implausibility of Del's sudden transformation, and the awkwardness of

Rodney's late bid for social respectability, would be lit up as if by a lighthouse beam whenever old Albert wandered waffling into frame.

One other aspect of this world that did change, but only unofficially, was the location of Nelson Mandela House and its nearby streets and scenes. The on-screen Peckham had never actually been Peckham: rather than any part of south London, it had mainly been bits and pieces of west London. The reason why the production team had never simply gone off and set up their cameras in Peckham itself was down to the fact that they were based at the BBC's Television Centre in White City, W12, and the amount of time and money it would have taken for them to have travelled back and forth every day across London to complete all or most of the external scenes for an entire series in and around SE15 would have proven prohibitive. When the time came to film the sixth series, however, even the area around Television Centre no longer seemed a viable option.

One reason was that the local markets had become much harder to use, because the regular workers resented all of the disruption that was usually caused (this was one of the things that had ended up discouraging John Sullivan from writing many fly-pitching scenes for Del). Another factor was that some of the areas within the district of Acton – which was often passed off as Peckham – were no longer appealing or particularly safe, with the presence there of major local drug gangs sometimes prompting the police to discourage any further visits to certain familiar locations. The third and final problem was that there was a sense in which the show had become a victim of its own success, because there was now so much interest from the fans that the actors were in danger of being mobbed while they were in character and out and about in the capital city.

The solution arrived at jointly by the producer Gareth Gwenlan, the director Tony Dow and the writer John Sullivan, was to hurry up and find somewhere else to film. After considering a number of possibilities, the trio went down to Bristol for a 'recce', and were delighted with what they found there: architecturally, the city seemed to have everything that was required, including the right old-fashioned pub exteriors, suitable streets, houses, markets and shopping centres as well as an appropriate block of flats. The original tower block, which would still be seen in the opening title sequence, had been Harlech Tower at Park Road East in Acton, but this now became Whitemead House on the Duckmoor Road Estate in the Ashton Gate area of Bristol. With this and other places relocated, all that was left for the team to do was to bring down a couple of red London buses to drive up and down in the background.

With these various alterations in place, the production moved on and (although John Sullivan was still working on the last two scripts[6]) the sixth series was ready to commence. It began at 7.15 p.m. on BBC1 on Sunday, 8 January 1989 with a very strong theme-setting episode entitled 'Yuppy Love'.

Rodney is determined to complete a diploma course in computing at the local Adult Education Centre, while Del – having seen and studied *Wall Street* several times – has gone all 'high-powered and trendy' and is now looking to take advantage of one Thatcherite policy by buying his own council flat and then selling it on for a profit to some or other middle-class chinless wonder. Albert, on the other hand, is still sitting back as usual in his easy chair, munching on a sandwich and watching TV.

A memorable sign of how hopelessly deluded Del now is

comes when he follows a couple of yuppies to a local wine bar and promptly embarrasses himself. After ordering a bottle of Beaujolais Nouveau – 'a '79', he specifies, smugly – and then mixing it up with some 'funny' mineral water to create a 'spitzer', he meets up with a disoriented Trigger. Eager to impress his old drinking partner, Del flicks through his Filofax while flirting with a few young women, and then, just as the barman props up the bar flap to take out some drinks, Del smiles at someone in the distance, leans back nonchalantly, sticks out an elbow and falls down sideways where the bar flap should have been. 'Drink up,' he tells the dazed Trigger, as he gets back up, brushes himself down and picks up his aluminium case. 'Drink up – we're leaving!'

It was another defining, classic sitcom moment for *Only Fools and Horses* – another scene to impress itself firmly on the memory – perfectly timed by David Jason. Like the 'wrong' chandelier incident in the second series, this was one more painfully believable calamity that had its roots in truth. John Sullivan had recently seen someone do something very similar in a real-life wine bar ('I was waiting for someone in The George, on the top of Balham Hill, and this guy leant forward to light his cigarette from his mate's lighter just as the barman came out. He didn't actually fall. He stumbled, and then gave a big cheesy grin as if he meant it'), and, like any good script-writer, he committed it to memory and waited patiently for the right moment to re-release it as comic fiction. The gag relied on the element of surprise – the audience needed to be distracted as the bar flap went up – and would have been ruined had a second take been required. David Jason also needed to plan his physical routine so that he would not do what came naturally and glance towards where he was falling.

Everything, therefore, had to be 'blocked' and positioned so precisely that he felt able to leave most things to trust and appear completely spontaneous. The result was a comic incident that is still voted one of TV's funniest moments: a sharply observed, sublimely choreographed, painfully plausible scene of human ineptitude whose humour survives no matter how many times it is repeated.

The other significant event in this episode occurred when Rodney, after attending one of his evening classes, meets a rather modern-minded young middle-class businesswoman called Cassandra Parry. This, it would later turn out, was the character to whom Rodney would become inextricably linked.

The role of Cassandra could have gone to the twenty-three-year-old Elizabeth Hurley, who auditioned for it enthusiastically, but she was deemed by Tony Dow to be too 'model-like' to suit someone like Rodney. 'It was quite extraordinary,' the director would say, 'because she looked even more amazing then than she does now, but I just couldn't believe that she could be Rodney's girlfriend; it seemed too much for this plonker to be dating this stunningly beautiful woman.'[8] The decision was eventually made to choose another actor, called Gwyneth Strong, whom Dow was keen not to describe as 'plainer' than Hurley in terms of looks, but, nonetheless, it was felt that she could engage more effectively with Nicholas Lyndhurst as a performer.

Strong, who was born in East Ham in 1959 and had been working in the profession since the tender age of ten, had auditioned for the part without much expectation of winning it. She had only given birth to her first child four months before and was, by her own admission, still 'wrapped up in the baby world'. The audition, however, could not have gone any better, and, much to her surprise and delight, she was soon confirmed as Cassandra. There had been no guarantees that the first appearance would lead to anything more, but, as things turned out, she was called straight back for the next episode, and, by the end of the sixth series, she would find herself one of the regulars.

She would, at times, have a thankless task playing the role, because, of all of John Sullivan's main characters in *Only Fools*, Cassandra is surely the least coherent, and most inconsistent, when seen over the course of all the shows that followed her arrival. In some early episodes she would seem to oscillate bewilderingly rapidly between snobbishness and egalitarianism, and in others she could appear cold and aloof in some situations and then vulnerable and needy in others. To John Sullivan, however, she represented the best chance that Rodney would have to develop a serious and lasting relationship (and, to be fair to the writer, his depiction of her would eventually acquire greater balance and clarity), so her introduction at the start of the sixth series was a vital sign of the move towards the sitcom–soap.

The first episode saw her character drawn into yet another storyline summoned from John Sullivan's own memory. Years before, when the writer was still single, he had met quite a posh-looking woman at a party, and she had offered him a lift home in her car. Not wanting her to see where he really lived, he took her to a large house on the middle-class Clarence Avenue, waved her off and then walked the two miles home in the rain.

In the actual episode, Rodney meets Cassandra in a cloak-room, where, once again, the combination of his gaucheness and his big brother's mischievousness threatens to sabotage any opportunity he has of forming a relationship: when she makes a point of seeking him out, he congratulates her on being sufficiently 'liberated' to make the first move, but is then hugely embarrassed when she explains that she is merely pointing out that he has taken her coat by mistake – and she knows this because the name 'Rodney Trotter' has been written in ballpoint on the inside of the very similar coat now draped over her arm. Later on, he meets her again at a disco and she offers to give him a lift home, and, afraid of what she might think of Nelson Mandela House, he pretends that he lives instead in a smart-looking avenue. After giving her his telephone number, he gets out and stands anxiously by the door of a large house until, eventually, she drives away – and then, as he sets off to his real home in the rain, it is clear that, once again, he has picked up her raincoat by mistake.

Back at the flat, drenched to the skin, he is in no mood to listen to a knowing Del analyse where it all went wrong, so he retaliates by stuffing his brother's Filofax in the bin bag just before Albert chucks it down the rubbish chute. He then discovers that Cassandra telephoned earlier about her coat, now knows where he lives and is still interested in meeting up with him again. Surprised and excited, Rodney asks where Del wrote down her number. 'In my Filofax,' Del replies.

Watched by 13.9 million people,[9] 'Yuppy Love' was an effective advertisement for the new fifty-minute format, with separate storylines for Del and Rodney criss-crossing their way through the programme until they came together for the final scene, and Del's instantly iconic fall through the open bar flap (which was later voted second – behind the same show's even more impressive chandelier scene – in a poll of British TV's '50 Funniest Sitcom Moments'[10]) showed that there would still be some inspired comic conceits to counterbalance the more soap-like ongoing themes.

Arguably the most intriguing thing about the opening edition of the series was the high confidence now evident in John Sullivan's writing. Here was a writer fully cognisant of how experienced, skilled and mature he had become, and he was clearly enjoying making full use of his range of talents and expertise. An ambition was being realised, with a belief that all past lessons had been learned to justify the new risks that were to be run. One could see the two main strands that had grown throughout his writing career now being woven together with great care and pleasure. The gently romantic themes and scenes, which were being echoed here in the Rodney–Cassandra relationship, had been explored and developed ever since the arrival of *Just Good Friends*, where the emotional ties that bound together the working-class Vince Pinner and the middle-class Penny Warrender were tested time and again as the couple struggled to trust as well as they loved. The lighter comic moments, on the other hand, had been repeatedly polished and improved from the early days of *Citizen Smith*, with its sometimes cartoon-like scenarios, through to the recent *Dear John*, with its calmer, kinder and wiser insight into human fallibility via a support group for divorced and separated adults. In the new and more elaborate incarnation of *Only Fools and Horses*, however, both of these strands were now being combined with far more assurance (if not always with more success) than ever before.

The next episode, 'Danger UXD', was not quite so well-balanced, but it did provide viewers with another great comic talking point when Del suddenly discovers that the fifty faulty plastic dolls that he has taken off Denzil's hands turn out to have been designed for men instead of little girls. As he tries to distract himself by relaxing in the flat, a strange hissing sound is heard at the back near the hot-air duct, and, when he and Rodney lean over to where the sound appears to be coming, one of the dolls suddenly pops up and scares them out the door.

The show's properties buyer, Malcolm Rougvie, had selected the laughably odd-looking dolls from a sex shop in Soho. 'I just walked in and asked this girl, who was full of interest and enthusiasm, reading her magazine, if she had any blow-up dolls,' he later recalled. 'She showed me where to look and I noticed they had black ones and white ones, but I asked if she had any Chinese ones as well. Then I got one out and started blowing it up. She said: "You can't do that in here!" But I wanted to make sure it wasn't too horrific, which it wasn't, so I bought five of each.'[11]

The scene proved hugely popular with the studio audience, and soon became another great favourite with the fans, but the BBC did actually receive several complaints from viewers, including one letter from a woman asking how she was supposed to explain to her seven-year-old daughter what the dolls were actually for. David Jason and Nicholas Lyndhurst were thus obliged to take a break from their frantic rehearsal schedule early the following week in order to respond to such criticisms on daytime television. Any further attacks by the usual obsessively BBC-baiting tabloids were thus averted, but the brief controversy reminded the team of how broad its audience had now become. The content would, in future, be checked a little more carefully for any hint that it might cause any unintended offence.

The remaining episodes in the series ranged from the tightly plotted if improbable 'Chain Gang' (which saw Del, Rodney,

Boycie, Trigger, Mike and Albert fall foul of an old-fashioned jewellery scam) to the more sprawling, 'streaky bacon'-style 'Sickness and Wealth' (in which Del experiences a health scare, Albert gets involved with a spiritualist, Marlene reveals that she is pregnant and Rodney gets engaged to Cassandra). Situated somewhere very near the middle of this spectrum was the very satisfying 'The Unlucky Winner Is . . .' – arguably the one episode in the series that consistently and successfully combined Rodney's continuing romantic storyline with a one-off comic plot.

The basic premise was that Del, as part of a desperate bid to win any free competition going, had surreptitiously entered some of Rodney's old paintings in an art contest, and won first prize for his younger brother: a free holiday for three at a five-star hotel in Mallorca. Rodney, initially, is delighted to hear this news until he, Cassandra and Del arrive at their destination, and, much to his horror, he discovers that the competition in question was in fact restricted to children aged under-fifteen. The result is that Del and Cassandra have to pretend to be his parents (enjoying themselves eating, drinking and taking in the sights), while he has no choice but to act as if he is their unusually tall young son (mingling grudgingly at the Junior Disco with the other kids in 'The Groovy Gang').

The series came to an end on 12 February with an episode that certainly seemed to complete the sitcom's transmutation into a distinctive sitcom–soap. Entitled 'Little Problems', it saw Rodney finally progress from youthful 'plonker' to a proper adult, as he ends up marrying Cassandra. 'It was a very emotional one,' David Jason would say of the programme, 'because we realised that Rodney had become a man and that was quite an eye-opener for Del, and for me too because Nick and I had been together for years. It was the Simply Red song

"Holding Back the Years" that got me, and I shed a few tears for real when that started during rehearsals.'[12]

After promising Rodney a £2,000 wedding present so that he can pay for his share of the new flat that he and Cassandra are planning to buy, Del has no choice but to take a beating from the dreaded Driscoll Brothers (Peckham's answer to the Kray twins), to whom he owes £2,000, in order to ensure that the cash goes to the right person. Once Rodney has married, an emotional Del, still wincing from all of his hidden injuries, has a word before his brother sets off with Cassandra on honeymoon:

DEL: Are you off, then, bruv?

RODNEY: Yeah, going in a minute.

DEL: Just wanted to ... er ... just wanted to say, Rodney, that I'm really *very* proud of you. You've got it all now, ain't you? New job, new flat, new wife, new life.

RODNEY: Yeah. We had a few good years, eh?

DEL: Yeah, we've had some good times.

RODNEY: Some right laughs, eh?

DEL: And a couple of tears. Still, that's what it's all about, innit? I just wish that ... I just wish Grandad and Mum ...

RODNEY: Oh, no, shut up! You'll have *me* going!

[They now just look at each other. Rodney embraces Del. Del shouts out in pain.]

DEL: *Ooohhh!*

RODNEY: What's wrong?

DEL: I got a bit of a bruise. I don't know how I got it.

It was an assured end to the first series of the new-style *Only Fools and Horses*. Watched by an average weekly audience of 16.7 million,[13] the show's popularity seemed stronger than ever, and there were no noticeable complaints about either the longer running-time or the greater role for romance.

An eighty-five-minute Christmas special followed at the end of the year. Called 'The Jolly Boys' Outing', it pushed on down the sitcom–soap road, with Rodney's new marital experiences being complemented by Del's unexpected reunion with Raquel. Although the character had slipped away the year before, John Sullivan had been planning for some time to bring her back as a plausible partner for Del. 'We began thinking that maybe Del was getting a bit too old for hanging around discos,' he would explain, 'and I didn't want him to become a dirty old man.'[14] Appearing in the 1988 special 'Dates', Tessa Peake-Jones had invested the character of Raquel with such an engaging mixture of vulnerability and independence, and had worked so well with David Jason, that Sullivan reasoned it now made good sense to bring her, and her character, back as Del's regular love interest.

Peake-Jones, who was born in Harrow, Middlesex, in 1957, had been working steadily in television for ten years prior to getting her big break with *Only Fools*, appearing in such productions as the BBC's 1980 adaptation of *Pride and Prejudice* (in which she played Mary Bennett) and Keith Waterhouse's delightful cricket-themed comedy–thriller series *Charters & Caldicott* in 1985. When she first started work as Raquel, she understood more or less immediately how interesting the character could become: 'Raquel was a little bit lost and was trying to make enough money to keep herself going. She wanted to be an actress and she had a heart of gold and then she met a similar man, in a way. The script touched on things like loneliness and marital problems and seemed to me to have real depth.' She also knew instinctively how to bring the woman to life: 'The costume designer and I made up her "look" together, but having lived in the East End for a few years, I knew exactly how she should look and act and we bought a lot of her clothes at the market.'[15]

Called back for 'The Jolly Boys' Outing', she knew that the latest appearance would be significant. She was going to become part of the family.

As far as the title's sitcom lineage was concerned, the notion of a 'Jolly Boys' troupe could have been traced back to the American radio of the 1940s, where 'The Jolly Boys' social club was a regular feature of the hugely popular NBC show *The Great Gildersleeve*.[16] The more immediate inspiration, however, came via John Sullivan's sister-in-law, whose father had gone off on such annual 'boys only' trips. 'They used to have an event called the Jolly Boys' Outing,' Sullivan would say. 'It seemed a silly name for a beano, but I just loved it. I also remember going on outings when I was younger, but I'd never written about them, so I thought it would be good to do something about Southend or Margate. The setting started off as Southend but I opted for Margate because by then I'd got to know the singers Chas & Dave, who'd written that great song "Margate", and I hoped they could record the closing music for it.'[17]

In 'The Jolly Boys' Outing', Rodney is now working as head of the computer section for Parry Print Limited – the company owned by Cassandra's father, Alan. In his absence from Trotters International Traders, Uncle Albert has been promoted by Del to the lofty position of 'Executive Lookout' on the market.

Rodney, however, is feeling like a misfit in his new office environment, and, with his first wedding anniversary imminent, he is also feeling insecure about Cassandra, as her commitment to her career at the local bank strikes him as far more intense than her concern for him. She is being encouraged by her father to ingratiate herself with her 'yuppie' boss, Stephen, which prompts Rodney to invite Del and Albert round to the flat for a comforting family dinner. The problem is that Cassandra has already arranged a dinner party that evening for Stephen and her parents, so the ensuing culture clash proves uncomfortable for everyone but Del.

In the circumstances, Rodney does not think twice before agreeing to join all of his old friends on the annual 'Jolly Boys' Bank Holiday outing to Margate. Setting off with Del, Albert, Boycie, Trigger, Denzil, Mickey Pearce, Mike and all the rest of the Peckham posse, the mood is bright and boozy until the coach driver passes out midway through the journey, Rodney falls foul of the law after a accidentally hitting a policeman with a football and his father-in-law gets sick from eating too many jellied eels. The day out then goes from bad to worse when the coach – thanks to one of Del's faulty Albanian radios – explodes, leaving the Jolly Boys stranded in Margate for the remainder of the Bank Holiday.

As the group splits up in search of temporary accommodation, Del, Rodney and Albert eventually end up in a local nightclub. It is there that they encounter Del's ex-girlfriend, Raquel, who has returned from the Middle East to work as a magician's assistant. The reunion goes well until, back at her place, Del spots the magician, Raymondo, decides he is up to no good and punches him on the nose. A furious Raquel explains that the magician is gay and just a flatmate.

When Rodney returns home to his own flat, he finds Cassandra with her boss, Stephen. Jumping to the worst conclusion, he punches his supposed rival and breaks his nose, only to then discover that Stephen's wife is also in the flat. A furious Cassandra throws him out and, shamefaced, he turns up back at Nelson Mandela House.

The show was certainly a tremendous success in terms of ratings, as it won its biggest audience so far with 20.12 million viewers[18] tuning in on Christmas Day afternoon for a bit of 'streaky bacon' after the turkey. It probably helped, given the fact that so many families around the country had settled down together in front of the set, that the show contained such a mixed set of ingredients, offering something for everyone, of all ages, as it juggled elements of a light-hearted comic romp, a bitter-sweet domestic melodrama and a playful Aldwych farce. Not all of the critics liked it – The *Guardian*'s Nancy Banks-Smith, for example, dismissed it as a 'small show' that had been 'monstrously inflated' like a hot-air balloon, 'with the cast gesturing desperately from their crammed baskets'[19] – but most were generally positive, and it was the spectacular viewing figures that featured in the eye-catching headlines.

The BBC, delighted with the impact of the show, was eager to commission not only another Christmas special but also another full-length series. It was quite a challenge to arrange, simply because so many members of the *Only Fools* team were now increasingly busy with other projects. In the year or so since completing the last series, David Jason, for example, had starred in David Nobbs' popular comedy–drama series *A Bit of a Do* and also appeared in the feature-length adaptation of Michael Wall's play *Amongst Barbarians*, as well as contributing to numerous other productions; Nicholas Lyndhurst had been similarly industrious, working on not one but two separate series of ITV sitcoms (the final run of *The Two of Us* and the soon-to-be-launched *The Piglet Files*); and John Sullivan had spent some time in America helping to adapt his *Dear John* sitcom for US TV, and had also been working on developing other possible programmes back in Britain. Everyone involved with *Only Fools*, however, remained so enthusiastic about the show that the team was able to reassemble in time to make the new episodes.

Still eager to develop further the soap-style ongoing storylines, the plan was to use the seventy-five-minute 1990 Christmas special to set up the dramatic and romantic themes that would then run all the way through the seventh series. Entitled 'Rodney Come Home', it would focus on the various tensions that were developing within Rodney and Cassandra's new marriage, and also introduce Del and Raquel as a 'proper' couple.

The show (which was watched by 17.97 million people[20]) began with Del in a very happy mood now that Raquel has returned from a tour of America and agreed to move in with him, but Rodney is depressed because his marriage to Cassandra is in trouble. He has felt for some time that she cares more about advancing her career than improving their relationship, and, when she appears to rate playing badminton at the bank's social club higher than spending time with him over dinner, he snaps and moves back to Nelson Mandela House.

His sudden reappearance in the flat strikes Del as a great inconvenience, as he was just about to propose marriage to Raquel. When Rodney appears to expect to resume his old living arrangements, Del takes him to one side and makes it clear that, until his own romance with Raquel ceases to be chaste, some things will have to change.

Usurped from his own bedroom by Raquel, Rodney has to make do with sleeping on the settee. Del looks on for a few days as his younger brother tries to distract himself with drink, but then he resolves to intervene: unwilling to see Rodney throw away his marriage, and unhappy at the prospect of losing the perks that come from having a brother working at his in-laws' printing company, he proceeds to play cupid.

The task proves more complicated than he expected, as Rodney takes the van down for repairs at the Peckham Exhaust Centre and invites the attractive young receptionist there, Tanya, out on a date. Rodney ignores the attempts by Del and Albert to talk him out of the move and heads off to take Tanya to the cinema. Improvising a hasty 'Plan B', Del visits Cassandra in the hope of making her jealous, but, after offering some dubious advice – 'There's none so blind as them as what won't listen' – ends up reducing her to tears.

Back home, Del gets a call from Rodney, who took his advice, cancelled his date and has decided to wait at his flat for Cassandra so that they can kiss and make up. Hanging up before Del can warn him, Rodney greets Cassandra with a smile but is stunned when, once again, she throws him out of their home. Del arrives too late to clear up the confusion, so Rodney, reluctantly, has no choice but to return with his brother to the old family flat.

'It was quite a downbeat episode,' the producer Gareth Gwenlan would later reflect, 'but that was down to John moving the characters on a couple of gear changes. The episodes that followed were only possible because we'd done "Rodney Come Home". John and I had long conversations about it because it wasn't a conventional episode but it was very pivotal to what happened afterwards'.[21] The majority of the reviewers of the time seemed to support such an approach, with one of them writing: 'Rather than keep the Trotter brothers in a time warp, their creator John Sullivan has taken the risk of moving them on with the times. By doing so, and getting Rodders hitched, he's been able to tackle relevant issues.'[22]

The seventh series, which began on Sunday, 30 December 1990 at 7.15 p.m., would therefore be the most soap-like of all, with a cluster of domestic hopes, fears and tears persisting from one episode to the next more stubbornly than a spot of Duncan's blood in *Macbeth*. Rodney and Cassandra would oscillate between estrangement and reunion, Del and Raquel would grow closer and more contented with their first child on the way, and Marlene and Boycie would fuss over their newborn son. Along with the stronger strand of dramatic realism, however, came some isolated but very effective comic sequences, so those fans who preferred the 'old' *Only Fools and Horses*, with its more conventional sitcom structure, still had plenty of moments to savour.

Arguably the two most thoroughly enjoyable episodes – certainly in terms of their clear and coherent comic structure – arrived in the middle of the run, with 'Stage Fright' and 'The Class of '62'. Both of them boasted a cleverly crafted plot, plenty of bright and funny dialogue, a memorable climax and some superb ensemble acting.

'Stage Fright' saw Del attempt to revive Raquel's dormant stage career by talking her into accepting a booking – arranged by his night club manager mate Eric – at The Starlight Rooms. Appreciating that she is too nervous to perform solo, he finds her what he thinks is the perfect partner: an old friend of Trigger's who has adopted the stage name of Tony Angelino ('The Singing Dustman'). Posing as a Tom Jones/Elvis Presley type, sporting dark sunglasses, a permed wig, a fake tan, an electric-pink shirt half undone to expose a garish gold medallion, tight white trousers, elevator boots and a salami shoved down the front of his underpants, Angelino (played with artful relish by Philip Pope) is cheesier than a lump of Cheddar, but his version of 'Delilah' seems guaranteed to get elderly members of the Women's Institute swaying and screaming with pleasure. Del is confident that he has spotted a star, and – although Tony protests that he can only sing certain songs – wastes no time in signing him up to appear alongside Raquel, with Del as their manager and Rodney their roadie.

Del's burgeoning confidence suffers a sudden blow when he hears from Boycie that the owner of The Starlight Rooms is actually local gangster Eugene McCarthy, who bought the club from Eric in return for not nailing his head to the door. A further blow comes when Del discovers that Raquel and Tony are due to make their debut on the night when McCarthy is hosting a party at the club for his eighty-two-year-old mother, and that if McCarthy dislikes an act he is known to get very angry indeed.

When the big moment arrives, the music starts, Raquel walks out on to the stage and starts singing the old Roy Orbison ballad 'Crying'. Hesitant at first, she seems to gain in confidence as the song begins to build, causing the watching Del to beam with pride and satisfaction. Then Tony Angelino emerges and takes over for the second verse, snapping out the lyrics like the pub performer that he is. Del is even more pleased, puffing on his cigar and contemplating his new career as a manager and impresario. Then comes a terrible shock: Tony, it transpires, suffers from rhotacism, which means that he cannot pronounce the letter 'r', so he proceeds to repeat the word 'Cwying' over and over again until the duet dies a painful and belated death. The room is silent. Del is stunned. Fearing the wrath of Eugene McCarthy, he decides it is time to protect himself. 'I'll see you later,' he tells Rodney, and scarpers.

Back at the flat, a furious Raquel returns to let Del know exactly how much more she had to suffer after his cowardly exit, listing the rest of the set: 'Please Welease Me', 'Congwatulations' and 'The Gween Gween Gwass of Home' (followed, according to a tactlessly amused Rodney, 'by a medley of wock 'n' woll'). When the doorbell rings, Del is terrified it might be Eugene McCarthy, ready to inflict his revenge, but it turns out to be a defiant Tony Angelino, pointing out that he signed a 'contwact' and is now eager to collect his half of the money. '*Crudités à la plat!*' Del exclaims, raging at the unfairness of the situation. He hands over the money and Tony leaves. The telephone rings: it is McCarthy, informing Del that his mother thought Raquel and Tony's act was the funniest thing she had seen in her entire life, and so he wants to sign them up for a five-week contract. Del thanks him for calling – '*Bonjour!*' – and then rushes off to the balcony, where he shouts down at the departing Angelino: 'Tony! Hey, just a minute, I've got some more bookings for you! Stick with me son – I'll make you *WICH!*'

'The Class of '62' featured the welcome return of Jim Broadbent as the slimy Roy Slater. Lured to a back room at The Nag's Head for a supposed reunion party of the members of Class 4C (1962) from Peckham's Martin Luther King Comprehensive, Del, Trigger, Boycie and Denzil, with Rodney tagging along, suddenly find themselves in the company of their old enemy Slater. Insisting that, since his release from prison, he has changed his ways and is now desperate to wipe the slate clean, his former schoolmates take pity on him and, as he is paying, join him for a few drinks, first at the pub and then back at the flat.

Some hours later, Raquel returns. She is alarmed enough by the sight of several drunks slumbering in the lounge, but is horrified to find that Slater is among them, because, as she soon points out to a suddenly sobered-up Del, Roy Slater happens to be her estranged husband. When Slater wakes up, he cheerfully tells Del that the other reason for his visit is the fact that he has heard from his solicitors that his wife wants him to agree to a divorce. He then notices a picture of Raquel (*'That's my wife! That's my Rachel!'*), explains that 'Raquel' is merely her stage name, and then Rachel/Raquel appears, heavily pregnant. It is now Slater's turn to be horrified: 'This woman – my lawful wedded wife – has been fertilised by a *Trotter!* You had the whole world to choose from, Rachel. You could have had Pol Pot or a Siberian pimp with gingivitis and a wart on his nose! But oh no, not you, you decided to go down-market!'

As the recently woken Uncle Albert listens, increasingly puzzled, while Slater continues to infuriate Del with comments about 'my Rachel', Albert's repeated question, 'Who's *Rachel?*' allows Buster Merryfield – often sidelined since the show slipped towards soap-style storylines – a rare opportunity to show his skill with some beautifully timed interjections. Slater goes on to reveal that he is due to inherit a 'nice few grand' and had hoped that he could share it with his Rachel, so that they could have a fresh start. This is too much for Del, who ushers Raquel away and prepares to deal with Slater. 'Who's *Rachel?*' asks Albert once again. '*OH SHUT UP, ALBERT!*' everyone else shouts.

Slater decides to blackmail Del, knowing that his notoriety as 'the most loathed and hated person on the parish' would attach itself to Del should their mutual connection to Raquel be revealed. Del feels trapped ('How d'you think my business associates and clients would feel knowing that I was going case-o with the ex-wife of an ex-copper?') until Rodney finds a 'post-nup' agreement in Slater's wallet, along with a letter from a diamond merchant, showing that the real reason for his return is actually to ensure that Raquel waives all of her rights to his money. Del realises (in a reference to the plot of the 1985 Christmas special 'To Hull and Back') that Slater's so-called 'inheritance' must be the diamonds he managed to squirrel away just before his arrest. It is at that moment that Slater reappears, reclaims his wallet and appears to have recovered the upper hand.

The next day at The Nag's Head, however, Del dupes Slater into agreeing a deal. Although Slater points out that the damning documents are now back safely in his wallet, Del counters by claiming that he has used one of his slow-moving stock of fax machines to photocopy them. Slater wriggles until he realises that the game is up, and so, reluctantly, he leaves Peckham for good. As soon as he is gone, Mike the landlord complains to Del about the fax machine he sold him; apparently the photocopier facility fails to work. 'That's funny,' says Del, with a triumphant smile, 'it don't on ours either!'

The rest of the series was skewed strongly in the direction of domestic drama: Rodney – rather improbably – gets himself sacked from his father-in-law's business, Uncle Albert wanders off feeling unwanted, and Cassandra complains that Rodney has become too much like Del. The final episode, 'Three Men, a Woman and a Baby', was probably the most openly, and self-consciously, dramatic and emotional edition of the show so far, with Rodney and Cassandra seemingly splitting up for good and then getting back together (via a painfully weak fake ponytail/rat incident that did neither character, nor actor, any favours), and Del and Raquel witnessing the birth of their first son, Damien.

Some of the tense exchanges between Del and Raquel, once they are inside the hospital, had been inspired by John Sullivan's own memories of when his wife, Sharon, gave birth to their children. When, for example, Raquel screams in pain and says, 'Don't you ever come near me again, Trotter!' it echoes a line from real life: 'Sharon had said that to me and then she asked to hold my hand and she dug her nails in and I said "ahh" and she said, "Now you know what it bloody feels like!" So I used that too.'[23]

The team had wanted the climactic scenes in 'Three Men, a Woman and a Baby' to appear as realistic as possible, so filming took place in a recently closed ward at West Middlesex Hospital in Hillingdon, and the cast was given special advice by one of the midwives from the open ward on the floor below, including a very graphic video of a woman giving birth. Tessa Peake-Jones had not yet had a child of her own, so she found the sights that she was shown sobering enough, but her male co-stars were left pale and queasy by the experience. When it came for the child to appear, Gareth Gwenlan rushed down to the lower ward and said: 'Hands up who's had a baby in the last hour who's prepared to lend it to the BBC?' One young mother (a Mrs McManus), delighted to think that her child would make his TV debut so quickly, happily lent him to Gwenlan.

In the final moment of the show and the series – realised quite brilliantly by the peerless combination of John Sullivan's writing and David Jason's acting – Del cradles the new-born baby in his arms, takes him over to the window and, in the moonlight, speaks to his son for the first time:

Oh, you are such a lovely little boy, you really are. You've got a mummy and daddy who think you're the most precious thing in the whole wide world. You've got a lovely family around you. Yes, you have, look. You've got your Uncle Rodney there to play with. Great-Uncle Albert. He'll tell you about all the places in the world he's been to – and sunk. And there's me. And you're gonna have all the things your Daddy couldn't afford. 'Cos I've been a bit of a dreamer, you know. Yeah, I have. I mean, you know, I wanted to do things, and *be* someone, but I never had what it took. But you, you're different, you're gonna live my dreams for me, and you're gonna do all the things that I wanted to do, and you're gonna come back and tell me about them. Tell me if they're as good as I thought they'd be. You're gonna have *such* fun. You are. And then when you get the hump, 'cos you're bound to get the hump sometimes, I'll muck about and make you laugh. 'Cos I've mucked about all me life, and I never knew the reason why until now. This is what it's all about. I was born for this moment. Yes. Oh, we're gonna have such fun, we are, you mark my words. This time next year, we'll be millionaires.

It was usually John Sullivan's strategy to slip in a joke to shake the audience out of one mood and straight back into another, but, on this occasion, he decided against it. 'I just thought, when I'd finally written that, and we'd rehearsed it, and spoken about "Maybe should we do something at the end?", David played it so well we just said: "Let's leave it. That's nice."'[24] The result was, indeed, so effective that even those fans who much preferred the earlier *Only Fools and Horses* episodes had to acknowledge that they had witnessed an exceptional piece of television.

No one really knew, at the time, that this would be the final series of the show. It had performed extremely well in the ratings – averaging a higher number of viewers (18.9 million[25]) than any previous run – and received an impressive range of critical plaudits and three more BAFTA nominations (with David Jason deservedly winning the 'Best Light Entertainment Performance' award). It could be argued that the soap-com style had not always been particularly satisfying, because, if one is going to add soap elements to a great sitcom, they really do need to be *great* soap elements, and the soap strand in *Only Fools* had sometimes seemed to border on the insipid: while the character of Raquel, for example, engaged very strongly and effectively with Del, the character of Cassandra, once again, had often appeared frustratingly insubstantial, and there were times when her and Rodney's on-off-on-again marital life had risked boring (or even irritating) those viewers who were more interested in good plots and great comic dialogue. What was undeniable, however, was that the show's current fan base was bigger and broader than ever, and the BBC was determined to continue capitalising on its exceptional appeal.

With the chances of everyone being available for another time-consuming series looking fairly slim for the foreseeable future, the BBC was happy, for the time being, to settle for the odd feature-length special. This decision, however, would create a problem all its own. Extended specials, with a few diegetic bells and whistles, had been reasonably practicable when *Only Fools* had still been a conventional sitcom: so long as a strong enough self-contained storyline was found, the programme could just about cope with both the greater length and the singular format. By the start of the 1990s, however, *Only Fools* was as much of a soap as a sitcom, and, by the very nature of soaps as 'continuing dramas', the show was no longer suited to being served up in lengthy and isolated annual instalments. During the next few years, therefore, the show and its various ongoing storylines would be obliged to continue in a discontinuous manner. While this would at least please the BBC by keeping its valuable franchise going, it arguably compromised the integrity of a show that had won its great reputation by making people laugh on a weekly basis. The new era of *Only Fools* as a hugely hyped annual treat would thus see it lose a little of its old charm, becoming much less neat and intimate and far more bloated and grandiose, straining to be both an unpretentiously entertaining comedy show and a bright and shiny BBC Behemoth.

Christmas was when *Only Fools and Horses* was deemed most likely to deliver the largest audience of the year, so a seasonal special was duly commissioned for the 1991 festive schedules. John Sullivan and the rest of the team were now more conscious than ever of the need to live up to all the lofty expectations, so it was proposed that, rather than produce another prosaic piece of comedy–drama in Peckham, the Trotters would venture abroad for a much more adventurous sort of story, spread out in the schedules between Christmas Eve and Christmas Day. The BBC duly agreed, and, in October of 1991, filming began in Miami, Florida, on a two-part £2 million project entitled 'Miami Twice'.

The technical conceit of the two programmes was that David

Jason would have to play two characters: himself and a lookalike gangster. This fairly familiar gimmick was in vogue at the time – a month or so before, Lenny Henry had appeared in a limp and laboured Hollywood movie entitled *True Identity*, in which he had to play both an African–American actor and a white mafia hit man[26] – and, as a technical challenge for David Jason, the appeal of the project was obvious, but it still made for a difficult dramatic enterprise. With the combined length of the episodes planned at well over two hours, and with the storylines from the seventh series continuing, the artistic risks seemed high.

The story began in Peckham, with Damien Trotter's christening. After the ceremony, Del sneaks off to strike a deal with the Vicar to market pre-blessed wine around the country.

Rodney, acting on the advice of a Relate counsellor, is now staying at Nelson Mandela House during the week and visiting Cassandra at weekends. Del arranges a '2 for 1' holiday for him and Rodney in Miami, knowing that Cassandra's career concerns will prevent her from joining her estranged husband.

Once the two brothers have arrived in Miami, their visit seems set to be the usual kind of chaotic affair until they encounter members of the Ochetti family, who appear more than happy to extend traditional 'American hospitality' to them. The reality is that the men belong to a local mafia family, and they have realised that Del bears a striking resemblance to their *capo*, Vincenzo Ochetti. As the Don is facing a trial that will probably see him sent down for a life sentence in prison, his men plan to lure Del into a public place and then have him shot, thus faking the death of their boss.

Sure enough, a bullet narrowly misses Del's head at a beach-side restaurant and he is then persuaded to drive a faulty jet ski miles out to sea, only for the coast guard to bring him back, but Del, like Rodney, remains strangely trusting of his shady hosts. It is only when he wanders around the mansion in search of his brother that Rodney mistakes the mafia boss for Del, and then bumps into Del himself, that the penny finally drops.

Shaken, Del then finds himself mistaken for the Don by a couple of Columbian drug barons who turn up at the mansion. Terrified, the Trotters climb out of a window and over the wall to freedom. On the run, they end up eventually in the Everglades, where they dodge a dangerous alligator and then bump into, of all people, the vacationing Boycie and Marlene. The four of them elude the gangsters, and Del pins details of the drug delivery to the park ranger's office and heads off for the airport. Back home in Peckham, they find Albert and Raquel stuck in the flat with piles of crates of unwanted Romanian wine.

'Miami Twice' was a very slow-moving and rather self-indulgent special that seemed far removed from what had made the show so popular. The believable working-class London milieu was largely ignored in favour of an unfamiliar and thoroughly implausible American setting, Del and Rodney were plunged into a convoluted plot that strained anyone's credulity and, shining out like beacons of creative exhaustion, there were even pointless cameos for Richard Branson (so wooden he deserved to be creosoted) and a dazed-looking Bee Gee, Barry Gibb. Scheduled to avoid David Jason's popular new ITV series *The Darling Buds of May*, the first, heavily hyped, part of the special (watched by 17.7 million people[27]) dominated the schedules on Christmas Eve to such an extent as to cause a massive 700-megawatt power surge on the National Grid, but met with decidedly lukewarm reviews from the critics. The second part screened on Christmas Day, however, attracted a somewhat smaller audience (14.88 million[28]) and another set of underwhelming reviews.

The suspicion that the team had returned to the well once too often seemed to be confirmed when it was announced in some newspapers a few days later, on 3 January 1992, that the 'Game is up for Del Boy'.[29] Reports said that, with both David Jason and Nicholas Lyndhurst now very busy with other projects, and John Sullivan also committed to writing a new sitcom called *Sitting Pretty*[30] and planning a wartime comedy–drama entitled *Over Here*,[31] there were no plans for any more series of *Only Fools and Horses*.

Once again, however, the business of broadcasting intervened: the BBC still needed the big name, the huge fan base, the powerful franchise. The jewel had to remain in the crown. Another Christmas special, therefore, was set in preparation for the end of that year.

In a rare festive season–themed edition entitled 'Mother Nature's Son', it began, unlike its over-inflated predecessor, on reassuringly familiar ground with Del and Rodney back in Peckham, feeling strapped for cash. To make matters worse, baby Damien is emitting strange smells, Raquel is suffering from post-natal depression, Albert is suffering post-Naval depression, Rodney is suffering from impotency, Del's plan to buy the flat has landed him mortgage payments double the cost of the rent and Grandad's old allotment has accumulated so much rubbish it has been declared a health hazard.

Del, it soon becomes clear, has lost his old drive. As Raquel points out, he has filled the spare room with boxes of Bros LPs, Charles and Di commemorative plates, 'Free Nelson

Mandela' T-shirts, 'scuba' deep-sea diving outfits and 'communion' Riesling wine. Rodney advises him to kill two birds with one stone by clearing Grandad's allotment and then lodging some of his own rubbish in the shed.

Down at the allotment, Del, Rodney and Albert find several barrels of noxious-looking yellow liquid. Enlisting the assistance of the ever-gullible Denzil and the even more gullible Trigger (who is no longer a humble roadsweeper but has now been upgraded by the council to the position of 'environmental hygienist'), they manage to dump the barrels at night. Apart from now having hands that glow yellow in the dark, Denzil and Trigger escape unscathed.

The following morning, a trip to the organic supermarket with the environmentally aware Rodney plants an entrepreneurial seed in Del's head. Noting that they are selling bottles of mineral water there for what he considers to be wildly inflated prices, he decides, via a hidden hosepipe on Grandad's allotment, to start marketing 'Peckham Spring Water'.

A few weeks later, the Trotter household has become a busy bottling factory, selling public water back to the public. When a guilt-ridden Rodney confesses to Cassandra, she is horrified – not just for him, but also because she was the innocent party who loaned Del the capital to fund the enterprise. Finding herself implicated in the scam, she has no choice but to keep quiet as the business continues to boom.

Back in the money, both couples decide to enjoy a romantic evening away at a plush hotel in Brighton. All goes well until, unheard in the background, a news flash comes on the TV: apparently a major case of water contamination has been reported in Peckham, caused by abandoned barrels of unidentified liquid. Blissfully ignorant, Del turns out the bedside light. A bottle of Peckham Spring Water glows yellow in the dark.

As a self-contained fiction the story ran out of ideas after a very promising build-up, and as a briefly resumed continuing drama it seemed unsure of what it wanted to say, but this was a high-profile Christmas special aimed at a very well-briefed and loyal (20.14 million-strong[32]) audience and it served its purpose in the schedules extremely impressively. It came as no great surprise, therefore, when the BBC, once again, worked so hard to persuade the team to attempt to repeat the achievement the following year. With the various participants now busier and more popular than ever, the prospect of reuniting to put their – and their show's – precious reputation on the line for the third year running must have seemed more than a little daunting, but, eventually, all concerned relented to make one more – and probably final – feature-length special.

Entitled 'Fatal Extraction', the 1993 edition appeared as the most soap-oriented edition of all, with the domestic issues overshadowing the comic incidents. It is Christmas time again, and Raquel is worried that Del is spending too much time drinking and gambling down at the 121 Club to provide Damien with any presents. Rodney – whose marriage to Cassandra is now, at long last, going so well that the two of them are trying for a baby – intervenes on Raquel's behalf, and discovers that Del, apart from nursing a sore tooth, is brokering a big deal at the club to buy and sell some ex-Russian military camcorders.

Raquel eventually becomes so angry with Del's distracted attitude that she takes Damien with her to stay with Rodney and Cassandra until Del apologises. He ends up instead at the dentist, where he loses a tooth but sets up a date with a receptionist named Beverley.

Back at the flat, Rodney points out that the Russian camcorders are not only too heavy but also use videos that fail to fit UK video players, and he and Albert persuade Del to cancel his date. Unable to contact Beverley by telephone, he leaves a message on her answer machine and stays in the flat. By the end of the following night, while they drink at The Nag's Head, Rodney's nagging finally wears Del down and he calls Raquel to apologise. Relieved to have saved his marriage, he orders champagne and celebrates.

On his way home, drunk and staggering, he starts singing so loudly that he sparks a mini riot on the estate. Albert summons Rodney to help him get Del safely inside, but then Del goes back out to flog the rioters some of his ski gear.

The following day, Del returns from work to find Beverley in the flat, enquiring about trading her answer machine for Damien's old high chair, which she claims she wants for her own son, also called Damien. Having heard rumours that she used to be a patient at a psychiatric hospital, Del panics, convinced he is being stalked by the woman he snubbed. It turns out, eventually, that Beverley thought that he was stalking her, and she used to be a nurse, not a patient, at the hospital. Relieved, he agrees to leave her alone and sorts out the trade that she requested.

The Trotters then settle down to celebrate Christmas Day in the flat. All goes well until Raquel plugs in their new answering machine, and hears Del's message. Del returns to the lounge, only to be hit by various ornaments thrown at him by Raquel. Outside, by the large Christmas tree, a group of carol singers sing 'Silent Night', and Beverley is among them, looking up at Del's flat, smiling knowingly.

Once again, the show did its job in the ratings, dominating the Christmas Day schedule with an audience of 19.59 million viewers,[33] and ended up as the third most-watched programme of the entire year.[34] It still seemed, however, a strangely subdued way for the sitcom, or the soap, or the sitcom–soap, to bow out, but it was doing so – at least as far as the television industry was concerned – at the top.

There had been twelve years of remarkable twists and turns, and near disasters and joyous triumphs. Now, as far as anyone involved could tell, it was all coming to an end.

CHAPTER TEN

The Long Goodbye

That spells like the end of it. But it don't, does it?

The end came not with a bang, nor with a whimper, but with a decade-long pause at the open exit door. Following the completion at the end of 1993 of the 'Fatal Extraction' special, the producer of *Only Fools and Horses*, Gareth Gwenlan, assumed that the show had finally come to a close. David Jason was now tied to an eighteen-month contract with Yorkshire Television to make the ITV police drama *A Touch of Frost*, and Nicholas Lyndhurst was starring in the new BBC1 sitcom *Goodnight Sweetheart*. There remained, however, a sense of some unfinished business.

No one involved in *Only Fools and Horses* was particularly comfortable with the idea of 'Fatal Extraction' being seen as the finale of the show. It had been a decent enough programme, but, with its soap-style obsessions and somewhat peculiar denouement, it had not left viewers with a suitably vivid memory of what had always made the show so impressive. The nagging feeling was that it had deserved a neater valediction.

Eventually, a couple of years later, Gareth Gwenlan broke the ice, contacting John Sullivan to say: 'It would be a shame if we just let it bleed away. Shouldn't we try to do just one final one?'[1] Sullivan said that he would be delighted to write another script, but it depended on Gwenlan getting David Jason and Nicholas Lyndhurst to take part. The producer knew that it would still be some time before Jason would become available again (as the actor had recently committed himself to another series of *Frost*[2]), but Lyndhurst assured him that he would drop just about anything else, at any time, in order to do another show. The dream then drifted on until the spring of 1996, when Gwenlan was busy overseeing the pilot episode of John Sullivan's new comedy–drama about minicab drivers, *Roger, Roger*. It was then that Gwenlan heard the news that David Jason was due to have a two-month gap in his work schedule during the autumn. An opportunity had finally arrived.

Gwenlan wasted no time before arranging for Jason, John Sullivan, the director Tony Dow and himself to reunite for dinner at The Greenhouse restaurant in Mayfair (Nicholas Lyndhurst was unavailable on that day, but, as he had already made his enthusiasm known, the meeting went ahead with his blessing). The four men ate, drank and reminisced about the show, and then Sullivan sketched out his ideas for how best to round off the saga. Sullivan had always wanted to tie things up in a satisfying fashion and have the Trotters end up as millionaires, and this time it seemed as if the energy was there to make it happen. The following morning, Gwenlan called Jason's agent and was delighted to discover that the actor had already cleared that section of his schedule and committed himself to the project.

The next step involved the producer contacting the BBC's new Head of Comedy, Geoffrey Perkins, to get official confirmation that another *Only Fools and Horses* Christmas special would be welcome. Perkins, unsurprisingly, jumped at the proposal.

John Sullivan was now free to sit down and work on a storyline. After a week of writing, however, he called Gwenlan and said that he had encountered a problem: he could not fit everything he envisaged into one solitary episode. He said that he would need a two- or perhaps even a three-parter to tie all of the strands together in a truly satisfactory way. It was the old recurring *Only Fools and Horses* production dilemma: how to cram a quart into a pint pot. If Gwenlan went ahead with two or three episodes, he would have to find a way to film all of them within a two-month period, and would also have to persuade the BBC to boost the budget and convince the cast that it was worth all the extra work. When Sullivan sent in the scripts, however, their quality seemed too good to waste, and the BBC was happy to suddenly have the prospect of a high-profile trilogy to place at the heart of its Christmas schedules.

The show was not returning to quite the same comedy landscape that it had dominated during its time on screen. With broadcasters seeking to engage with a more youthful audience, new trends had already emerged, including the more irreverent kind of postmodern knowingness that had popularised sophisticated parodies of current affairs programmes (*The Day Today* in 1994), chat shows (*Mrs Merton* and *Knowing Me, Knowing You,* both also beginning in 1994) and games and quizzes (*Shooting Stars,* which started in 1993), and, more specifically, a few new sitcoms such as *Father Ted* (which began in 1995) were suggesting a more playfully ironic direction for the genre to explore. The comedy mainstream, however, was still more or less as *Only Fools* had left it three years before, with the most successful of the recent new sitcom arrivals, the unapologetically conventional *The Vicar of Dibley* (which made its debut in 1994), underlining how strongly the centre still held. In such a context, therefore, the revival of *Only Fools and Horses* seemed a perfectly prudent way for the BBC to pander to that broad family audience still eager for something resembling a traditional festive TV viewing event.

The deal was complete by July, and it was not long after that the publicity machine cranked into action and tantalising stories started cropping up in the tabloids. 'Lovely Jubbly' said one headline, 'Del's back on the telly'.[3] Subsequent reports stressed the sacrifices that had been made to help the project to happen: Nicholas Lyndhurst, for example, had postponed the next series of *Goodnight Sweetheart* and David Jason had passed on an offer from Yorkshire Television to film an extra episode of *A Touch of Frost*. Everyone involved, it was noted, was determined to ensure that this *Only Fools and Horses* trilogy was going to live up to the high expectations of the show's vast mass of fans. The sense of anticipation was thus building steadily with several months still to go before the first instalment reached the screen.

Work, meanwhile, commenced on Thursday, 3 October with the start of location filming in Bristol. During the next month or so, the production team took great care to shoot all of the external scenes without giving the lurking press photographers any opportunity to snap 'spoilers' of the stand-out comic moments. One or two fairly innocuous pictures did find their way into the papers,[4] but the speculation that they provoked only added to the free publicity the project was provoking.

Once all of the location work was completed, the team returned to London and Television Centre to prepare for the recordings. There were some emotional moments during the sessions at the BBC's rehearsal block in north Acton, not just because of some powerful and dramatic scenes in the script but also because everyone realised that it would soon all be over – and this time probably for good. Nicholas Lyndhurst, for example, had first started appearing as Rodney when he was just twenty, and he was now thirty-five, so he felt as though he had 'grown up' in these rehearsal rooms, surrounded by the other members of the cast and crew, and, as he would later reflect, it seemed 'awful' to contemplate that the team was about to disband.

The three sixty-minute shows were filmed in front of studio audiences over three evenings, spaced out between Thursday, 14 November and Friday, 6 December. The intensity of the production process meant that, for much of the time, the actors had no time to pause and reflect on the experience, but, as the final scenes from the final episode were shot, the emotions returned and all of those concerned had to fight to retain their composure. Nicholas Lyndhurst was shaken when he saw the set lit up for the last time: 'It was really horrid. It was like seeing an old friend and thinking, "What have they done to you?" It was a shell. It didn't look like a flat any more. It looked like what it was – just a studio set. It was three walls propped up. It was very sad'.[5] Buster Merryfield cried before he made his final entrance, wiping away the tears just before he walked through the door. Even David Jason, by far the most experienced of the three, struggled to keep his feelings in check: it was, he knew, the last time that they would all be together, in character, the last time that it would all seem real. Once it was over, and the credits rolled down the screen on the studio monitors, he and his co-stars stayed on set and fully gave in to their feelings.

A sign of how emotional the evening had been for the

audience, too, came when they responded to the end by rising to their feet and giving the cast a standing ovation, which lasted several minutes. No one had witnessed anything like it in a television studio, and none of them would forget it.

After the audience dispersed, the crew started dismantling the sets, packing up all the costumes and props and clearing the studio. The lights went out, the last echo faded away, the place fell silent and there was nothing left but darkness. Even more so than turning off the TV set, this sudden emptiness brought home the evanescence of the actual experience. From this point on the individual memories would preserve what they could.

The evening ended with the cast and crew moving up to the Reception Suite on the Sixth Floor of Television Centre, where the current Controller of BBC1, Alan Yentob, hosted a party to congratulate them all for their efforts. Old friends and former members of the team, including Ray Butt, Martin Shardlow and Jim Broadbent, were also present as the end of an era was marked.

There was still some work to be done before the trilogy was ready for transmission. For Gareth Gwenlan, Tony Dow and John Sullivan, the next three weeks were as busy as ever as they edited the three recordings and tried to add a final polish to the production. The pressure, as Gwenlan would recall, was immense as he and Sullivan sat down on Christmas Eve to complete the final sound edit: they were all too aware that the BBC was billing the three shows as the Corporation's 'Christmas present to the nation', the previewers in the press were predicting a triumphant finale and the bookmakers William Hill were offering odds on the trilogy topping the TV ratings. 'I turned to John and I said, "What happens if they don't like it?", and he said, "I've been thinking about that."[6] Both men had known about enjoyable productions that had ended up as miserable failures on the screen, and seen 'sure-fire hits' dismissed as hopeless misses, and so, proud though they were of what they had done, they knew that the nerves would remain until the shows had actually gone out and prompted some kind of response.

The trilogy began at 9 p.m. on Christmas Day with 'Heroes and Villains'. At about 9.30 p.m., Gwenlan, who was watching at home with his family, felt sufficiently relaxed to pick up the telephone and call John Sullivan. As he expected, he was put straight through to the answerphone, where he left the following message: 'John, I'm telling you, it's OK!'[7] It was indeed.

The trilogy returned to all of the soap-style storylines that had been relevant the last time around: Del and Raquel are still besotted with their son Damien, Rodney and Cassandra are still trying for a baby of their own, and there are preoccupations with the fragility of love and life and the material need for money. The new shows also contained several more of the stellar sitcom moments that had made previous specials so memorable to connoisseurs of classic sitcoms. Although there were no doubt some viewers who remained unconvinced by the hybrid that *Only Fools and Horses* had become, a much larger number would feel that the trilogy lived up to the hype.

In the first instalment, 'Heroes and Villains', the Trotters are back to leading lives of not-so-quiet desperation. Thatcherism is dead, the yuppies are now middle-aged and middle-class, John Major's Conservatives are hanging on limply to power and would-be working-class entrepreneurs like Del Boy are now, alas, all-too-closely attuned to the dominant ideology of the time: confused, frustrated and perfunctorily pragmatic. Inside the two Trotter households, a sense of aimlessness seems to have crept up and eclipsed the old ambitions.

Rodney's nagging unease about young Damien – the little 'antichrist' whom he fears will grow up to usurp him in the family business – is even intruding into his dreams. In a nightmare sequence, Rodney thinks that the year is 2026, the family firm is now the massive multinational corporation 'TITCO Global PLC', Del is 'Lord Trotter of Peckham' and the boss of all bosses is none other than 'Sir Damien Trotter'. Cassandra is a mere maid and Rodney himself is at the beck and call of his dreaded nephew. When he finally wakes up, he is back in the familiar surroundings of the flat in 1996, with all of the usual old problems to overcome – such as his and Cassandra's ongoing struggle to have a child.

Del appears unsympathetic. He has enough problems of his own. His latest gambles – which include investing in 125 Latvian radio alarm clocks 'that go off anytime they bloody want' and 200 aerodynamic cycling helmets 'that turn out to be horse-riding crash helmets that some git sprayed red' – have not paid off, the local council has turned down his application for a home-improvement grant, Raquel seems too embarrassed to take him and Damien with her to meet her parents and, on top of all of that, 'there's a gang of hoodlums mugging anyone who dares to put their head outside the front door'.

Uncle Albert, meanwhile, is tired of Damien bouncing a football off his head, is not very keen on the prospect of Rodney and Cassandra conceiving another 'little sod' to make his life even more of a misery, and he has just mistaken Cassandra's latest urine sample for a small pot of apple juice. It is no better elsewhere: Boycie is still relying on a strong dose of *schadenfreude* to get him through each day, Marlene is still dissatisfied, and Mike the landlord is staring at the unwanted items in his hot 'n' cold food cabinet and fretting about all the waste. The only person who seems in good spirits, somewhere behind his blank expression, is Trigger, who has just been awarded a medal by Councillor Murray – the official who blocked Del's application – for saving the council money by using an old broom to sweep the roads.

With their respective partners away visiting their parents, Del decides that he and Rodney need a break from the daily grind, so he persuades his brother to accompany him to the Annual Publicans' Fancy Dress Ball (which offers a good prize for the best costumes). Rodney's enthusiasm evaporates, however, once he discovers what outfits Del has chosen for them to wear: Batman for him and Robin for Rodders.

The inspiration for the particular comic sequence that follows – easily the highlight of the entire episode – originated, like so many earlier ones, from John Sullivan's own experiences. 'That came about because a friend of mine was saying to me that he and his wife were going to this "Vicars and Tarts" party. And to get there he had to go through an area of London that wasn't really a nice part. But he said, "The big gag is: she's going as the vicar and I'm going as the tart!" And I said to him, "Yeah . . . and all you need to do is break down in Stockwell, dressed like that!". "Yes," he said, "I didn't think of that." So that started me thinking. I thought, right, the Trotters are going to break down somewhere dressed as idiots!'[8]

In the episode, Del and Rodney set off, dressed up in their superhero costumes, in their battered old Reliant Regal 'Supervan', backfiring loudly, and promptly break down in one of the worst parts of Peckham. Fearful of being seen by all the drunks who will soon start spilling out of the pubs, they decide to run to their destination while the streets and alleys are relatively clear. As they do so, Councillor Murray emerges from her office on her way home, but is accosted by some muggers as she tries to unlock her car. The muggers, however, are stunned when they look down the lane and see two figures coming towards them from out of the fog: a short Batman and a tall Robin. Confused and alarmed, they spin around and run off, and Del just has time to introduce himself to the councillor before being urged on by Rodney.

The party turns out to be a disaster, because, when they finally burst in, singing the *Batman* theme, they discover that the host has died and the event is now a black-tie-only wake. 'I suppose the prize-giving's off now?' says Del, glumly. The following morning, however, while working at the market, Del manages to overcome yet another would-be mugger, earning himself a medal for bravery from the mayor in the presence of an awed Councillor Murray.

Back at the flat, Del serves everyone champagne as they celebrate his fifteen minutes of fame. Rodney and Cassandra then double the reasons for celebration by announcing that they are finally expecting their first child. Del adds yet another reason by revealing that a grateful Councillor Murray has reversed her decision about his application and sent him a cheque for £5,000. 'Not a bad old world is it, bruv?' asks Del. 'Getting better all the time, Del Boy,' Rodney replies. They clink their glasses. Del declares: 'Lovely jubbly!'

'Heroes and Villains' proved an enormous success in terms both of ratings and reviews. Seen by an estimated 21.3 million viewers,[9] the way that the show dominated the day's schedules made several newspaper front pages and attracted numerous admiring remarks. Gwenlan, Sullivan and the rest of the team could now sit back and enjoy the rest of the run.

The second episode, 'Modern Men', was a different kind of comedy–drama, but, in its own way, just as effective as its predecessor. The harshest of critics might have argued that it was fifty minutes of aimlessness followed by ten minutes of action, but, to most viewers, it was a consistently watchable hour of high-class entertainment, with some fine writing and exceptionally good acting. The first half of the show featured many good comic lines ('To Del, "Market Penetration" means sex under a barrow!') and plenty of very engaging ensemble acting, followed by a brief and rather cartoonish dream sequence, while the latter part lurched quite suddenly towards dark and dramatic soap-like concerns. It did, however, show how determined John Sullivan was to explore the more painful and unsettling aspects of ordinary life while still preserving a comic perspective.

Broadcast at 8 p.m. on Friday, 27 December, 'Modern Men' found the Trotters' finances strained but their spirits still bright as they looked forward to the birth of Rodney and Cassandra's baby. Both brothers are looking to change their ways at least a little: Del is reading a guide to the 'new', more sensitive and caring man (but still behaving like a very old-fashioned one), while Rodney is thinking of getting a proper job (while still relying on Del to tell him what to do).

Del's solution is to have a vasectomy. Rodney's solution is to apply for the position Del has advertised to assist Rodney Trotter. All such plans are brought to a sudden halt when Rodney hears that Cassandra has been rushed to hospital after suffering a miscarriage. While he comforts his wife, a distraught Del wanders off and deals with a troublemaker in the A&E waiting room.

This second instalment, like the first, attracted 21.3 million viewers[10] and had a similar kind of impact. Assured in its purpose, it concentrated on its characters, allowing their ordinary interaction to propel the episode along until its climax. One of the most satisfying aspects of the programme, in this sense, was the much-improved and better-integrated presentation of the Rodney–Cassandra relationship, with Gwyneth Strong – in her best performance so far – finally getting a more well-rounded version of her character to embody, and Nicholas Lyndhurst once again making Rodney seem amusingly naive, touchingly vulnerable and effortlessly authentic.

A good sign of the positive reception elicited by the first two episodes came when the final part of the trilogy, 'Time On Our Hands' (broadcast at 8 p.m. on Sunday, 29 December), drew in the even larger audience of 24.35 million[11] – the biggest audience of the entire year on any channel (beating the second-placed episode of *Coronation Street* by 5 million[12]) and a new record for a British sitcom (eclipsing the previous top performer, a 1979 episode of *To the Manor Born*, by almost half a million[13]). If anyone had still doubted the extent of the show's success, this extraordinary achievement surely disabused them.

The inspiration for the storyline of 'Time On Our Hands' came in two stages. The first was simply the desire that John Sullivan had to end *Only Fools and Horses* with the Trotters finally becoming millionaires; the second was the result of a careful and assiduous search for the item or event that could help them to secure such wealth. Sullivan did not want anything so obvious as a win on the football pools or the lottery; he wanted something unusual, unexpected but plausible.

Mona Adams, an historical consultant employed by the BBC,

was thus asked to supply the writer with some thought-provoking ideas. She soon believed that she had come up with something suitable when she imagined Del discovering some ivory tusks buried in the mud on a Docklands rubbish tip: this fitted in with the Trotters' *modus operandi*, searching some of London's most insalubrious areas for scraps that might be sold on for a profit, as well as with the need for verisimilitude, as such tusks were indeed imported to London in previous centuries and some could well have been lost while being unloaded from the ships. The problem was that Adams had, if anything, done her job too well, because a few days later she was stunned to hear a report on the evening news announcing that builders had just discovered some ivory tusks buried deep in the mud at the London Docklands. Reality had intruded rudely on fiction, and Adams was back to square one.

Her next idea – prompted by a conversation with Jane Bendall, a friend who worked at the National Maritime Museum in Greenwich – was to seek advice from Jonathan Betts, the Museum's Curator of Horology, regarding genuine rare and missing artefacts that could, conceivably, be rediscovered and sold for a massive amount of money. 'It was all very "hush hush",' Betts would recall. 'I was not told which programme it was for. I was only told that the item should be worth millions rather than thousands and actually could be found.'[14] Betts suggested one particular timepiece, designed by the celebrated eighteenth-century horologist John Harrison, which was indeed believed to be missing and would certainly fetch the finder a fortune.

It was an intriguingly topical notion, because Dava Sobel's best-selling book *Longitude*, which told of Harrison's quest for an accurate way to determine where seafarers were on the globe, had only been published the previous year, and, along with a tie-in Channel 4 documentary, it had brought the man's work into contemporary popular consciousness. Harrison created four clocks in his pursuit of the Longitude Prize,[15] and then made another, the H5, as a gift to George III in 1772 to highlight the fact that the longitude problem had indeed now been solved. Harrison's surviving notes and drawings, however, suggested that he had also built a so-called 'lesser watch', the H6 pocket timekeeper, but it has never been found. Betts noted that Harrison scholars still dreamed of one day uncovering the unique H6 in some or other dusty attic, so the idea of Del Boy picking it up unwittingly along with various other pieces of 'junk' seemed an ideal scenario for John Sullivan to exploit. Mona Adams agreed, and the background details were passed on to the writer, who was delighted with the suggestion and promptly began work on the script.

'Time On Our Hands' begins a fortnight after Cassandra's miscarriage with the Trotters still failing, but not yet failing better. Rodney is grieving over the loss of a child, Del is preparing to meet his in-laws for the very first time and Albert is struggling to find new ways of introducing the subject of the Second World War ('During the 1939–1945 conflict with Germany . . .').

As the two Trotter brothers attempt a quick inventory of all the rubbish that is piled up in their garage – it includes boxes of batteries, electrical plugs, smoke detectors, sunglasses, super-glue, frying pans, ladies' tights, bits of cars and dented bicycle frames – Del, desperate to cheer his brother up, tries to claim that such detritus is someone else's treasure, but Rodney is having none of it: 'Derek, we have got a pile of Showaddywaddy LPs under a tyre for a Triumph Herald and an artificial limb.

These are *not* gonna make big news on *The Antiques Roadshow!*' Del still seems to think he can find a positive, but Rodney can only see negatives. The future, as far as he is concerned, seems bleak, and yet, as he longs for a change in fortune, it is Del, not him, who is the most realistic:

RODNEY: I'd love a bit of good luck, Del. Not just for me. For all of us. I just wish something good would turn up.

DEL: So would everyone, Rodney. That's why they're all out there doing the lottery, ain't they? I mean, look, if it were up to me, right, what *I'd* like to do, I'd like to be able to say . . . *[He points at a tray of bits and pieces on top of an old tea chest]* say this, say *that*, was life's lucky dip, what I'd like to do, I'd love to just go, *da daaa!* *[Lifts out an old pocket watch]* There it is, look: *that* is going to change our lives! *[Looks at the watch sadly and then tosses it over into a frying pan]* But it won't, will it? 'Cos life is not like that.

The good luck comes, in spite of everything, after the visit from Raquel's parents. Raquel's father, James, is an antiques dealer, and, when he comes to pick up his car from Del's garage, his eye spots the pocket watch in the frying pan. Inspecting it more closely, he notices the name 'Harrison, AD 1774' engraved on the face. Del blithely explains that he picked it up years ago at a house clearance in Deptford. James, however, is shaking with anticipation: this could be, he gasps, John Harrison's 'lesser watch', which has been missing for about 300 years.

It duly goes to auction at Sotheby's and, after hearing the

opening bid of £150,000, Del faints. Upon recovering, he
and Rodney rush back into the auction room, with the
bidding still progressing. The latest bid is revealed to be
£4,000,000 and Rodney, too, faints. It then emerges that the
final bid was at £6,200,000. When the Trotters are back in
the Reliant van, Rodney re-reads the Sotheby's statement,
Del says, 'Well, we've had worse days,' and then the two
brothers begin whooping hysterically, rocking the little yellow
van with their excitement.

The remainder of the episode sees them tease Boycie, celebrate
with the other regulars of The Nag's Head and buy new houses
(a mansion for Del and Raquel, a luxury riverside apartment
for Rodney and Cassandra and a riverboat for Albert). Returning
to the now empty flat at Nelson Mandela House for the final
time, Del looks around and recalls all the memories, and some
words from his mother, his father and Grandad. Rodney turns
up, and so does Albert, both of them keen to take one last look
at the old place. Del, especially, is reluctant to leave the building,
and the life, behind, but, after taking and being tempted by a
call from Lenny Morris offering him 250 carpet steamers, Rodney
tells his older brother that they are no longer in business. Del,
with a little sadness, agrees, and tells Lenny: 'Trotters Independent
Traders has ceased trading. Bonjour.'

As they leave Nelson Mandela House in search of a Chinese
meal, a subdued Del suddenly becomes animated again:

DEL: *Mon Dieu, Mon Dieu!* What a *fool* I've been!
RODNEY: What's wrong now?
DEL: Well, here I am thinking now we've got all
           this money, you know, that spells like the end
           of it. But it *don't,* does it? It's like the *beginning!*

Because for the first time in our lives we've got money to *invest!*

RODNEY: No!

ALBERT: Dangerous business, investment!

[The three begin walking away, arguing.]

DEL: Oh, come on, Rodders, you remember all those years you used to say to me: 'Del Boy, we should be investing!'

RODNEY: No, I *never* said that!

DEL: Well, it must have been me, then. I remember it was one of us who got it right. Now we can invest big-time in the futures market! Hey, we can get into Hong Kong, Singapore, Peking . . .

RODNEY: I don't want to invest – all right?

[Now the three men walk on, as the tower block fades away and the road ahead starts to be framed by a warm red glow, and they walk off into the sunset.]

DEL: Rodders, have I ever let you down?

RODNEY: *Yes!* Like a couple of years ago when you told me I'd won a holiday in a painting competition but forgot to mention that, for the entire week, I would have to pretend to be fourteen!

DEL: That's always been your problem, Rodney, you're always dwelling on the past. Mum said to me on her deathbed . . .

RODNEY: Oi, now don't start on about Mum and her deathbed!

DEL: She said to me on her deathbed: 'Del Boy, if you and little Rodney become rich, you must invest in the futures market!'

RODNEY: You liar! 'Cos there wasn't a futures market
            when Mum was alive!

DEL: Ah, no, but then, you see, that shows you how
            visionary she was! Come on, Rodney, this is
            our big chance, eh? He who dares, wins! This
            time next year we could be *billionaires!*

The credits then rolled, and the trilogy, and *Only Fools and Horses*, was over. The actors had shed some tears after the recording, and so, by all accounts, did some viewers after the transmission.

There had been some memorable moments during the past hour of television, including a splendid ensemble scene in Del's flat with his in-laws, and another beautifully judged and modulated exchange between Del and Rodney in the lift, but the ending was the most poignant of all, bringing a great programme to a close with genuine sensitivity, good grace and fine taste. The original idea had been for Del, Rodney and Albert to have left the tower block for the last time and then walked off down the Yellow Brick Road, turning into cartoon characters as we watched them go: 'I felt that once they were cartoons,' John Sullivan would later explain, 'they were no longer real and couldn't return.'[16] The director Tony Dow, however, decided against such a gesture and opted instead to simply show the real figures walk away from the camera, and the audience, into the distance. It was a wise choice, because, for a show that over its years had come to value realism and emotional truth more and more, only flesh and blood deserved that final focus.

The remarkable success of the Christmas trilogy left the team with a rare sense of elation. Proud not just of what had been achieved over the entire run, but also of how it had all been brought to a close, there were no regrets – just count-less warm memories, and many lasting friendships. Awards would follow early in the following year, including BAFTAs for the show itself and for the performance of David Jason (as well as another richly deserved nomination for Nicholas Lyndhurst) and a couple of British Comedy Awards, but, by that time, everyone had moved on. This time, it really did seem right.

The cast did get back together, very briefly, to film a short contribution to the 1997 Comic Relief fundraising campaign, but otherwise the individual members of the team got on with their careers: Gareth Gwenlan, in addition to his numerous other projects and responsibilities, continued his association with John Sullivan by producing two more of his series, *Roger, Roger* (1998–2003), and *Heartburn Hotel* (1998–2000); David Jason and Nicholas Lyndhurst remained extremely busy with such popular series as the former's *A Touch of Frost* (which would continue until 2010) and the latter's *Goodnight Sweetheart* (running until 1999); and most of the other former members of the cast remained very active on the stage and the screen. Life went on.

Many people, however, still wanted *Only Fools and Horses* to live on. There had been no tailing-off of interest or affection during the show's final few years – indeed, the opposite had been the case, given the gradual rise to that last record-breaking edition – and, while some appreciated and accepted the deci-sion to stop, there were plenty of others who remained eager for more. Repeats were watched avidly; sales of videos and tie-in books rose rapidly; Del, Rodney and Albert lookalikes were found and hired out; battered old yellow three-wheeler vans started chugging out for charity events; Steve Clark's very informative official celebration, *The Only Fools and Horses Story*, was published by BBC Books in 1998 (to be followed a few years later by Richard Webber's similarly invaluable *The Complete A–Z of Only Fools and Horses*); and the *Only Fools and Horses Appreciation Society* (which had been established by the devoted fan Perry Aghajanoff in 1994) found that its membership continued to increase long after it seemed that the show had ended.

The programme also remained firmly entrenched in the popular cultural consciousness, with innumerable references in the media, society and politics about 'Del Boy' types and 'real-life' *Only Fools and Horses* scenarios.[17] The most egregious example of such allusions came shortly after the trilogy had ended, when Chris Woodhead, the Government's then-Chief Inspector of Schools, made a bizarre public attack on the show for having an impact upon the country's schoolchildren, arguing that 'if Del Boy and Rodney are the only role models available to the young then we have a problem'.[18]

While many people pondered how the Chief Inspector of Schools (who seemed to be channelling the spirit of that old pop-cultural paranoiac Queenie Leavis) could ever have come to the conclusion that Del Boy and Rodney were the sole role models available to the youth of the day, *The Sunday Times* commissioned a response from John Sullivan, who defended his show with rather more rigour than Woodhead had used to attack it. According to Sullivan, the fact that schoolchildren had long been able to study Shakespeare's *Romeo and Juliet* without feeling compelled to commit suicide, or Charles Dickens's *Oliver Twist* without needing to pick a pocket or two, should reassure Woodhead as to the infinitesimal chances of Del Boy driving fifth formers to save up for Reliant Regals and start working on a market. He went on to say: 'Throughout the series I have tried to emphasise the basic decency of the Trotters. They are not violent, they don't take drugs and they don't drink and drive. They respect the old and the very young. More importantly, they have strong family values, loyalty and love and the ability to laugh at themselves. If more people followed their example, Britain might be a happier place.'[19]

The continuing interest in the show was by no means limited to the United Kingdom. *Only Fools and Horses* had been sold to numerous other countries, and, as a consequence, it now had a large and loyal international following. The Netherlands, in addition to screening the original UK series, had also made a version of its own – *Wat schuift 't?* ('What's It Worth?'), starring Johnny Kraaykamp Jr as Stef (Del), Kasper van Kooten as Robbie (Rodney) and Sacco van der Made as Granpa[20] – and in America, after NBC had tried and failed to adapt the show as a new vehicle (called *This Time Next Year*) for the actor Henry Morgan (Colonel Sherman Potter in *M*A*S*H*), the production company Castle Rock took over the rights in 1999 and started planning another version.[21] Fan letters were pouring in from all over the world, and many of them were urging the BBC to bring the show back.

There were many people at the BBC who wanted to bring it back. Television in the late 1990s had never been so tensely competitive, as not only had the four terrestrial channels now grown to five (with Channel Five being launched in 1997), but there was also the additional challenge from the rapidly proliferating satellite channels (including UK Gold, whose audience, somewhat ironically, had been boosted since the autumn of 1997 by the daily reruns of such classic BBC shows as *Only Fools and Horses*).[22] BBC1, in particular, had seen its annual audience share decline steadily from 39 per cent in 1981 (when there were three channels in total) to 28.4 per cent in 1999 (when there were eighty-four).[23] The pressure to hold on to guaranteed ratings winners, therefore, was ever more intense, and, when a broadcaster has such a hugely popular and record-breaking show like *Only Fools and Horses* on its books, the temptation is to keep bringing it back for one more special, or even another series, that dominates the schedules.

It was the *Only Fools* team itself that remained, at best, ambivalent about an on-screen reunion. Apart from continuing to be preoccupied with other projects, they were also understandably wary about the prospect of possibly tarnishing the show's hard-won reputation. 'I wondered whether we should leave it alone,' David Jason would say. 'I also dragged my heels about returning to the character [of Del Boy], not because I wondered if John could do it, that wasn't a problem, it was whether Nick and I could as older characters.'[24]

John Sullivan arguably had more reason than Jason and Lyndhurst to be tempted by the idea of a return, because, while the two actors were currently enjoying considerable success with their latest respective starring vehicles (Jason with *A Touch of Frost* and Lyndhurst with *Goodnight Sweetheart*), Sullivan was beginning to regret what was for him the novel experiment of trying to collaborate with another writer, Steve Glover, on his latest sitcom, *Heartburn Hotel*. Launched on BBC1 in the summer of 1998, the project, about an irascible veteran of the Falklands conflict who is now the landlord of a Midlands hotel, was performing disappointingly in terms both of viewing figures and critical reviews, and Sullivan was finding the experience of working with a co-writer distinctly uncomfortable ('To have somebody else in the room,' he would say, 'was at times like an invasion of my privacy'[25]). Even Sullivan, however, was doubtful about reviving *Only Fools*, because he was already busy planning another, long-cherished, project – an adaptation, co-starring David Jason as Mr Micawber and Nicholas Lyndhurst as Uriah Heep, of one of his favourite Charles Dickens novels, *David Copperfield* (which, following a row with the BBC Entertainment Department, would eventually reach the screen in 2001 on ITV, radically revised as a mini-series, featuring Jason but not Lyndhurst, entitled *Micawber*[26]).

Sullivan was also, by this stage in his career, far less interested than the BBC in the notion of writing something expressly to top the ratings: 'You think,' he said of his other current (solo-written) show, *Roger, Roger*, 'OK, we're doing six million, which compared with *Fools* is no big shakes, but it's warm and nice and people are enjoying it. The letters are coming in . . .'[27] He was reasonably content to carry on with what he was doing.

One further, and seemingly decisive, reason for the team to resist the various requests to return then arrived at the end of the decade with the sad loss of a much-loved member of the cast: Buster Merryfield.

Merryfield had marked the show's 1996 finale by publishing his autobiography, *During the War and Other Encounters* (which, with a characteristic mixture of good humour and old-fashioned financial pragmatism, he took to selling around the country from a suitcase[28]), and then, quite happily, carried on seeking work as an ordinary jobbing actor while enthusiastically supporting various charitable ventures. 'Who knows what's round the corner,' he had said soon after completing his very last appearance as Uncle Albert. 'Of course, I'm in the enviable position of being an actor with a pension. The most pleasurable thing is that I can walk down any street and people smile at me and say, "There's Uncle Albert." That's magic.'[29] The last, somewhat unnerving, sight that television viewers had of him was at the British Comedy Awards in December 1997, when he fell over while walking up the stairs to collect an award for the otherwise-engaged David Jason. He died in Poole General Hospital, Dorset, on 23 June 1999, shortly after being treated there for a brain tumour. He was seventy-eight. Both David Jason (who described him as a 'joy to work with') and Nicholas Lyndhurst (who called him 'a gentle, sweet-natured man' who had made the character of Uncle Albert into a 'national institution') attended the funeral in Verwood, near Bournemouth, along with many other members of the cast and crew.[30]

Even after Merryfield had been mourned, however, the speculation continued about the return of *Only Fools*. John Sullivan put it down to a throwaway remark that Gareth Gwenlan had made a few years before: 'Gareth, off his own bat, said: "Maybe we'll do a special for the Millennium." Although it was three or four years off we started receiving more and more interest.'[31] Sullivan had suspected that such enthusiasm would soon die down, but it never did. It actually intensified after a casual comment from David Jason at a press conference for *A Touch of Frost* was blown out of all propor-tion: 'A reporter asked why he wasn't doing any more *Fools and Horses*,' Sullivan would recall, 'and he was reported as saying something like: "Oh, I haven't been asked." Of course, that kicked it off like crazy. The phone kept ringing, and my agent said: "Don't let it be you who killed the series off." So the process started there, really, although, of course, we all had other work to finish.'[32]

Gareth Gwenlan did try to find a block of time when both David Jason and Nicholas Lyndhurst would be available, but Jason was still under contract with Yorkshire Television, and (although newspapers had reported the plans[33]) the Millennium came and went without anything being done. With no obvious 'hook' remaining upon which to hang a high-profile reunion, that seemed to be that for *Only Fools*, but the BBC was still extremely keen for something to happen (especially at Christmas), and, by this time, the key members of the team had been sufficiently intrigued by the idea to keep the possibility alive.

Gwenlan knew that his Millennium idea had at least galvanised John Sullivan to the extent that he had sketched out a storyline, just in case, so the producer arranged for the two of them to meet up for dinner with David Jason and Nicholas Lyndhurst to discuss what might be done. 'As soon as John explained the ideas he had,' Gwenlan later recalled, 'David got excited and became Del Boy. He'd come in looking like Frost, which he was working on at the time, and within five minutes was animated and looking just like Del, it was remarkable. David told us that he was available between November 2001 and March 2002, and Nick said he'd make himself available, so it looked as if we finally had a chance.'[34]

Gwenlan then called the other members of the cast, including John Challis, Sue Holderness, Tessa Peake-Jones, Gwyneth Strong, Roger Lloyd Pack and Paul Barber to alert them to what was happening and to check on their availability. Apart from Buster Merryfield, another actor who would now be missing was Ken MacDonald, who played Mike, the landlord of The Nag's Head: he died of a heart attack, on 6 August 2001, while on holiday with his family in Hawaii, aged just fifty. It was another genuinely sad loss to the old team, but, by this time, momentum was building rapidly and the project went ahead.

The next step saw Gwenlan discuss the project with the BBC. John Sullivan, once again, found that his plans were already outgrowing the notion of a single seventy-five-minute special, so Gwenlan proposed that the BBC commission three programmes, to be spaced out over a three-year period, instead. 'Of course, they were interested,' he would say, 'although they swallowed a bit hard when I told them what the budget was going to be [about £1 million per episode], but then David, Nick and John don't come cheap and we've always made [*Only Fools*] with high production levels, which has helped distinguish it from other shows.'[35] The BBC, excited by the prospect of a major event for each of the next three festive seasons, rubber-stamped the idea, dates were duly arranged in various diaries and John Sullivan was told to go ahead and start writing the scripts.

He was only a few days into work on the first episode, however, when, on 11 September, al-Qaeda terrorists in the United States hijacked four commercial passenger jet airliners and crashed two of them into the Twin Towers of the World Trade Center in New York City. As Sullivan stopped and watched all the non-stop coverage via the rolling news channels, and saw how the sense of shock, outrage and horror stretched far across the Atlantic and deep into the British public, the prospect of writing comedy shows suddenly seemed in dubious taste. In the days that followed, he came close to abandoning the project completely. 'Then,' he would recall, 'someone said to me how the country needed a laugh, and he was so right; I thought that, perhaps, through *Fools* I could do my bit to help: maybe I could put a smile back on people's faces. That simple statement inspired me to carry on with the script.'[36]

Apart from working on the plot, Sullivan also had to respond to the enforced changes in the cast. Following the loss of Buster Merryfield and Ken MacDonald, he decided to acknowledge (at some stage) the death of Uncle Albert on the screen, but merely send Mike the landlord to prison for attempting to embezzle the brewery (replacing him in the pub with the character called Sid – played by Roy Heather – who had previously been seen as the owner of the local greasy spoon café). An existing character who now needed fleshing out was that of Del and Raquel's son, Damien, who did feature in the 1996 trilogy but only as little more than a very diminutive bystander (played quite sweetly but rather shyly by the three-and-a-half-year-old Jamie Smith). In the first of the new episodes he would be aged ten and developing into a distinctive personality in his own right, so a new child actor (Ben Smith, no relation to Jamie) was recruited and Damien was 'updated' as an irritatingly spoilt and cocky little brat whose vocabulary is peppered with gangsta slang.

While Sullivan was preoccupied with the scripts, Gareth Gwenlan oversaw the other aspects of the production. Some members of the old crew were now committed to other projects, so several new people were enlisted to help bring the world of the Trotters back to life. Jacky Levy, for example, assumed responsibility for costume design, dealing with the difficult job of dressing the central characters so that they now looked like millionaires without seeming too different, in terms of taste, from their previously impecunious incarnations.

Similarly, as Sullivan was planning a dramatic return to

Peckham and Nelson Mandela House for the Trotters, the very experienced set designer David Hitchcock was brought in to recreate their old flat. After studying the files and previous recordings, Hitchcock set about searching for some identical wallpaper (not an easy task, as it turned out, because the original tacky pattern had long since ceased production), reclaimed the old curtains from the BBC's stock rooms, and also introduced a few subtle revisions of his own. A pair of net curtains, for example, was put up over the normally bright window at the back of the set, partly because Hitchcock reasoned that Raquel would by now have added it as a 'feminine' touch to the flat, and partly because it would be much easier to light the room without the window being permanently exposed to 'daylight'. He also planned for the balcony to get more use, as although it had only figured previously on a couple of brief occasions, it would provide the team in future with a welcome additional option in terms of place and action. As the flat was to now accommodate not only Del, Raquel and Damien but also Rodney and Cassandra, the bedrooms and kitchen were also opened out and decorated to provide more space for certain scenes.

The actors also had to do some preparation in order to reacquaint themselves with their roles. 'We have had to watch old episodes to get our characters right,' John Challis said at the time. 'You can do a rough impression, but it needs practice to really sink into the part.'[37] For David Jason and Nicholas Lyndhurst in particular, it was a case of considering how their respective characters had changed, now that Del was fifty-six and Rodney forty-one, and how they now interacted as brothers. The two men thus thought long and hard about what might have happened during the years since 1996. They wanted

Del and Rodney to reappear in front of the cameras looking the same but different: older, not necessarily much wiser, but in some sense definitely affected by the time that has passed.

Location filming, on this occasion, would take place in two lengthy sessions, first in the autumn of 2001 and then during the early spring of 2002. It took the cast and crew to a wide range of areas both in Britain and abroad. Bristol, once again, provided the external shots of 'Peckham', while other scenes were shot in such disparate places as a town hall in Weston-super-Mare, a wine warehouse in Cherbourg and the Hotel de Paris in Monte Carlo. An unexpected complication came late on at Pinewood Film Studios when a plan to feature Del taking part in the popular game show *Who Wants to Be a Millionaire?* had to be hastily rethought after ITV declined to grant the rights for it to be used on repeat runs of the episode,[38] so a fictional quiz show called *Goldrush* was created instead. The race to get everything completed on time was, as usual, both frantic and nerve-wracking.

John Sullivan, meanwhile, was putting the finishing touches to his new trio of scripts. The main narrative problem he had faced with the return of *Only Fools* was that it unravelled the neat completion of the 1996 trilogy: the various strands then either had to be left hanging limply where they were, or they would have to be pulled back far into the past. As it happened, the latter decision was made. As far as Sullivan was concerned, money would have had as much impact on the Trotters as upper-class diction would have had on Eliza Doolittle: in other words, purely superficial. 'The guys just wouldn't change,' he would say, 'and would always return to Peckham some day because it's where their roots are.'[39]

The most unfortunate consequence of this was that it made

the first part of the new trilogy – 'If They Could See Us Now', which was broadcast on 25 December 2001 – seem uncomfortably like a Victorian parable: not this time, alas, by Dickens, but rather by a reactionary critic of the masses. The sequence thus developed rather like a lecture on the folly of encouraging the vulgar working classes to better themselves. We saw the Trotters acquire a fortune, and then squander it with a mixture of tastelessness, capriciousness and rank stupidity. Ticking off all the old clichés about the in-built limitations of the 'lower orders', the Trotters learn absolutely nothing, and do little except get excited about hobnobbing with the poshest of nobs, buy garish designer clothes, fly everywhere on Concorde, drive in grotesquely ostentatious stretch limousines, enjoy long and fecklessly glamorous holidays, gamble away huge sums at the roulette wheel and invest in a Central American venture that they clearly do not understand. When their investment is duly lost and they end up back in London in the Bankruptcy Court, one half expects the ghost of George Gissing to pop up, tap the camera lens and order all the common people back into the gin palaces to play push-pin and skittles.

The comeuppance of the Trotters, while leaving a nasty taste in the mouth, at least sets up some predictable but reliable comedy in what follows. Back in the old flat inside Nelson Mandela House, the familiar routine is resumed: everyone sitting around surrounded by boxes of unwanted stock, dreaming idly of ways to make some money. Albert's death is marked via the rather elderly gag of his family turning up at someone else's funeral by mistake, and then everyone's attention turns away from mortal thoughts and back to material matters.

Del's desperate attempt to win back some cash involves him taking part in a TV quiz show called *Goldrush*. He does surprisingly well until a question on classical music stumps him and he has to phone a friend: Rodney. Although Rodney is confident that he knows the answer, when Del accepts it he is told that it is wrong and he is out of the show. Later on, back at the flat, the embarrassed *Goldrush* producers call to explain that the answer was actually correct and he is entitled to the prize money. Del – suspecting it is yet another prank call from someone at The Nag's Head – announces sarcastically that he is giving it all to charity. The episode then ends as Del declares triumphantly to Rodney: 'We're the Trotters, and we're back!'

There were a few good things about this opening show. The Rodney–Cassandra relationship, once again, was a much more believable and better balanced affair, with Gwyneth Strong now interacting very effectively with Nicholas Lyndhurst. The 'new' Damien was also surprisingly promising, goading Rodney at every opportunity and using a cod-Jamaican gangsta rap accent to irritate his mother ('Don't fuzz me, bitch, me gun is hungry!'). There was surprisingly little, however, to convince the 20.3 million people[40] who watched the show (it would be the biggest audience of the decade[41]) that the return, as a whole, had been particularly wise.

BBC1's current Controller, Lorraine Heggessey, came out with the kind of comments that showed how much television executives now sounded like patronising politicians, claiming that the programme had been 'full of the comic panache we've come to expect from *Only Fools and Horses*',[42] but, as far as the reviewers were concerned, the majority were distinctly underwhelmed. Thomas Sutcliffe, in the *Independent,* lamented that the show was 'beginning to feel its age',[43] and David Stephenson, in the *Sunday Express*, complained that it had seemed 'under-cooked',[44] while another paper dismissed the episode as 'the biggest letdown' of the Christmas period[45] and *The Sunday Times* accused the BBC of 'flogging a dead horse for the ratings'.[46] The *Daily Mirror*'s TV critic offered the most trenchant response of all, arguing: 'From David Jason's bad dye job to the toe-curling creakiness of the gags and plot lines, this was a huge Christmas disappointment.' The same critic added that it was also striking how 'unlovable everyone has become', with Del Boy 'now an embittered buffoon', Rodney 'so stupid he shouldn't be allowed out' and the denizens of The Nag's Head now with 'no redeeming features'.[47]

The most peculiar thing about the episode was that it had seemed so cavalier about what, on its own terms, was surely a tragic–comic situation. After trying for so long to be millionaires, Del and Rodney have lost everything in the most irrational and irresponsible of ways, and now, at the ages of fifty-six and forty-one respectively, they find themselves right back where they used to be – much to the apparent amusement of all their so-called friends. Given the sympathy and compassion shown towards these characters in the past, especially since the show evolved into a sitcom–soap, there was something jarring about this episode's near-indifference to the nature of their plight. It was as though, after spending so long making us care about these people, the show, quite suddenly, just wanted us to laugh at them. As a supposed comic–drama, therefore, this was not so much streaky bacon, but more like an unappetising chunk of mechanically reformed ham.

In the ruthlessly competitive business of broadcasting, however, none of this really mattered. All that did matter was that the show had done its job spectacularly well in the ratings, easily dominating a pale and plucked turkey of a festive schedule whose other supposed 'highlights' included various soaps and hospital dramas, a couple of nostalgic documentaries, an ITV *Stars in Their Eyes* 'special', an over-blown CGI-reliant adaptation of the Sir Arthur Conan Doyle story *The Lost World* and the other disappointing John Sullivan/David Jason collaboration *Micawber*. In the absence of newer, fresher, better mainstream entertainments, even a mediocre edition of *Only Fools* struck the BBC as invaluable, and its executives, salivating over their spreadsheets, simply looked forward to seeing a similar result the following year.

The second instalment, 'Strangers on the Shore', was duly screened on Christmas Day 2002. While this was a much more conventional, almost 'old-fashioned' edition of *Only Fools*, it still seemed strangely aimless. Now that it had been established that the Trotters, even if they did become millionaires all over again, would be incapable of holding on to their wealth, any dramatic potential had been completely drained away from their future schemes, and all that was left was an expectation of 'more of the same'.

The episode began with the key characters struggling to adapt to their sudden change in fortune. The Trotters' precarious financial situation has reduced Del, humiliatingly, to earning some extra cash by acting as Boycie's part-time chauffeur. Rodney, meanwhile, is stuck at home, trying and failing to outstare the diabolic young Damien. Cassandra is pregnant and Raquel is waiting patiently for Del to come up with a bright idea to raise some money and save their flat.

A welcome distraction arrives when a letter from the Seamen's Association comes through the door, inviting Albert to a reunion for the remaining members of the crew that spent some time during the war based in a little village in Normandy.

Rather than merely reply that Albert has passed away, Del and Rodney decide to go as their Uncle's representatives. Del also plans to multi-task by getting Denzil and Trigger to follow them over to France to pick up a large quantity of alcohol from a wine warehouse and then sell it on to Sid at The Nag's Head for a handsome profit.

Soon after arriving at the village, they learn that Albert was driven out of the country because of his over-amorous ways, and that makes them suddenly notice how many of the locals are sporting big and bushy mariner's beards ('Good God,' gasps Rodney, 'it's like a geriatric village of the damned!'). Once the low-key festivities are over, they set off home via the warehouse and help Denzil and Trigger stock up on crates of Saint-Omer beer for the trip back to Britain.

That night, back at Nelson Mandela House, Denzil and Trigger find a stowaway, who speaks no English, hiding in the back of their lorry. The Trotter brothers head down to the garage to investigate, and end up bringing him up to the flat and introducing him to everyone as 'Gary', supposedly a friend whom Rodney met at evening school, although Raquel real-ises more or less immediately that 'Gary' is actually an illegal immigrant. Boycie also shows up, because a gas leak from Del's Slovak log-effect gas fires has caused an evacuation from his own mansion by order of the fire brigade.

A few days later, Boycie is able to go home, but 'Gary' has disappeared while playing football with Damien and his friends. As Boycie, who is on his way to an important meeting in Paris, and the Trotters, who are planning another trip to the wine warehouse, head to France in an old white van, there is a news report back in the UK featuring 'Gary', in which his real name is revealed as Rashid Mamoon, a young man claiming that he was 'kidnapped and held hostage by a south London organisation known as the Gary Gang'. When Del, Rodney and Boycie arrive in France, they meet with Boycie's Iranian business partner, Mr Mamoon, who introduces them to his son, whom they realise is actually Rashid. The young man panics and claims that Boycie and the Trotter brothers are his kidnappers. Mr Mamoon calls the police and Del, Rodney and Boycie are arrested on suspicion of kidnapping.

Watched by about 16.3 million viewers[48] – a decent enough figure in itself, but still 4 million down on the previous year's effort – the episode had seemed very stretched at seventy-five minutes and strikingly devoid of fresh ideas, with far too much reliance on the laboured 'Gary' catchphrase as a means to generate laughs. Most of the critics, by this stage, were clearly finding it hard to maintain their patience with a programme that, in the past, they had admired so much. Charlie Catchpole, writing in the *Daily Star*, complained that he had 'rarely felt so cheated, seeing a much-loved programme lamely and lazily going through the motions',[49] and Nancy Banks-Smith probably spoke for many when she wrote in the *Guardian*: 'I would like to thank *Only Fools and Horses* warmly for all they have done, and urge them to stop doing it now.'[50]

Once again, the television executives were the only ones who appeared genuinely and completely content with how things had turned out. The show, for the second year running, had been the most successful entertainment programme on offer over Christmas, and, in an era in which the number of available channels was now listed as 148 and still rising rapidly,[51] even a fading *Only Fools* was clearly still highly prized as a potent ratings weapon. Those independent observers who felt that the major terrestrial broadcasters, and particularly the BBC, should be aiming to achieve rather more than merely dominate a deeply disappointing festive Top Ten, probably felt like echoing the *Daily Record*'s thoroughly disenchanted TV reviewer Bob Shields, who advised like-minded viewers to take down their television aerial and, 'if you happen to be in the presence of the BBC's Director-General or the programming head of ITV, I suggest you stick it up as far as possible'.[52]

By the time that the final part of the *Only Fools* trilogy was due to be broadcast the following year, the common expectations were noticeably lower, but the programme still received a great deal of pre-publicity from the BBC, and some newspaper TV previewers were still prepared to describe the imminent arrival of another episode as an 'event'.[53] While the general view was that the return of the Trotters had so far been a disappointment, the hope was that the final instalment would end on a high.

Entitled 'Sleepless in Peckham', and broadcast on BBC1 at 9.20 p.m. on Christmas Day 2003, the episode began with Cassandra heavily pregnant, Rodney reading up on 'creative writing', Damien – very reluctantly – attending school, and Del deep in denial. Things are rather more serious than they first seem, because it soon transpires that the Trotters only have two weeks to find £53,000 to pay the Inland Revenue, or they will be evicted from their home in Nelson Mandela House. After twenty-two years in the flat, it could all be over.

Rodney's response is to try to write a commercially appealing movie. It involves a team of scientists landing on a remote island to investigate 'strange goings on'. Mel Gibson is earmarked for one of the leads, and Julia Roberts for the other. Once he falls asleep, however, the project draws to a halt.

Del's response is to study the *Financial Times* and dream up even more dramatic, racy and wildly improbable movies for Rodney to write up and get filmed. He also decides to hide all the letters he and Rodney have been receiving from the Official Receiver, threatening to auction the flat in ten days' time.

Marlene, meanwhile, has disappeared, and the locals at The Nag's Head are speculating that she has either run off with Denzil or been murdered by Boycie. Denzil, however, is soon spotted on his own at the local pizza parlour, recovering from an operation for piles. Intrigued, Del and Rodney then pay a visit on Boycie, whose awkwardness makes them even more suspicious. Del opts for the subtle approach: 'I hope you won't take offence by what I'm about to say, but me and Rodney think you've murdered Marlene and buried her in the garden.' Boycie is appalled: 'You know how much I've spent on that garden – do you think I'm going to dig a *hole* in it?' It turns out that Marlene has merely been away to have a couple of breast implants. '*Entente cordiale!*' gasps Del when he sees the finished results.

Back at the flat, however, Raquel has discovered what Del has been hiding, and she is furious with him. He responds by pointing out all that he has been through over the years, looking after Rodney in the absence of their parents, and urges her to sympathise and lend him some support. Unimpressed, she goes off to the bedroom and he goes out to the balcony, where Rodney joins him. Hurt and angry, he vows to leave her, until she calls him to join her in bed.

Rodney, however, has worries of his own. He has borrowed an old photograph of a 1960 'Jolly Boys' Outing' with which to embarrass Del, but, once he has had it blown up, he spots someone in it, from the year of his birth, who looks eerily like him. It is Freddie 'The Frog' Robdal. Rodney realises now that Freddie was his biological father. Del knows, too, and has done for years – ever since Uncle Albert got drunk and told him at a party. Neither brother, however, will tell the other, reasoning that it would break his heart.

The next morning, Del and Rodney are called to see a solicitor named Mr Cartwright, thinking that it is about their failure to pay the Inland Revenue. Mr Cartwright, however, explains that he has been writing to both of them for three months now without receiving any reply, and he reveals that they are the beneficiaries of their Uncle Albert's will. As they gave him a large sum of money when they became millionaires, and he went on to lead a relatively simple life making a few sensible investments, he has left them the sum of £145,000 each.

Before they can celebrate, they have to rush to the hospital, where Cassandra has gone into labour. When they get there, however, she has already had the baby by caesarean section, and he and Cassandra finally have a daughter.

Some days later, Rodney takes the baby out to his mother's grave. He stands in front of her monument and speaks to her:

Did you love him? Did he love you? I hope he made you happy. You know, a few laughs. I've got two photos of you. But that's it. That's my past. My history is two photos. One of 'em's blurred. Don't matter. [Looks over at his daughter and then back at the monument] I hope she'll be as lovely as you. Well . . . she will. I wish I'd known you. I wish we'd had . . . well, you know, something to . . . just something. If you bump into Uncle Albert, say thanks.

Del arrives in the old yellow van. When he goes to visit the monument and looks at the dedication, he is touched to see that it has been altered to include his mother's new grand-daughter, whom Rodney has named after her: Joan. As the two brothers walk away, Rodney asks Del a question:

RODNEY: Other than looks, was he like me in any way?
DEL: Who?
RODNEY: You know who. Freddie Robdal. My father.
DEL: Freddie 'The Frog' was a professional burglar. He was disloyal to his friends. He was a womaniser, a home breaker, a conman, a thief, a liar and a cheat. So, no, Rodney, you're nothing like him.

Del puts his arm around Rodney's shoulder. 'Come on, let's go home, bruv.'

The episode thus ended strongly and aptly, with good acting, believable emotions and meaningful gestures. An audience of 16.37 million – the biggest of the year for anything other than a soap – saw it,[54] and liked it enough to help it top the poll for a special BAFTA voted for by the viewing public. Just as on that September night back in 1981, an episode of a sitcom, on this Christmas night in 2003, had left its audience not only laughing at the comedy but also, and most importantly, genuinely caring about its characters.

After so many false notes and forced scenes over the past three years, the second trilogy had come to the kind of conclusion that did justice to *Only Fools and Horses*. It had been quite a while, but, as the show finally went out through the door for the final time, it seemed itself again: a very special, and greatly cherished, television show.

EPILOGUE

Long live Hooky Street.

Après moi le déluge . . .

'Never say never,' John Sullivan remarked when asked, shortly before the 2003 Christmas special was screened, if there would ever be any more editions of *Only Fools and Horses*.[1] David Jason would say much the same thing seven years later, in 2010, when he responded to yet another question about the possibility of the programme returning by admitting: 'I wouldn't rule it out.'[2] The prospect of another revival was only finally ruled out, once and for all, by the sad loss of John Sullivan himself the following year. In truth, however, after seven series and eighteen specials – sixty-three episodes in all – it was surely time for the show to stop. Arguably no other sitcom had grown so much, and changed so much, and yet retained such a strong hold on the public's imagination and affection. It had more than earned the right to go out at the top.

What had it achieved? Apart from all the critical plaudits, awards and record-breaking audience figures, it had rearranged, subtly but profoundly, the landscape of television comedy. First it enriched the British sitcom from within, bringing in a deeper, darker, sense of mortality, fragility and truthful humour that paved the way for the likes of *One Foot in the Grave*, *The Royle Family* and *Rev*. It then went beyond the boundaries of that genre to create a new kind of comedy–drama format, blending elements of the conventional episodic sitcom with aspects of a soap or 'continuous drama', and in doing so helped to establish a new tradition that would nourish such future shows as *The Office, Gavin and Stacey* and *Shameless. Only Fools and Horses* did not just entertain and amuse the people who watched it; it also made a lasting difference to what they expected of, and wanted from, a situation comedy.

The achievement of John Sullivan (who was awarded an OBE in 2005 for services to drama) was not only to develop the show so much but also to write every single episode of it himself. There was never any writing partner, let alone a large writing team, to lighten the load, contribute ideas and share some of the strain. He did it all on his own. Probably only Eddie Braben, who similarly took sole responsibility for the vast majority of scripts that made *The Morecambe & Wise Show* such a success, invested so much of himself in the creation, and maintenance, of one of the nation's favourite television programmes.

The achievement of David Jason and Nicholas Lyndhurst was to set an extraordinarily high standard, extraordinarily consistently, of top-quality character acting. Along with the likes of Harry H. Corbett and Wilfrid Brambell in *Steptoe and Son*, Arthur Lowe and John Le Mesurier in *Dad's Army* and Ronnie Barker and Richard Beckinsale in *Porridge*, Jason and Lyndhurst showed how the sitcom, or any comedy–drama, could encourage acting just as strong, affecting, engaging and real as any performance seen in any so-called 'straight' or 'dramatic' production. Knighted in 2005 for services to drama, David Jason, deservedly, received several awards for his work in the show; Nicholas Lyndhurst should certainly have been given just as many. Together, the two actors combined to produce a partnership that was a credit to their profession: a funny, touching, complex on-screen relationship, stretching out over twenty-two years, that never once seemed inauthentic.

The achievement of the production team behind the scenes was, in its own way, similarly impressive, battling against all kinds of obstacles in terms of time and space and budget to ensure, on the vast majority of occasions, that what reached the screen represented everyone at their best. Whether it be episodes lasting half-an-hour or fifty minutes, or feature-length specials, all those involved helped to provide viewers with a properly polished production.

Only Fools and Horses deserved all of the awards. It deserved all of the attention. It deserved to be respected, admired and loved.

It also deserves to be remembered and treated with due care by the television schedulers. As early as 2003, even before the last special was broadcast, the BBC was already repeating as many as forty-seven episodes each year,[3] and, since the original run came to a close, the back catalogue has been exploited so ruthlessly, and routinely, by the so-called 'gold' satellite channels that it has often seemed as though viewers were being challenged to keep revering the programme in spite of the remorseless repetition.

Nostalgia channels should be there to serve classic shows – not the other way around. Genuinely great television programmes should never be used as mere padding in otherwise threadbare and unimaginative schedules. Past episodes of *Only Fools and Horses*, alas, tend not only to be over-exposed but also shown out of their correct sequence. Something that once was organic and meaningful is now all too frequently rendered artificial and trivial. Here, for example, is the main part of UK Gold's schedule (unedited) for Saturday, 26 March 2011:

9.50 a.m.	*Only Fools and Horses* (Series 1, episode 4)
10.30 a.m.	*Only Fools and Horses* (1990 Christmas Special)
12.10 p.m.	*Only Fools and Horses* (1982 Christmas Special)
12.50 p.m.	*Only Fools and Horses* (Series 3, episode 4)
1.30 p.m.	*Only Fools and Horses* (1993 Christmas Special)
3.20 p.m.	*Only Fools and Horses* (Series 5, episode 4)
4.00 p.m.	*Only Fools and Horses* (Series 1, episode 4)
4.40 p.m.	*Only Fools and Horses* (1990 Christmas Special)
6.15 p.m.	*Only Fools and Horses* (1982 Christmas Special)
6.55 p.m.	*Only Fools and Horses* (Series 3, episode 4)
7.35 p.m.	*Only Fools and Horses* (1993 Christmas Special)
9.25 p.m.	*Only Fools and Horses* (Series 5, episode 4)

Over the course of the following month, April 2011, no fewer than forty-two repeats of the show were screened on the same channel – and that was by no means an unusually large monthly quantity.

No great work of literature, music, film or television can hope to remain fresh, charming and engaging when it is depicted, day after day, month after month, year after year, more like an unavoidable obstacle than an appealing treat. Such careless ubiquity dulls the mind and saps the soul. It repackages something precious as something prosaic. One may as well play the 'best bits' of Mozart in a musty lift.

The opposite kind of danger to such routine carelessness, however, is that strange mixture of punctiliousness and proprietorialism that now seems to be seeping into the celebration of each and every classic sitcom. One of the unintended consequences of the modern preservation and marketing of the comedy past (in stark contrast to the previous era when so much that was prized was wiped) is that it has engendered an irascible insatiability that drives some fans deep into the most humourless of moods.

Everything has survived, everything is available, except the precious novelty of the original moment. What started out as the simple and innocent enjoyment of a comedy programme can now all too easily end up as a world-weary addiction to over-analysis and increasingly bad-tempered debate. On-screen repeats and DVDs are studied and reassessed, filming locations are logged and rights-related edits are listed, internet forums are formed and filled, and, slowly but surely, fan communities are shaped and structured into tighter and tighter cliques until they calcify into curiously po-faced and pompous hierarchies headed by a tiny network of worshipful masters.

What tends to be so sadly long-forgotten, as the dourest of these obsessives continue to jostle among themselves to gnaw on the dry bones of the comedy carcass, is that the original shows actually used to make them *laugh*. It is quite an achievement, of sorts, to turn so much unforced amusement into such a burdensome chore, but it is surely not one that requires any outside encouragement.

An appropriate celebration of a classic show should therefore not be aimed primarily at these self-proclaimed know-it-alls, because, quite frankly, they probably already do know it all. No doubt, like the spectacularly corpulent trencherman Mr Creosote in *Monty Python*'s *The Meaning of Life*, they may well think that, even at this late belt-straining stage, they can still find room inside for one more wafer-thin detail, but it would surely be better for their health if they just abstained and asked for the bill.

None of this is meant to malign the most ardent and good-natured of individual full-time fans. Commercial culture makes such chronic commitment love's line of least resistance. It is simply to acknowledge that there is no need to interfere with how they attend to their own avidity.

The team responsible for *Only Fools* would be, understandably, ambivalent about such diametrical and divisive trends. On the one hand, some of them were uneasy about the threat of overkill (they cared far too much about the sitcom to countenance loving it either not wisely or too well). On the other hand, all of them were pleased and proud to see the show still so prevalent on the screen ('I just think it's amazing,' said Tessa Peake-Jones, 'that the programmes are shown so often on any channel'[4]), and were grateful for the lustre that John Sullivan's glorious creation continued to lend them ('He changed my life in 1984 when he gave me Marlene,' Sue Holderness recalled fondly. 'Twenty-seven years later I am still being employed because of Marlene'[5]).

John Sullivan himself never ceased to be astonished by the sheer persistence of the show's popularity. 'It still surprises me,' he admitted not long before he died. 'We now have a new generation of kids writing to us who weren't born when we started in '81. But we also now have another generation writing to us who weren't born when we finished in 2003. It just keeps on going.'[6]

One of the ways that, in later years, he chose to engage imaginatively with this interest was via spin-off shows. There had been media interest in such ventures since before the final trilogy of *Only Fools* had been broadcast, when a national newspaper urged Sullivan and the BBC to create a series called *The Nag's Head,* featuring all of the familiar characters apart from the Trotters.[7] After the original run was over, and the demand remained strong, he started responding to such requests. First, he launched *The Green Green Grass* – a culture-clash style of sitcom featuring the characters of Boycie and Marlene, uprooted from Peckham to the relative wilds of Shropshire after learning that the Driscoll Brothers, who were sent to jail on Boycie's supergrass evidence, have now been released and are seeking revenge. It ran for four fairly successful series and three Christmas specials between 2005 and 2009. Sullivan then developed something with which he had been toying for a number of years, first as a potential novel and then as a possible television programme: *Rock & Chips.* Set in the early 1960s and inspired by the storyline in the final episode of *Only Fools* (in which Rodney realised that the late local jewel thief Freddie Robdal was his real father), it reached the screen in January 2010 on BBC1, billed as a 'one-off prequel',[8] but it performed well enough to lead to two more specials.

Such projects were welcomed by most of the diehard fans, and had their own particular charms, but nothing would ever replace the special appeal of *Only Fools and Horses* itself. While some admirers distracted themselves with the random rotation of repeats, and others gorged themselves on the expensive DVD box sets, the vast majority who loved the show the first time around simply went on with their lives while remembering all of the wonderful, funny and sometimes moving moments: the plummeting chandelier; the loss of Grandad; the hang-gliding incident; the sudden space in the counter at the bar; the uncontrollable blow-up dolls; the club singer who 'cwied'; the birth of Del's son; the improbably shaped and placed Batman and Robin; and the joyous, though short-lived, experience of being millionaires. Most people were happy just to keep hold of those cherished memories. They really did mean so much. They still inspired a smile.

Great shows like *Only Fools and Horses* will not be fatally diminished or demeaned even by careless repeats or obsessive over-analysis. They will continue to inspire such striking extremes, but, much more importantly, they will also remain available and appealing to those who simply want to enjoy something truly exceptional.

'At the end of the day,' John Sullivan once sat back in his home and said of the warmth that he felt from the fans of *Only Fools*, 'it's those people who go into the post office and buy a TV licence – they pay my wages, they pay the heating in this place. And if I'm not keeping them happy, I'm not doing a good job, I feel like I'm cheating. It's nice to get that response from them. So I think, OK, I'm doing a decent job.'[9]

He did so much more than a good job. This remarkably talented, modest and much-missed man left behind a rich and enlightening legacy that will continue to inspire comedy writers, and delight comedy fans, for as long as anyone can imagine.

There will always be English underdogs, there will always be close but combative families, there will always be little men with high hopes and gangly ones with deep doubts. Someone, somewhere, will always be waiting patiently to catch that precious cut-glass crystal, only to see the other one at the opposite end of the room crash straight down to the ground. Someone, somewhere, will always be striving to impress, only to fall through the open bar flap. Someone, somewhere, will always have moments when he or she is caught acting like a proper plonker. That is life. That is us.

This classic comedy will continue to elicit such keen feelings of recognition. This time next year, and for many, many, years after that, people will still be enjoying *Only Fools and Horses*.

Episode Guide

Series One (1981)

No.	Title	Producer	Director	Original Air Date	Audience	Running Time
1	**Big Brother**	Ray Butt	Martin Shardlow	08.09.81	9.2 million	30 mins

Del Boy – the self-appointed chairman of Trotters Independent Traders – decides to employ his younger brother Rodney, a budding financial adviser, as a key cog in his business machine. Later on, in The Nag's Head pub, Del buys twenty-five executive briefcases from Trigger. When he discovers that none of them actually open, he is rattled by Rodney's advice to throw them in the river.

No.	Title	Producer	Director	Original Air Date	Audience	Running Time
2	**Go West Young Man**	Ray Butt	Martin Shardlow	15.09.81	6.1 million	30 mins

Searching for bargains, as usual, Del and Rodney visit Boycie's car lot, where they spot a Mark II Cortina that is being used as a part-exchange for a Vanden Plas. Del negotiates the price of the motor down to £25, in return for housing an E-type Jaguar that Boycie is planning to give as a gift for his 'bit on the side'. After persuading a customer to purchase the clapped-out Cortina for £199, Del and Rodney jump in the Jag and head off for a celebratory night on the tiles. After a poor start, the two brothers manage to get the telephone numbers from a couple of young women. Rodney, however, contrives to lose the piece of paper on which the numbers are written, and then something terrible happens to the car.

3	**Cash and Curry**	Ray Butt	Martin Shardlow	22.09.81	7.3 million	30 mins

Always keen to establish new business contacts, Del befriends a wealthy Indian businessman called Vimmal Malik. It does not take long before Del becomes caught up in a dispute between Malik and his fierce rival, Mr Ram. It transpires that Vimmal currently possesses a precious porcelain heirloom that Ram claims belongs to his family – and they want it back. In order to make a positive impression, Del offers to mediate between the two men, especially because Mr Ram is willing to pay a generous sum for the heirloom's return. Not everything, however, is quite as it seems.

4	**The Second Time Around**	Ray Butt	Martin Shardlow	29.09.81	7.8 million	30 mins

Del is surprised to hear that Pauline Harris, one of his ex-fiancées, is back in Peckham – twelve years after she left for America. In spite of the reservations expressed by Rodney and Grandad, it is not long before the former couple are engaged all over again. Pauline's past, however, then comes back to haunt her, and scare Del.

5	**A Slow Bus to Chingford**	Ray Butt	Martin Shardlow	06.10.81	7 million	30 mins

Del's latest moneymaking scam is 'Trotters Ethnic Tours': a scenic tour around Chingford and Croydon, taking in such enticing sights as the Lee Valley Viaduct. Rodney is persuaded to drive the bus and Grandad agrees to distribute the publicity leaflets. What follows, however, is not what Del envisaged.

| 6 | **The Russians Are Coming** | Ray Butt | Martin Shardlow | 13.10.81 | 8.8 million | 30 mins |

Del, quite by accident, has managed to buy a DIY nuclear fall-out shelter. As Rodney is already fearful about the prospect of a Third World War, Del is persuaded into putting a survival plan into action.

Christmas Special 1981

| 7 | **Christmas Crackers** | Bernard Thompson | Bernard Thompson | 28.12.81 | 7.5 million | 35 mins |

The turkey is burnt to a crisp, the Christmas pudding is charred hard, the same old shows are on television, and Rodney is bored stiff. Even Grandad would rather depart for an OAPs' party instead of remaining stuck in the flat, so the Trotter brothers decide to head off to The Monte Carlo Club in search of romantic distractions.

Series Two (1982)

| 8 | **The Long Legs of the Law** | Ray Butt | Ray Butt | 21.10.82 | 7.7 million | 30 mins |

Del and Grandad are appalled to discover that the woman Rodney is dating, called Sandra, is actually a police officer. At the end of their first date, Rodney brings Sandra back to the flat for a nightcap. With all the dodgy merchandise on view in the lounge, she is the last person the Trotters need inside their home – and Del has noticed something incriminating about the watch Rodney has just given her.

| 9 | **Ashes to Ashes** | Ray Butt | Ray Butt | 28.10.82 | 9.8 million | 30 mins |

Trigger's grandmother has passed away, and the Trotters gather round to offer their condolences. Del spots a couple of antique urns that he fancies selling on for a handsome profit. The only problem is that they currently contain the ashes of Trigger's grandad.

| 10 | **A Losing Streak** | Ray Butt | Ray Butt | 04.11.82 | 7.5 million | 30 mins |

Del is struggling financially, and his gambling is only making things worse – even his double-headed coin cannot help him win. He cannot resist, however, when Boycie challenges him to a winner-takes-all poker game.

| 11 | **No Greater Love** | Ray Butt | Ray Butt | 11.11.82 | 8.6 million | 30 mins |

Rodney has fallen for a woman twice his age – and she is married to a hoodlum who is about to be released from prison. Fearing for his brother's safety, Del decides to intervene. One or other Trotter, however, will be facing retribution for the ill-advised dalliance.

| 12 | **The Yellow Peril** | Ray Butt | Ray Butt | 18.11.82 | 8.2 million | 30 mins |

Del has got a job redecorating a Chinese restaurant, so he enlists the assistance of Rodney and Grandad. He also plans to sneak some of the gold-coloured paint off to the cemetery to smarten up his mother's monument. This turns out to be one bright idea that, if anything, is too bright for its own good.

| 13 | **It Never Rains . . .** | Ray Butt | Ray Butt | 25.11.82 | 9.5 million | 30 mins |

Prolonged summer showers have forced the Trotters off the streets and into the pub. Alex the travel agent is also drowning his sorrows indoors, moaning that business is so slow he cannot even give holidays away. Del proposes a scheme that ought to be mutually beneficial, but only ends up getting him, Rodney and Grandad as far as a run-down hotel in Benidorm. Once they arrive, things go from bad to worse, thanks to Grandad's misdemeanours.

14	**A Touch of Glass**	Ray Butt	Ray Butt	02.12.82	10.2 million	30 mins

Returning from an auction in the country, the Trotters stop to help a woman whose car has broken down. It turns out that she is Lady Ridgemere, the wife of Lord Ridgemere who owns the Ridgemere Hall Estate. Having taken her back to the stately home, Del overhears the Lord of the Manor complaining to the firm that has been hired to clean their chandeliers, so he wastes no time in offering the Trotter's own 'expert' services for a bargain price. What happens next is not what anyone expected.

Christmas Special (1982)

15	**Diamonds are for Heather**	Ray Butt	Ray Butt	30.12.82	9.3 million	30 mins

It is Christmas, but Del Boy is depressed, drinking alone at The Nag's Head. It is there, however, that he meets a woman named Heather, with whom he is instantly smitten. Romance soon blossoms, and before long Del is ready to propose. There is at least one complication, however, that he will have to resolve: Heather's estranged husband.

Series Three (1983)

16	**Homesick**	Ray Butt	Ray Butt	10.11.83	9.4 million	30 mins

It seems that the strain of climbing the twelve floors in Nelson Mandela House every day is taking its toll on Grandad's legs. Fortunately, Rodney has just been elected Chairman of the Housing Committee, and, following a little pressure from Del, he uses his influence to arrange for the family to move into a three-bedroom bungalow nearby. The plan appears to be going very smoothly – until the welfare co-ordinator decides to pay the Trotters a visit.

17 **Healthy Competition**	Ray Butt	Ray Butt	17.11.83	9.7 million	30 mins

Rodney is taking stock of his life: now aged twenty-four, he is frustrated by the fact that he has not yet moved beyond acting as a look-out while Del sells dodgy goods. He decides that the way forward is to team up with Mickey Pearce and set up a rival business. A shocked Del warns him that, if he really wants to stand on his own two feet, the price will be total independence from the TITCO cash flow – including beer money. Rodney goes ahead, and, at a local auction, the brotherly battle commences.

18 **Friday the 14th**	Ray Butt	Ray Butt	24.11.83	9.7 million	30 mins

The Trotters take a trip down to Cornwall to borrow Boycie's country cottage for a spot of salmon poaching. A bad storm is the first sign that things are not set to go swimmingly, and then they discover that an axe-wielding murderer with a fierce hatred of salmon fishermen has just escaped from the local insane asylum. Only Del Boy seems to remain confident that all will be well.

19 **Yesterday Never**	Ray Butt	Ray Butt	01.12.83	10.6 million	30 mins

Del Boy ventures into the world of fine art when he attempts to pull the wool over the sharp eyes of a glamorous antiques dealer. He fails to convince her that his battered old wooden cabinet is in fact a 'Queen Anne' original, but, even though she insists it is 'worthless', she does take a shine to a painting that is hanging on Del's wall. The question is: who is tricking who?

| 20 **May the Force Be With You** | Ray Butt | Ray Butt | 08.12.83 | 10.7 million | 30 mins |

Peckham's least-favourite policeman, Detective Inspector Roy Slater, is back in town sniffing on the scent of some missing microwaves. Having known Del since they were at school together, he knows who to suspect. After duping Rodney into taking him back to the flat for a 'reunion' meal with Del, Slater pounces and sets about turning the Trotters into informers. Del, however, is determined to resist.

| 21 **Wanted** | Ray Butt | Ray Butt | 15.12.83 | 11.2 million | 30 mins |

Rodney's attempt to help a drunken woman on the street back-fires when she accuses him of man-handling her and promptly cries 'rape!' Convinced by his mischievous brother that the police are looking for 'The Peckham Pouncer', Rodney disappears, fearing he is now a fugitive from justice. Realising that the prank has gone too far, Del tries to track him down.

| 22 **Who's a Pretty Boy?** | Ray Butt | Ray Butt | 22.12.83 | 11.9 million | 30 mins |

Del plans to get revenge on the decorator Brendan O'Shaughnessy for supplying him with 'apple white' paint that was actually battleship grey. Upon learning that the Irishman is painting Denzil's flat for £200, Del persuades his friend that he and Rodney can do the job for far less money. Denzil agrees, despite his wife Corrine's suspicion that the Trotters can never be trusted. Problems arise more or less immediately when Rodney leaves a kettle on the boil and steams the whole apartment, not only wrecking the kettle but also, it appears, killing Corrine's pet canary with paint fumes. The race is now on to make things right before she returns.

Christmas Special (1983)

23	Thicker than Water	Ray Butt	Ray Butt	25.12.83	10.8 million	30 mins

Del Boy receives the least welcome Christmas present imaginable when his father, Reg, turns up after eighteen years' absence. Explaining that he has been diagnosed with an hereditary blood disorder, Reg claims that he has come to do the right thing and warn his two boys. After both brothers go for tests, however, it appears that Del and Rodney have different blood types. Their father has some explaining to do.

Series Four (1985)

24	Happy Returns	Ray Butt	Susan Belbin	21.02.85	15.2 million	30 mins

After stopping a young boy, named Jason, from running into the road, Del strikes up a friendship with him. Del then discovers that Jason's mother, June, is an old flame whom he last saw about nineteen years ago. Rodney, meanwhile, is dating a young girl called Debby. When it transpires that Debby is none other than June's daughter, and it is coming up to her 19th birthday, Del and Rodney soon put two and two together and decide that Debby may well be Del's daughter and Rodney's niece. It is clear that Del and June need to have a serious talk.

25	Strained Relations	Ray Butt	Susan Belbin	28.02.85	14.9 million	30 mins

Grandad has died, and among the mourners is his brother, an old navy man named Albert. Back at the flat, after the wake, Del and Rodney are surprised to find that Albert has been left behind. Del, apparently in no mood for any further familial complications, wants him gone as soon as possible, but Rodney cannot believe that his brother can be so callous.

26 Hole in One Ray Butt Susan 07.03.85 13.4 million 30 mins
Belbin

The Trotters are in trouble. Rodney has invested £500 in suntan lotion during one of the worst winters in living memory, and the deep-fat fryer that Del sold to the landlord of The Nag's Head has just been reported as faulty. The brothers are in a bad mood, but Uncle Albert assures them that their luck will change soon enough. Sure enough, he accidentally falls through an open cellar door at the pub, and the Trotters come up with a quick way to get some cash – by suing the brewery for damages.

27 It's Only Ray Butt Susan 14.03.85 13.6 million 30 mins
  Rock and Belbin
  Roll

Rodney has joined a new rock band, and Del responds by appointing himself as their manager, arranging for them to get some instruments and equipment, and then booking them into The Shamrock Club to play at the St Patrick's night festivities. The gig, however, results in chaos.

28 Sleeping Ray Butt Susan 21.03.85 18.7 million 30 mins
  Dogs Lie Belbin

Seizing on to an easy way to make £60 a week, Del persuades Boycie and Marlene to entrust him and Rodney with the care of their Great Dane puppy, Duke, while they are away on vacation. When Duke proves strangely docile during what is supposed to be his first morning run with the Trotters, the brothers rush him off to the vets. As they have been eating the dog's expensive steaks while feeding him cheap cuts of 'freshly reheated' pork, the vet concludes that Duke has probably contracted salmonella poisoning. When they get home and discover that Albert has eaten the rest of the pork with some pickles and crusty bread, they really start to panic.

| 29 | **Watching the Girls Go By** | Ray Butt | Susan Belbin | 28.03.85 | 14.4 million | 30 mins |

Tired of being teased about his imaginary girlfriends, Rodney is desperate to find a date to take to a party at The Nag's Head. When Del discovers that Mickey Pearce has bet Rodney that he will turn up alone, he vows to help his brother out – and pocket a share of the winnings.

| 30 | **As One Door Closes** | Ray Butt | Susan Belbin | 04.04.85 | 14.2 million | 30 mins |

The painter and decorator Brendan O'Shaughnessy has asked Del to provide him with enough louvred doors to refit an entire housing estate in Nunhead. The problem is that Del's own supplier, Teddy Cummings, only stocks and sells in bulk, so it is up to the Trotters to find £2,000 by the next day or the deal will be off. When Del hears about Denzil's redundancy money, it does not take him long to redirect it his way, but then O'Shaughnessy informs him that the doors are no longer required – leaving the Trotters to deal with Denzil and his five very angry brothers.

Christmas Special (1985)

| 31 | **To Hull and Back** | Ray Butt | Ray Butt | 25.12.85 | 16.9 million | 90 mins |

Boycie and his shady associate Abdul are planning a diamond scam. Del Boy becomes involved after they offer him a £15,000 cut of the estimated £150,000 sale of the stones on the UK market to act as the courier between Holland and Britain. Del soon discovers that his old foe DI Slater is already hot on Boycie and Abdul's trail, so he must find an unexpected way to travel if he is to have any chance of eluding detection.

Series Five (1986)

32 From Prussia   Ray Butt   Mandie   31.08.86   12.1 million   30 mins
With Love   Fletcher

Del and Rodney take pity on a tearful young – and heavily pregnant – German girl called Anna who has turned up at The Nag's Head after being thrown out by the family she had been serving as an au pair. Rodney is charged with the task of finding her a hotel, but ends up taking her back with him to the flat. Stuck with another one of his brother's waifs and strays, Del ponders what can be done with Anna's unwanted baby – and the first people he thinks of are Boycie and Marlene, who have been trying for a child for years. Del proposes that they adopt Anna's child as their own.

33 The Miracle   Ray Butt   Mandie   07.09.86   14.2 million   30 mins
of Peckham   Fletcher

Del suddenly seems to be experiencing pangs of guilt about his dubious lifestyle, and so he heads to the confession booth of his local Catholic church to speak with Father O'Keith. While chatting with the priest, Del discovers that the local hospice urgently requires a £185,000 renovation. After his confession is over, Del is about to put some money into the collection box when Father O'Keith exclaims that the statue of the Virgin Mary is weeping holy tears. Del wastes no time in hatching a plan that he assures the priest will exploit this 'miracle' and raise precious funds for the hospice.

34 The Longest   Ray Butt   Mandie   14.09.86   16.7 million   30 mins
Night   Fletcher

Del, Rodney and Albert, out shopping at their local supermarket, are mistakenly apprehended as shoplifters by an officious security guard and taken off to the manager's office. Shortly after, the security guard brings a 'proper' shoplifter into the office, and he promptly pulls out a gun and demands all the money from the safe. Unfortunately for him, however, he is wearing one of Del's faulty watches, has thus mistimed his arrival, and the safe has a time lock that will not open again until tomorrow morning. Everyone, it seems, is in for a long night.

35 Tea for Three   Ray Butt   Mandie   21.09.86   16.5 million   30 mins
                                             Fletcher

Trigger's attractive young niece, Lisa, is in town for a while. Del and Rodney immediately start competing for her affections when they invite her round to their flat for tea. Del gains an advantage when he sabotages Rodney's snooze on the sun bed by cranking up the power and leaving him to turn bright red. Determined to gain his revenge, Rodney then convinces Lisa that it would be a nice surprise for her to arrange a hang-gliding session as Del's birthday treat.

36 Video Nasty   Ray Butt   Ray Butt   28.09.86   17.5 million   30 mins

Rodney has been given a council grant to make a film about the local community. While he suffers from writer's block, Del dreams of turning the project into a big commercial blockbuster, and Mickey Pearce fancies filming a blue movie for the back room at The Nag's Head.

37 Who Wants   Ray Butt   Ray Butt   05.10.86   18.8 million   30 mins
to Be a
Millionaire?

Del's old business partner from the 1960s, Jumbo Mills, is back in the UK to sort out a deal with Boycie. Having made a fortune for himself in Australia, Jumbo asks Del to become the new face of his new import business – but it means a move Down Under. After being assured that Rodney and Albert can come with him, Del agrees to the move – but then things get complicated.

Christmas Specials (1986–88)

38 A Royal Flush Ray Butt   Ray Butt   25.12.86   18.8 million   76 mins

Rodney has met Vicky, a seemingly struggling artist who it turns out is the daughter of a duke. Eager to impress, Rodney invites her to the opera, but the experience is spoilt by the presence there of Del and his noisy date. It seems as though a romance is still possible when Vicky invites Rodney to a party at her father's country home, but then, once again, comes Del's rude intrusion.

39 The Frog's   Ray Butt   Ray Butt   25.12.87   14.5 million   60 mins
Legacy

The Trotters are in trouble: Uncle Albert's badly acted bouts of lumbago down at the market are failing to help sell a batch of massage gadgets, and the flat is full of faulty RAJAH computers. It is at the wedding of Trigger's niece that they hear the tale of Freddy the Frog, a bank robber who became such a close friend of the boys' mother that he left everything to her in his will – including missing gold bullion. Suddenly, it seems, they might finally be on the verge of becoming millionaires.

40 Dates   Gareth   Tony Dow 25.12.88   16.6 million   80 mins
          Gwenlan

It will soon be Uncle Albert's birthday, and Del is planning a surprise party for him at The Nag's Head. Both of the Trotter boys, meanwhile, are busy pursuing women to take to the occasion: Rodney by affecting a mean and moody persona, and Del by posing as a big shot businessman via a dating agency.

Series Six (1989)

41 Yuppy Love   Gary   Tony Dow 08.01.89   13.9 million   50 mins
Gwenlan

Del, having studied the film *Wall Street*, has decided the time is right for him to become a yuppie. He starts dressing differently, takes his Filofax everywhere he goes and mixes sparkling water with vintage Beaujolais Nouveau. Rodney, meanwhile, is trying to complete a computing diploma course at the Adult Education Centre. Things do not go smoothly for either brother: Del abandons The Nag's Head for a trendy bistro only to embarrass himself at the bar, while Rodney tries to impress a posh young woman called Cassandra by lying about where he lives.

42 Danger UXD   Gareth   Tony Dow 15.01.89   16.1 million   50 mins
Gwenlan

Del thinks he is on to a good deal when he agrees to help Denzil by taking fifty dolls off his hands. He only finds out later back at the flat that the items are actually inflatable sex dolls, filled with explosive propane gas. He and Rodney need to get them out of the building as discreetly as they can.

43 Chain Gang   Gareth   Tony Dow 22.01.89   16.3 million   50 mins
Gwenlan

When Del is offered a case of eighteen-carat gold chains by an ex-dealer called Arnie, he agrees to buy them for £12,500. Quickly forming a consortium with Boycie, Trigger, Mike, Albert and Rodney, he can only see huge profits for everyone. When Arnie collapses at a business lunch and is whisked away by ambulance to an unknown destination, Del and his anxious colleagues realise that both the jewellery and cash are still on his person.

44 The Unlucky Gareth   Tony Dow 29.01.89   17 million   50 mins
    Winner Is. . . Gwenlan

Del has entered every competition available in the hope of winning some lucrative prizes. Rodney discovers that Del has entered some of his old work for an art competition, and won them a holiday for three in Spain. Setting off excitedly with Cassandra and Del, it is only when he arrives at the five-star hotel in Mallorca that Rodney learns that his prize was for the under-fifteen category – so while Del and Cassandra relax with the other parents, Rodney has to endure the company of all the kids in The Groovy Gang.

45 Sickness Gareth   Tony Dow 05.02.89   18.2 million   50 mins
    and Wealth Gwenlan

Del is suffering from stomach cramps, but he is too scared to visit a doctor. In an attempt to distract himself with business projects, he decides to promote Uncle Albert's spiritualist lady-friend, Elsie Partridge, by setting up a séance in a back room at The Nag's Head. When some of the messages from 'the beyond' start to come through, Del is not the only one who is in for a surprise.

46 Little Gareth   Tony Dow 12.02.89   18.9 million   50 mins
    Problems Gwenlan

Rodney is depressed. Although he has just got engaged to Cassandra, he fears he has failed his Diploma in Computer Science, which could cost him a good job at the company owned by his future father-in-law. As if that is not bad enough, he is also unable to come up with his share of the cash for the new flat he and Cassandra plan to buy. Del, however, is keen to do what he can to help his kid brother – even if it hurts.

Christmas Specials (1989–90)

47 The Jolly Gareth   Tony Dow 25.12.89   20.12 million   85 mins
    Boys' Outing Gwenlan

It is Rodney and Cassandra's first wedding anniversary, but as she seems more interested in advancing her career than spending much time with him, Rodney decides to join his old mates on the annual Jolly Boys' Outing to Margate. Things start out well, but then one disaster follows another.

48	**Rodney Come Home**	Gareth Gwenlan	Tony Dow 25.12.90	17.97 m	75 mins

The Trotters appear to have found domestic contentment: Rodney has a wife, a job at his father-in-law's printing company and a home of his own; Del has been reunited with Raquel, who has moved in with him at the flat. Rodney's marriage, however, is already in trouble, and Del decides that it is down to him to make things right.

Series Seven (1990–91)

49	**The Sky's the Limit**	Gareth Gwenlan	Tony Dow 30.12.90	15 million	50 mins

The flat at Nelson Mandela House suddenly seems very cramped: not only is Del living there with Raquel and Albert, but Rodney has returned there after separating from Cassandra. Del, once again, wants to help out his brother – and is also keen to get him off the couch – so he plans to engineer a romantic reconciliation as soon as Cassandra flies back from a break abroad.

50	**The Chance of a Lunchtime**	Gareth Gwenlan	Tony Dow 06.01.91	16.6 million	50 mins

In a bid to revive her theatrical ambitions, Raquel has decided to audition for a production of Shakespeare's *As You Like It*. Rodney, meanwhile, seems intent on throwing away not only his job but also his marriage. Del is bemused by both of them, but he is in for a shock of his own.

51 Stage Fright   Gareth   Tony Dow 13.01.91   16.6 million   50 mins
                     Gwenlan

An old friend of Del's is putting on a cabaret night at The Starlight Rooms. Although Raquel is now pregnant, Del still cannot resist the chance to get her back on stage. When she protests that she needs a partner, Del hires a local crooner called Tony Angelino to share the singing duties and help dazzle the audience. As the big night approaches, not even the discovery that the club is now owned by an exceptionally irascible local gangster can stop Del from dreaming that it will all be a huge success.

52 The Class   Gareth   Tony Dow 20.01.91   16.2 million   50 mins
    of '62   Gwenlan

Raquel is unsettled when she receives a letter from her solicitor informing her that they have traced her ex-husband, who is considering her request for a divorce. Del, meanwhile, has set off to join the likes of Trigger, Boycie and Denzil for a school reunion at The Nag's Head, only to be confronted by a supposedly contrite ex-DI Roy Slater. Just when Del, after more than a few drinks, begins to believe that Slater really has changed for the better, he discovers the real reason for his return.

53 He Ain't   Gareth   Tony Dow 27.01.91   17.2 million   50 mins
    Heavy, He's   Gwenlan
    My Uncle

Del has decided not only to reinstate Rodney as a TITCO employee but also appoint him the new Director of Commercial Development. Uncle Albert, meanwhile, has taken to attending the Over-Sixties Club on the estate and appears to be courting a lady there named Dora Lane. One night, he arrives at the flat, bruised and shaken, claiming that he has been mugged. It is left to Del and Rodney to discover what has actually happened.

54	**Three Men, a Woman and a Baby**	Gareth Gwenlan	Tony Dow 03.02.91	18.9 million	50 mins

Del is due to become a father, but Rodney has never seemed so depressed: the polar ice cap is melting, the oceans are being polluted, the rainforest is dying, his marriage is still on the rocks and he has not 'had a bit' for months. He is so desperate he even finds Del's new stock of 'trendy' clip-on ponytails quite enticing.

Christmas Specials (1991–2003)

55	**Miami Twice**	Gareth Gwenlan	Tony Dow 24.12.91	17.77 million	35 mins

Del and Raquel's baby son, Damien, is being christened, and Del strikes a deal with the vicar to sell pre-blessed wine around the country. Rodney, meanwhile, is residing with Del, Raquel and Albert during weekdays, and visiting with Cassandra at weekends, on the advice of a Relate counsellor. Somewhat deviously, Del organises a 'two for one' holiday for him and his brother in Miami, sensing that both of them, for different reasons, could benefit from a bit of a break. It seems, at first, just what the two of them needed, but then they meet some members of the Ochetti family.

56	**Mother Nature's Son**	Gareth Gwenlan	Tony Dow 25.12.92	20.14 million	65 mins

It is Christmas, and the Trotter brothers are struggling financially. Although Cassandra has finally won her promotion, Raquel is suffering from post-natal depression, the rent for the flat is set to double, Grandad's allotment has been declared a health hazard and Rodney fears that Del has lost his old 'he who dares, wins' drive. It is while clearing the allotment that Del suddenly seems animated once again: spotting a gap in the market, he decides to bottle tap water and sell it as 'Peckham Spring Water'.

57 Fatal   Gareth   Tony Dow 25.12.93   19.59 million   85 mins
Extraction   Gwenlan

It is yet another downbeat Christmas in the Trotter household, as Raquel is worried that Del Boy is too busy down the 121 Club getting drunk to provide Damien with any presents. Rodney is concerned enough to question Del about his attitude, and Del explains that he is brokering a deal to get hold of some Russian ex-military camcorders to raise some funds to get him through the festive season. Raquel, however, is unimpressed, and suddenly it is Del's marriage that looks to be in trouble.

58 Heroes and   Gareth   Tony Dow 25.12.96   21.3 million   60 mins
Villains   Gwenlan

Cassandra is now so eager to conceive a baby that she has Rodney responding to a fertility schedule that has turned sex into a time-consuming chore. Del is frustrated that his home improvement grant has been rejected by the council. Eager to distract themselves on a rare boys' night out, the brothers dress up as Batman and Robin for a fancy-dress party held for a local publican. En route, they experience a peculiar incident, and then an acute embarrassment, before another set of unexpected events intervenes.

59 Modern Men   Gareth   Tony Dow 27.12.96   21.3 million   60 mins
Gwenlan

Del's sudden obsession with behaving like a 'modern man' is making him act more oddly than usual, and he is even thinking of having a vasectomy. Rodney is now waiting for Cassandra to give birth, and he wants more responsibility and a better job to provide for his family. It will not be long, however, before something far more dramatic intervenes in their lives.

60 Time On   Gareth   Tony Dow 29.12.96   24.35 million   60 mins
    Our Hands   Gwenlan

Rodney is still consumed by grief over the loss of his and Cassandra's child, and Del is struggling to distract him by sorting through the unsold stock in their garage. Both men are startled, however, when Raquel's antique-dealer father arrives and spots something potentially rather special amidst all the junk.

61 If They   Gareth   Tony Dow 25.12.01   20.3 million   71 mins
    Could See   Gwenlan
    Us Now

The Trotters have lost all their fortune in a bad investment and are declared bankrupt. They have no choice but to return to their flat in Nelson Mandela House. Desperate to raise some money, Del decides to take part in a TV game show.

62 Strangers   Gareth   Tony Dow 25.12.02   16.3 million   75 mins
    on the Shore   Gwenlan

Del and Rodney set off on a trip to France after agreeing to visit Uncle Albert's navy memorial ceremony. On the way back home, they join Trigger and Denzil to collect some duty-free booze to sell on to The Nag's Head. Upon arriving back in Peckham, they discover that an illegal immigrant has stowed away in their van.

63 Sleepless in   Gareth   Tony Dow 25.12.03   16.37 million   75 mins
    Peckham   Gwenlan

The Trotters now have only two weeks to find £53,000 to pay the Inland Revenue, or they will be evicted from their home in Nelson Mandela House. Rodney is trying to solve the problem by writing an ultra-commercial screenplay. Del is trying to solve the problem by urging Rodney to finish it. Boycie, meanwhile, is the subject of considerable gossip due to the mysterious disappearance of Marlene.

Mini Episodes (1982–97)

Christmas Tree	Ray Butt	Ray Butt	27.12.82	7.2 million	8 mins

A short sketch produced for the 1982 Christmas show, *The Funny Side of Christmas*, presented by Frank Muir. Del is trying to sell Christmas trees at the local market.

Licensed to Drill	Malcolm Taylor	Malcolm Taylor	1984	N/A	19 mins

In an educational short made in 1984 expressly for use in schools and colleges, Del, Rodney and Grandad discuss oil drilling and fossil fuels.

White Mice	24.12.85	N/A	3 mins

In a spoof consumer report, shown on BBC1's *Breakfast Time*, Del is investigated by a BBC consumer affairs specialist about a controversial deal with a pantomime character.

Royal Variety Performance	27.11.88	18.14 million	4 mins

While delivering a crate of dubious goods to a shady London club owner, Del, Rodney and Uncle Albert inadvertently walk in on the *Royal Variety Show*.

The Robin Flies at Dawn	Gareth Gwenlan	01.12.90	N/A	5 mins

In a special recording, Del, Rodney and Uncle Albert deliver a message to those British troops serving in the 1990–91 Gulf War.

Comic Relief	14.03.97	10.6 million	6 mins

A short scene, set exclusively in the flat. The first half features Del and Rodney slipping in references to other TV shows that featured David Jason and Nicholas Lyndhurst (including *A Touch of Frost* and *Goodnight Sweetheart*) before the duo come out of character and make an appeal to camera for donations for Comic Relief.

DVDs

Only Fools and Horses – The Complete Collection (released 2006: BBC Worldwide/2 entertain, catalogue number BBCDVD2272)

26 discs.

Only Fools and Horses Complete Series 1–7 Box Set (released 2010: BBC Worldwide/2 entertain, catalogue number BBCDVD3326)

9 discs.

Appreciation Society

http://www.ofah.net/blog/society/

Acknowledgements

The sad and sudden death of John Sullivan deprived me of the planned opportunity to interview him at length, but I am very grateful to those friends and former colleagues who shared their memories with me or offered advice, support and encouragement. I am particularly grateful to Lord Grade, James Gilbert, Sue Holderness, Tessa Peake-Jones, John and Carol Challis, Jonathan Betts and John Ammonds, as well as, from earlier projects, John Howard Davies, David Croft and the late Sir Bill Cotton. I am also indebted to Richard Webber, a fellow author who always behaves with great decency and enthusiasm.

I am grateful to the staff of the following institutions: the BBC Written Archives Centre; the National Archives; the British Library, Newspaper Library and Sound Archive; the British Film Institute Library; the Broadcasters' Audience Research Board; and the University of Cambridge Library.

Apart from thanking my excellent editor at Canongate, Nick Davies, I would like to express my gratitude to Norah Perkins and Jo Dingley for their invaluable encouragement, assistance and expertise. I am also pleased to acknowledge the admirable efforts of my copy-editor Octavia Reeve, and the usual sage and good-humoured advice of my agent Mic Cheetham. Their contributions could not have been more welcome.

Finally, my heartfelt thanks also go, as always, to Vera McCann, Richard McCann and Dick Geary for their kindness and company, and to Silvana Dean, without whose extra-ordinary belief and support I would never have seen the project all the way through to its conclusion.

Notes

Prologue

Frontispiece quotation: Samuel Beckett, *Worstward Ho* (London: John Calder, 1983).

1   'Getting Better', by Lennon and McCartney, The Beatles, *Sgt. Pepper's Lonely Hearts Club Band*, © 1967 Northern Songs.

2   Source: BARB. The *Only Fools and Horses* special of 1996 was the most-watched show of the 1990s; the special of 2001 was the most-watched show of the 2000s.

3   *Britain's Best Sitcom* was broadcast by the BBC in 2004. The top five were as follows: 1. *Only Fools and Horses*; 2. *Blackadder*; 3. *The Vicar of Dibley*; 4. *Dad's Army*; 5. *Fawlty Towers*.

4   The BFI TV 100 was a list compiled in 2000 by the British Film Institute, chosen by a poll of industry professionals, to determine what were the greatest British television programmes of any genre ever to have been screened.

5   The OnePoll survey was published in 2008 on the BBC website: http://news.bbc.co.uk/1/hi/uk/7184075.stm.

6   David Quantick, *Daily Telegraph*, 25 April 2011, p.17; Alan Yentob, quoted in numerous BBC broadcasts, 23 April 2011; Maurice Gran, *Daily Mail*, 25 April 2011, p.31.

Chapter One

1   The line was suggested by one of Thatcher's speechwriters, Sir Ronald Millar. After tactful explanations, a still-sceptical Thatcher delivered the line as written at the 1978 Conservative Party Conference. Her apparent ignorance of comedy was evident again at the 1990 Conference, when she only agreed to include a reference to *Monty Python*'s 'Dead Parrot' sketch after she had been assured that 'this Monty Python' was indeed 'one of us' (see Simon Hoggart, *A Long Lunch*, Edinburgh, John Murray, 2010, p.191).

2   Peter Fiddick, *The Guardian*, 2 May 1980, p.9.

3   John Sullivan, quoted by Richard Webber, *The Complete A–Z of Only Fools and Horses* (London: Orion, 2002), p.187.

4   Jim Trowers, speaking in *The Story of Only Fools and Horses*, first broadcast on BBC1, 20 December 2002.

5   Speight's pay was reported in the *Daily Mirror*, 20 January 1968, p.11.

6   John Sullivan, interviewed by Sanjeev Kohli for *Laughed Off the Page*, BBC Radio Scotland, 11 March 2010.

7   John Sullivan, speaking in *The Story of Only Fools and Horses,* first broadcast on BBC1, 20 December 2002.
8   John Sullivan, quoted by Webber, *The Complete A–Z of Only Fools and Horses, op. cit.,* p.188.
9   John Sullivan, interviewed by Sanjeev Kohli for *Laughed Off the Page,* BBC Radio Scotland, 11 March 2010.
10 John Sullivan, speaking in *The Story of Only Fools and Horses,* first broadcast on BBC1, 20 December 2002.
11 Bob Monkhouse, conversation with the author, 14 April 1998.
12 Dennis Main Wilson, interviewed by Alan Lawson with Norman Swallow in 1991 as part of the BECTU History Project.
13 James Gilbert, interview with the author, 30 May 2011.
14 *Ibid.*
15 The period of six weeks between commissioning and broadcast was reported by *The Guardian* on 2 December 1978, p.9. Some later accounts, more reliant perhaps on failing memories, have put the length of time at six or seven weeks.
16 James Gilbert, interview with the author, 30 May 2011.
17 See *Daily Mirror,* 21 September 1974, p.13.
18 Quoted by Stafford Hildred and Tim Ewbank, *Sir David Jason: A Life of Laughter* (London: John Blake, 2010), pp.32 and 44.
19 Simon Oates, quoted by Hildred and Ewbank, *Sir David Jason, op. cit.,* p.45.
20 David Jason, quoted in the *Daily Express,* 27 October 2003, p.33.
21 See, for example, *Daily Mirror,* 21 March 1968, p.19.
22 *Daily Mirror,* 21 September 1974, p.13.
23 *The Stage,* 9 September 1976, p.14.
24 Nicholas Lyndhurst, quoted by Frances Hardy, 'How Nicholas Lyndhurst tries to escape the "plonker" label,' *Daily Mail,* 7 September 2007, p.34.
25 Lennard Pearce, quoted by Kit Miller, 'Len's seven life-savers,' *News of the World,* 18 December 1983, p.13.

Chapter Two

1   According to Tommy Cooper's biographer, John Fisher (*Tommy Cooper: Always Leave Them Laughing,* London: Harper, 2007, pp.69–72), Cooper worked such markets as those in Leather Lane and Portobello Road during his early days trying to make a living after the war. One of his specialities to hold a crowd was something he called the Buddha Papers. A penny was placed in a small paper packet, which was in turn placed in another packet, which was then placed in another, and so it went on; when they were all unfolded the penny had disappeared.
2   John Sullivan, interviewed by David Bradbury and Joe McGrath, *Now That's Funny!* (London: Methuen, 1998), p.88.
3   *Ibid.*
4   John Sullivan, quoted by Jim Hiley, 'Black Market Comedy,' *Radio Times,* 5–11 September 1981, p.21.
5   See the report in *The Times,* 3 March 1980, p.4.
6   See *The Times,* 9 June 1980, p.15.

7   John Sullivan, interviewed by David Bradbury and Joe McGrath, *Now That's Funny!*, *op. cit.*, p.88.

8   John Sullivan, quoted in the *Daily Express*, 15 November 2002, p.50.

9   John Sullivan, by Richard Webber, *The Complete A–Z of Only Fools and Horses*, *op. cit.*, p.212.

10 The Employment Secretary, Norman Tebbit, responded to recent claims that rioting was an inevitable consequence of unemployment by asserting: 'I grew up in the '30s with an unemployed father. He didn't riot. He got on his bike and looked for work, and he kept looking till he found it.' (See *The Times*, 16 October 1981, p.4.)

11 John Sullivan, interviewed by David Bradbury and Joe McGrath, *Now That's Funny!*, *op. cit.*, p.88.

12 John Sullivan, interviewed by David Bradbury and Joe McGrath, *Now That's Funny!*, *op. cit.*, p.91.

13 John Sullivan, interviewed by Sanjeev Kohli for *Laughed Off the Page*, BBC Radio Scotland, 11 March 2010.

14 John Sullivan, quoted by Richard Webber, *The Complete A–Z of Only Fools and Horses, op. cit.*, p.96.

15 'Billericay Dickie' (1977), written by Ian Dury/Steve Nugent, published originally by Blackhill Music Ltd, now published by Templemill Music Ltd/Warner Chappell Music. 'Clever Trevor' (1977), written by Ian Dury and Chaz Jankel, published originally by Blackhill Music Ltd, now published by Templemill Music Ltd/Warner Chappell Music. 'This is What We Find' (1979), written by Ian Dury and Chaz Jankel, published originally by Blackhill Music Ltd, now published by Templemill Music Ltd/Warner Chappell Music.

16 James Gilbert, interview with the author, 30 May 2011.

17 *Ibid.*

18 Recalled by James Gilbert, interview with the author, 30 May 2011.

19 *The Morning Post*, 21 March, 1857, p.6. See also the *Manchester Guardian*, 9 August 1911, p.10: a court report quoted one William Windall, an aggressive Londoner charged with stealing a pair of boots, as saying: 'I am a tramp by profession; only fools and horses work.'

20 See, for example, the *Daily Mirror*, 13 September 1946, p.6.

21 Jimmy Gilbert was by no means the only executive to use such geographical reference points when judging how accessible comic material might be. His colleague Michael Mills, for example, sometimes used to ask those writers he deemed 'cerebral' if their dialogue would make sense to 'bus drivers in Stoke-on-Trent'.

22 James Gilbert, interview with the author, 30 May 2011.

23 John Sullivan, interviewed by David Bradbury and Joe McGrath, *Now That's Funny!*, *op. cit.*, p.93.

24 Gareth Gwenlan, quoted by Webber, *The Complete A-Z of Only Fools and Horses*, *op. cit.*, p.96.

Chapter Three

1   See my *Spike & Co.* (London: Hodder & Stoughton, 2006), p.283.

2   Michael Mills, quoted in my *Dad's Army: The Story of a Classic Television Show* (London: Fourth Estate, 2002), p.57.

3   See my *Frankie Howerd: Stand-Up Comic* (London: Fourth Estate, 2004), p.237.

4   John Cleese, quoted in my *Fawlty Towers* (London: Hodder & Stoughton, 2007), p.54.

5   Nicholas Lyndhurst, speaking in *The Story of Only Fools and Horses*, first broadcast on BBC1, 20 December 2002.

6   Nicholas Lyndhurst, speaking in *The Story of Only Fools and Horses*, first broadcast on BBC1, 20 December 2002.

7   John Sullivan, quoted by Clark, *The Only Fools and Horses Story*) London: BBC Books, 1998) p.15.

8   Lennard Pearce, quoted by Kit Miller, 'Len's seven life-savers,' *News of the World*, 18 December 1983, p.13.

9   Ray Butt, quoted by Webber, *The Complete A–Z of Only Fools and Horses, op. cit.*, p.97.

10 David Jason, quoted by Hildred and Ewbank, *Sir David Jason, op. cit.*, p.141.

11 Steve Clark, for example, would claim in his *The Only Fools and Horses Story*, (*op. cit.*, p17) that there was 'resistance' from Jimmy Gilbert, and others, to David Jason being cast as Del Boy because it was feared that his recruitment 'could jeopardise their relationship with Ronnie Barker' and 'the risk of offending Ronnie was deemed too great'. In an interview with me, however, Gilbert dismissed this assertion.

12 James Gilbert, interview with the author, 30 May 2011.

13 John Sullivan, *The Only Fools and Horses Story, op. cit*, p.17.

14 John Sullivan, quoted by Webber, *The Complete A–Z of Only Fools and Horses, op. cit.*, p.97.

15 See Webber, *The Complete A–Z of Only Fools and Horses, op. cit.*, p.8.

16 David Jason, quoted by Hildred and Ewbank, *Sir David Jason, op. cit.*, p.143.

17 Ray Butt, quoted by Webber, *The Complete A–Z of Only Fools and Horses, op. cit.*, p.98.

Chapter Four

1   Phoebe De Gaye, quoted by Webber, *The Complete A–Z of Only Fools and Horses, op. cit.*, p.56.

2   David Jason, quoted by Clark, *The Only Fools and Horses Story, op. cit.*, p.37.

3   David Jason, quoted by Johnny Black, 'Del Boy – nice work if you can get it,' *Radio Times*, 21–27 January 1989, p.20.

4   John Sullivan, notes for the script of the first ever episode of *Only Fools and Horses*, 'Big Brother'.

5   Later locations for The Nag's Head would include The Three Johns (now The Hobgoblin) near Chapel Market in Islington, London, and The Wagon and Horses in Stapleton Road in Bristol.

6   Tony Snoaden, quoted by Webber, *The Complete A–Z of Only Fools and Horses, op. cit.*, p.181.

7 Martin Shardlow, quoted by Webber, *The Complete A–Z of Only Fools and Horses, op. cit.,* p.175.

8 John Sullivan, interviewed by Bradbury and McGrath, *Now That's Funny!, op. cit.,* p.84.

9 John Sullivan, *ibid.,* p.84

10 John Sullivan, *ibid.,* p.84

11 'Only Fools and Horses', words and music by John Sullivan.

12 John Sullivan, interviewed by Bradbury and McGrath, *Now That's Funny!, op. cit.,* p.85.

13 Ray Butt, quoted by Webber, *The Complete A–Z of Only Fools and Horses, op. cit.,* p.193.

14 Ray Butt, *ibid.,* p.98.

Chapter Five

1 *Radio Times,* 5–11 September 1981, p.21.

2 Source: BBC WAC.

3 Stephen Biscoe, *Yorkshire Post,* 9 September 1981, p.21.

4 Source: BBC WAC.

5 Source: BARB: Top Ten Programmes of 1981.

6 Source: BBC WAC.

7 James Gilbert, interview with the author, 30 May 2011.

8 John Sullivan, quoted by Webber, *The Complete A–Z of Only Fools and Horses, op. cit.,* p.99.

9 John Howard Davies, interview with the author, 31 May 2007.

10 John Sullivan, quoted by Bradbury and McGrath, *Now That's Funny!, op. cit.,* p.83.

11 Ray Butt, quoted by Webber, *The Complete A–Z of Only Fools and Horses, op. cit.,* p.99.

12 John Sullivan, quoted by Webber, *The Complete A–Z of Only Fools and Horses, op. cit.,* p.99.

13 David Jason, quoted by Steve Clark, *The Only Fools and Horses Story, op. cit.,* p.34.

14 Chas Hodges, interviewed in the *Lancashire Evening Post,* 13 June 2008, p.23.

15 John Sullivan, quoted by Steve Clark, *The Only Fools and Horses Story, op. cit.,* p.82.

16 John Sullivan, quoted by Bradbury and McGrath, *Now That's Funny!, op. cit.,* p.85.

17 Nicholas Lyndhurst, quoted by Hildred and Ewbank, *Sir David Jason, op. cit.,* p.145.

18 John Sullivan, quoted by Bradbury and McGrath, *Now That's Funny!, op. cit.,* p.85.

19 Roger Lloyd Pack, quoted by Webber, *The Complete A–Z of Only Fools and Horses, op. cit.,* p.208.

20 John Challis, *ibid.,* p.62.

21 David Jason, transcribed by the author at a press preview, 24 May 2010.

22 David Jason would recall that, after filming this scene, he and the other actors adjourned to a nearby pub to have some lunch, and it was there that they were hugely amused to see a real-life Del Boy, dressed in his own camel hair coat, standing at the bar demonstrating a musical jewellery box with a rotating

Dresden lady on top. 'He'd obviously got a van load of them outside and he was giving the landlord all the patter – it was just too good to be true.' (*Radio Times*, 2–8 March 1985, p.13).

23   The building that was used as 'Ridgemere Hall' was actually Clayesmore School at Iwerne Minster in Dorset.

24   John Sullivan, quoted by Webber, *The Complete A–Z of Only Fools and Horses, op. cit.,* p.15.

25   John Sullivan, speaking in *The Story of Only Fools and Horses*, first broadcast on BBC1, 20 December 2002.

26   Andy Dimond, quoted by Webber, *The Complete A–Z of Only Fools and Horses, op. cit.,* p.206.

27   Nicholas Lyndhurst, speaking in *The Story of Only Fools and Horses*, first broadcast on BBC1, 20 December 2002.

28   Source: BBC WAC.

29   Source: BARB.

30   Source: BARB.

31   Source: BARB.

32   Source: BARB.

33   Source: BARB.

Chapter Six

1   See, for example, the *Daily Express*, 18 June 1983, p.1.

2   Source: BBC WAC.

3   John Sullivan, quoted by Webber, *The Complete A–Z of Only Fools and Horses, op. cit.,* p.99.

4   John Sullivan, speaking in *The Story of Only Fools and Horses*, first broadcast on BBC1, 20 December 2002.

5   John Sullivan, quoted by Webber, *The Complete A–Z of Only Fools and Horses, op. cit.,* p.99.

6   John Sullivan, quoted by Clark, *The Only Fools and Horses Story, op. cit.,* p.93.

7   David Jason, quoted by Clark, *The Only Fools and Horses Story, op. cit.,* p.95.

8   Jim Broadbent, interviewed by Michael Hellicar, *Daily Mail*, 19 November 2010, p.64.

9   Eva Mottley – who was also known for her work in the 1983 ITV drama, *Widows* – committed suicide on Valentine's Day, 14 February 1985, aged thirty-five.

10   Source: BBC WAC.

11   *Harty,* broadcast on BBC1, 21 December 1983.

12   See *The Times*, 25 November 1982, p.27; *Radio Times*, 5–11 November 1983, p.4; *Daily Express*, 2 January 1984, p.18.

13   See *The Times*, 18 April 1984, p.4.

Chapter Seven

1   Ray Butt, quoted by Clark, *The Only Fools and Horses Story, op. cit.,* p.100.

2   Nicholas Lyndhurst, quoted by Clark, *The Only Fools and Horses Story, op. cit.,* p.53

3 John Sullivan, quoted by Webber, *The Complete A–Z of Only Fools and Horses,* *op. cit.,* p.100.

4 Internationally, too, major characters very rarely died in sitcoms. Ignoring the countless 'incidental' deaths of peripheral figures in the long-running military medical sitcom *M*A*S*H* (1972–77) – which I think was more of a 'comedy–drama' than a conventional sitcom – the significant breakthrough in the US came when Edith Bunker (played by the still very much alive Jean Stapleton), the wife of Archie in *All in the Family*, was revealed to have died (off camera) from a stroke when Archie Bunker returned on his own in the second season of a spin-off sitcom called *Archie Bunker's Place* in 1980, but such instances would remain extremely rare. (It could be argued that three earlier examples occurred in the ABC comedy show *Soap*: first in 1977 when Peter Campbell is murdered with a knife, a brick and a gunshot in episode 12 of season 1; second in October 1978 when Tim's mother dies of natural causes in episode 5 of season 2; and then in December 1978 when Danny's wife, Elaine, is shot in episode 13 of season 2. In my opinion, however, *Soap* is more accurately described as a parody or 'spoof soap opera' rather than a sitcom, so I have not classed it as such.)

5 David Jason, in Webber, *The Complete A–Z of Only Fools and Horses, op. cit.,*p.10.

6 Buster Merryfield, *During the War and other encounters* (Chichester: Summersdale 1997), p.239.

7 Buster Merryfield, *ibid.*, p.240.

8 Susie Belbin, quoted by Webber, *The Complete A–Z of Only Fools and Horses,* *op. cit.,* p.33.

9 Source: BBC WAC.

10 See *Radio Times*, 16–22 February 1985, p.13.

11 Saul Bellow, *Humboldt's Gift* (Harmondsworth: Penguin Books, 1977), p.262.

12 Susie Belbin, quoted by Webber, *The Complete A–Z of Only Fools and Horses,* *op. cit.,* p.33.

13 Susie Belbin, *ibid.*

14 J. A. Sutton, *Radio Times*, 5 April 1985, p.80.

15 Buster Merryfield, *During the War, op. cit.*, p.242.

16 *Ibid,* p.243.

17 John Sullivan, quoted by Jim Hiley, 'Black Market Comedy,' *Radio Times*, 5–11 September 1981, p.23.

18 Sue Holderness, quoted by Webber, *The Complete A–Z of Only Fools and Horses, op. cit.,* p.39.

19 Sue Holderness, interview with the author, 7 May 2011.

20 Susie Belbin, quoted by Webber, *The Complete A–Z of Only Fools and Horses,* *op. cit.,* p.39.

21 Source: BBC WAC.

22 See my *Spike & Co., op. cit.*, pp.123–48 and 279–308.

23 Buster Merryfield, *During the War, op. cit.*, p.243.

24 Bilko dialogue, written by Arnie Rosen and Coleman Jacoby, from 'Bilko Saves Ritzik's Marriage,' *The Phil Silvers Show*, first broadcast 22 February 1958.

25 Source: BBC WAC.

Chapter Eight

1   Sir Bill Cotton, interview with the author, 6 June 2000.
2   See David Hewson, 'Will BBC1 make the grade?', *The Times*, 29 November 1984, p.11.
3   Michael Grade, interview with the author, 7 March 2011.
4   Source: BARB.
5   See, for example, the *Daily Express*, 24 December 1985, p.21.
6   Herbert Kretzmer, *Daily Mail*, 27 December 1985, p.27.
7   Maureen Paton, *Daily Express*, 27 December 1985, p.27.
8   *Daily Express*, 10 January 1986, p.3.
9   Source: BBC WAC.
10 *Daily Express*, 10 January 1986, p.3.
11 See *The Stage*, 21 August 1986, p.49.
12 Michael Grade, interview with the author, 7 March 2011.
13 Source: BBC WAC.
14 Source: BBC WAC.
15 *The Stage*, 30 October 1986, p.19.
16 Buster Merryfield, *During the War, op. cit.*, p.244.
17 Source: BBC WAC.
18 John Sullivan, quoted by Clark, *The Only Fools and Horses Story, op.cit.*, p.118.
19 Source: BBC WAC.
20 Gareth Gwenlan, quoted by Webber, *The Complete A–Z of Only Fools and Horses, op. cit.*, p.100.
21 John Sullivan, interviewed by Bradbury and McGrath, *Now That's Funny!, op. cit.*, p.84.
22 Source: BBC WAC.
23 David Jason, in Webber, *The Complete A–Z of Only Fools and Horses, op. cit.*, p.10.
24 John Sullivan, quoted by Bradbury and McGrath, *Now That's Funny!, op. cit.*, p.93.
25 David Jason, in Webber, *The Complete A–Z of Only Fools and Horses, op. cit.*, p.11.

Chapter Nine

1   John Sullivan, *Radio Times*, 23 December 1989 – 5 January 1990, p.5.
2   John Sullivan, interviewed by Bradbury and McGrath, *Now That's Funny!, op. cit.*, p.87.
3   Charles Dickens, *Oliver Twist* (London: Wordsworth Editions, 2000), p.106.
4   Mark Lawson, 'The Nice Man Cometh' (1991), in *Bloody Margaret: Three Political Fantasies* (London: Pan Macmillan, 1992), p.188.
5   Del Boy's year of birth is, predictably enough, a rather contentious subject among the most obsessive of fans, because the details are contradicted in several episodes. In 'Sleepless in Peckham' (2003), for example, Rodney points to an old picture and says that Del was aged 15 at the time, which would have made his date of birth about 1945. In 'Go West Young Man' (1981), however, Del claims to be 35, making his birth year 1946. In 'A Losing Streak' (1982) and 'Thicker than Water' (1983), Del claims that their father, Reg, left them in 1965 on his 16th birthday, making his year of birth 1949. In 'Tea for

Three' (1986), Rodney tells Trigger's niece Lisa that Del's forty-sixth birthday is coming up, making Del's year of birth 1940. The episode 'The Class of '62' (1991) saw Del and friends attending a class reunion, suggesting a birth year of 1946 or 1947.

6   See *Radio Times*, 21–27 January 1989, p.20.

7   John Sullivan, interviewed by Brian Viner, 'The Spirit of Christmas Present,' *Independent*, 21 December 2001, p.7.

8   Tony Dow, quoted by Webber, *The Complete A–Z of Only Fools and Horses, op. cit.*, p.102.

9   Source: BBC WAC.

10   The poll of the '50 funniest sitcom moments' was compiled in 2000 from the votes of a panel of comedy writers, actors and producers that included Ronnie Barker and Victoria Wood. The top ten was as follows:

1. The chandelier scene from *Only Fools and Horses*
2. The bar flap scene from *Only Fools and Horses*
3. Edina falls into a flowerbed in *Absolutely Fabulous*
4. Mainwaring shouting 'Don't tell him, Pike!' in *Dad's Army*
5. Alf Garnett explaining that Jesus must have been English in *Till Death Us Do Part*
6. The scene where a demanding guest provokes Basil by complaining to him that she had asked for a room with a view in *Fawlty Towers*
7. The 'a pint?' scene in 'The Blood Donor' episode of *Hancock's Half-Hour*
8. Frank Spencer's roller-skating scene in *Some Mothers Do 'Ave 'Em*
9. The scene where Captain Mainwaring wears a toupée in *Dad's Army*
10. The 'don't mention the war' scene in *Fawlty Towers*
     Source: *Radio Times*, 19–25 August 2000, pp.18–22.

11   Malcolm Rougvie, quoted by Webber, *The Complete A–Z of Only Fools and Horses, op. cit.*, p.170.

12   David Jason, quoted by Clark, *The Only Fools and Horses Story, op. cit.*, p.125.

13   Source: BBC WAC.

14   John Sullivan, quoted by Webber, *The Complete A–Z of Only Fools and Horses, op. cit.*, p.101.

15   Tessa Peake-Jones, interview with the author, 24 April 2011.

16   *The Great Gildersleeve* – itself a spin-off of another very popular 1940s radio show called *Fibber McGee and Molly* – starred Harold Peary (and later Willard Waterman) as Throckmorton P. Gildersleeve, a pompous but well-meaning local official who was also responsible for his orphaned niece and nephew. The show ran for 13 years (1941–1954), with over 550 shows produced. The Jolly Boys was a social club consisting of Gildersleeve, the local druggist Mr Peavey, Judge Hooker and two additional regulars, the barber Floyd Munson and police chief Gates.

17   John Sullivan, quoted by Webber, *The Complete A–Z of Only Fools and Horses, op. cit.*, p.21.

18   Source: BBC WAC.

19 Nancy Banks-Smith, *The Guardian*, 27 December 1988, p.22.

20 Source: BBC WAC.

21 Gareth Gwenlan, quoted by Clark, *The Only Fools and Horses Story, op.cit.*, p.129.

22 Pam Francis, *Today*, 27 December 1990, p.19.

23 John Sullivan, quoted by Clark, *The Only Fools and Horses Story, op. cit.*, p.131.

24 John Sullivan, interviewed by Sanjeev Kohli for *Laughed Off the Page*, BBC Radio Scotland, 11 March 2010.

25 Source: BBC WAC.

26 Other recent examples of actors appearing in dual or multiple roles included Eddie Murphy's four roles in *Coming to America* (1988), Michael J. Fox's three roles in the first two *Back to the Future* sequels (1989 and 1990) and Meg Ryan's trio of characters in *Joe Versus the Volcano* (1990).

27 Source: BBC WAC.

28 Source: BBC WAC.

29 See Clark, *The Only Fools and Horses Story, op. cit.*, p.136.

30 *Sitting Pretty* (1996) was a story of the wartime conflict between the RAF and the recently arrived US Air Force on an English air base in 1942.

31 *Over Here* (1992–3) was the story of a wayward daughter (played by Diane Bull) returning to live on the family farm in Kent.

32 Source: BBC WAC.

33 Sources: BBC WAC and BARB.

34 Source: BARB.

Chapter Ten

1 Gareth Gwenlan, quoted by Clark, *The Only Fools and Horses Story, op. cit.*, p.138.

2 See the *Daily Mirror*, 29 August 1995, p.3.

3 Steve Clark, *Daily Mirror*, 18 July 1996, p.9.

4 Pictures included ones of Del in a Rolls-Royce (*Daily Mirror*, 16 October 1996, p.15) and Albert on a luxury yacht (*The People*, 17 November 1996, p.15).

5 Nicholas Lyndhurst, *ibid.*, p.140.

6 Gareth Gwenlan, *ibid.*, p.141.

7 Gareth Gwenlan, *ibid.*, p.141.

8 John Sullivan, interviewed by Sanjeev Kohli for *Laughed Off the Page*, BBC Radio Scotland, 11 March 2010.

9 Source: BBC WAC.

10 Source: BBC WAC.

11 Sources: BBC WAC, and BARB.

12 Source: BARB.

13 Source: BARB.

14 Jonathan Betts, interview with the author, 7 May 2011.

15 The Longitude Prize – established through an Act of Parliament (The Longitude Act) in 1714 – was a reward offered by the British Government for a simple and practical method for the precise determination of a ship's longitude.

16 John Sullivan, quoted by Webber, *The Complete A–Z of Only Fools and Horses,*
    op. cit., p.242.

17 See, for example, Michael Ancram's comments during a House of Commons
    debate 25 July 1997 (*Hansard*, 25 July 1997, Column 1135): 'The more I listen
    to the Secretary of State speaking about his proposals, the more I am reminded
    of Del Boy in *Only Fools and Horses* trying to sell his latest doubtful wares.'

18 Chris Woodhead made his remarks during a speech on 21 January 1997;
    quoted in the *Sunday Times*, 26 July 1997, 'News Review,' p.2.

19 John Sullivan, 'Trust them: Del and Rodney are model citizens,' *Sunday Times*,
    'News Review,' 26 January 1997, p.2.

20 *Wat schuift 't?* was the Dutch adaptation of *Only Fools and Horses*. Running
    for one series in 1995, it changed the surname of the Trotters to 'Aarsman'
    but otherwise stayed fairly close to the original situation and characters.

21 *This Time Next Year* was the first attempt by US production companies to
    remake *Only Fools and Horses* for American network television. Ed Weinberger
    (a writer for, among other programmes, *The Cosby Show*) turned producer to
    prepare a pilot of this show, renaming the Trotters the 'Flanagans' (apparently
    because he envisaged casting the family as either Irish or African–Americans)
    and changing Rodney's name to 'Marlon'. Because it was intended as a vehicle
    for the already fairly elderly Harry Morgan, the role of Grandad was set to
    be made the lead, with the two brothers as supporting characters. The project,
    however, failed to progress as far as the making of the pilot, and the US rights
    were passed on to a succession of other companies. Ed Weinberger did,
    however, collaborate successfully with John Sullivan on the US remake of
    Dear John, which ran for four seasons between 1988 and 92. See Janine Gibson,
    'Del and Rodney to strike it rich in the US,' *The Guardian*, 1 May 1999, p.6.

22 Sky Television had begun a four-channel service of general entertainment
    (Sky Channel), movies (Sky Movies), sport (Eurosport) and rolling news (Sky
    News) on 5 February 1989, and British Satellite Broadcasting (BSB) brought
    several more channels to the air early on in the following year, but in
    November 1990, a 50:50 merger was announced to form a single company,
    operating as British Sky Broadcasting (BSkyB), but marketed as Sky. For UK
    Gold's early use of *Only Fools and Horses*, see *New Media Markets*, 16 October
    1997, p.3.

23 Source: BARB.

24 David Jason, writing in Webber, *The Complete A–Z of Only Fools and Horses,*
    op. cit., p.11.

25 John Sullivan, interviewed by David Bradbury and Joe McGrath, *Now That's
    Funny!, op. cit.,* p. 90.

26 Sullivan's involvement in the BBC's new adaptation of *David Copperfield*
    was announced in the spring of 1998. In June 1999, however, Sullivan was
    reported as having 'stormed' out of the project, having objected to a new
    suggestion that the adaptation be made to resemble more of a traditional
    costume drama. 'If they wanted that,' Sullivan was quoted as saying, 'they
    shouldn't have asked me to do it. I was pushed around – their behaviour
    is quite astonishing' (*Mail on Sunday*, 20 June 1999, p.22). He then took his
    scripts away with him and told Yorkshire Television's then-controller of

comedy drama, David Reynolds, that he and Jason still wanted to explore the character of Micawber, and the four-part mini-series *Micawber* was the result. Charting the further adventures of Dickens's verbose, impecunious lawyer, with new storylines, the series was broadcast on ITV over the Christmas period in 2001. The critics, in general, disliked the production, and it was eclipsed in the ratings by the first instalment of the *Only Fools* trilogy.

27 John Sullivan, interviewed by David Bradbury and Joe McGrath, *Now That's Funny!*, *op. cit.*, p. 95.

28 See Clare Raymond, 'Laughing All the Way to the Bank,' *The Mirror*, 1 July 1999, p.3.

29 Buster Merryfield, quoted in *The Independent*, 24 June 1999, p.22.

30 David Jason and Nicholas Lyndhurst, quoted in the *Mirror*, 24 June 1999, p.11.

31 John Sullivan, quoted by Webber, *The Complete A–Z of Only Fools and Horses*, *op. cit.*, p.242.

32 John Sullivan, *ibid.*, p.242.

33 See *The Mirror*, 28 January 1997, p.3.

34 Gareth Gwenlan, quoted by Webber, *The Complete A–Z of Only Fools and Horses*, *op. cit.*, p.242.

35 Gareth Gwenlan, *ibid.*, p.242.

36 John Sullivan, *ibid.*, p.242.

37 John Challis, quoted in the *Radio Times*, 22 December 2001 – 4 January 2002, p.7.

38 ITV wanted the BBC to allow it to repeat the entire programme on its own channel because the *Who Wants to Be a Millionaire?* format was to be featured during a five-minute sequence. The BBC rejected the proposal and the fictional game show was used instead.

39 John Sullivan, quoted by Webber, *The Complete A–Z of Only Fools and Horses*, *op. cit.*, p.242.

40 Source: BBC WAC. This Christmas special would end up as the most-watched British television show of the decade.

41 Source: BARB.

42 Lorraine Heggessey, quoted in the *Daily Mirror*, 27 December 2001, p.7.

43 Thomas Sutcliffe, *Independent,* 30 December 2001, p.8.

44 David Stephenson, *Sunday Express*, 30 December 2001, p.56.

45 *Daily Mirror*, 1 January 2002, p.11.

46 *The Sunday Times*, 'Culture' section, 15 December 2001, p.60.

47 Christina Smith, *Daily Mirror*, 27 December 2001, p.7.

48 Source: BBC WAC. (This figure was also the most widely reported total at the time, although BARB later measured the show at 17.4 million.)

49 Charlie Catchpole, *Daily Star*, 30 December 2002, p.13.

50 *Guardian*, 27 December 2002, p.18.

51 Source: BARB.

52 Bob Shields, *Daily Record*, 28 December 2002, p.15.

53 See the *Daily Mail*, 24 December 2003, p.55.

54 Source: BARB. The most watched programme of the year was an edition of *Coronation Street,* which drew an audience of 19.43 million.

Epilogue

1   John Sullivan, quoted in the *Daily Mail*, 24 December 2003, p.55.
2   David Jason, quoted in the *Daily Mirror*, 24 March 2010, p.30.
3   See *Daily Mail*, 4 October 2003, p.19.
4   Tessa Peake-Jones, interview with the author, 24 April 2011.
5   Sue Holderness, interview with the author, 7 May 2011.
6   John Sullivan, interviewed by Sanjeev Kohli for *Laughed Off the Page*, BBC Radio Scotland, 11 March 2010.
7   See Gary Bushell, *The People*, 15 July 2001, p.17.
8   See the *Daily Telegraph*, 16 January 2010, p.11.
9   John Sullivan, interviewed by David Bradbury and Joe McGrath, *Now That's Funny!*, op. cit., p.95.

Bibliography

Only Fools and Horses

Adams, Jane, 'Why Del can bank on Albert,' *Daily Mail*, 24 December 1985, p.30

Bellamy, Guy, 'From the horse's mouth,' *Radio Times*, 5–11 November 1983, p.4

Black, Johnny, 'Del Boy – nice work if you can get it,' *Radio Times*, 21–27 January 1989, p.20

Clark, Steve, *Only Fools and Horses: The Location Guide* (London: Seaspite Publishing, 1993)

The Only Fools and Horses Story (London: BBC, 1998)

Dugdale, John, 'King of Comedy,' *The Guardian*, 17 May 1993, p.15

Fraser, Nicholas, 'How the Beeb bets on fools and horses,' *Observer*, 18 March 1990, p.63

Gibson, Janine, 'Del and Rodney to strike it rich in the US,' *The Guardian*, 1 May 1999, p.6

Greaves, William, 'Fools for Love,' *Radio Times*, 22 December 1990 – 4 January 1991, p.9

Hattersley, Roy, 'Fools in paradise,' *Mail on Sunday*, December 16, 2001, p.27

Hildred, Stafford & Tim Ewbank, *The Dream Team* (London: John Blake, 2000)

Hiley, Jim, 'Black Market Comedy,' *Radio Times*, 5–11 September 1981, pp.21–3

Household, Nicki, 'Del keeps it in the family,' *Radio Times*, 2–8 March 1985, p.13

'Get a load of this!' *Radio Times*, 3 August – 5 September 1986, p.3

Hyland, Ian, 'The Luvvly Jubbly Life of John,' *Sunday Mirror*, 5 July 1998, pp.14, 16 and 17

Merryfield, Buster, *During the War and other encounters* (Chichester: Summersdale, 1997)

Murphy, Rachel, 'Nobody's Fool,' *The Mirror*, 14 December 2002, p.8

Paton, Maureen, 'The Man Who Makes the Queen Laugh,' *Daily Express*, 22 February 1986, p.19

Raymond, Clare, 'Laughing All the Way to the Bank,' *The Mirror*, 1 July 1999, pp.3 and 32

Rees, Jasper, 'The Star of Christmas Present,' *Radio Times*, 15–21 December 2000, pp.31–2

Saunders, Kate, 'The Other Side of Del Boy,' *The Sunday Times* (Section 5), 23 December 1990, pp.2–3

Sullivan, John, *The Bible of Peckham,* Vol. 1 (London: BBC, 1999)
   The Bible of Peckham, Vol. 2 (London: BBC, 2000)
   The Bible of Peckham, Vol. 3 (London: BBC, 2001)
   'Trust them: Del and Rodney are model citizens,' *The Sunday Times*, 'News Review,' 26 January 1997, p.2
   'Fool's Gold,' *Mail on Sunday*, 21 December 2003, p.15

Viner, Brian, 'The spirit of Christmas present,' *Independent*, 21 December 2001, p.7

Webber, Richard, *The Complete A–Z of Only Fools and Horses* (London: Orion, 2002)

General

Allen, Steve, *The Funny Men* (New York: Simon and Schuster, 1956)

Barfe, Louis, *Turned Out Nice Again* (London: Atlantic Books, 2008)

Black, Peter, *The Biggest Aspidistra in the World* (London: BBC, 1972)
   The Mirror in the Corner (London: Hutchison, 1972)

Bradbury, David & Joe McGrath, *Now That's Funny!* (London: Methuen, 1998)

Brandreth, Gyles, *Brief Encounters* (London: Politico's, 2003)

Briggs, Asa, *The History of Broadcasting in the United Kingdom* (Oxford: Oxford University Press, 1961–1979):

Vol. 1: *The Birth of Broadcasting*, 1961

Vol. 2: *The Golden Age of Wireless*, 1965

Vol. 3: *The War of Words*, 1970

Vol. 4: *Sound and Vision*, 1979

Cardiff, David, 'Mass middlebrow laughter: The origins of BBC comedy,' *Media, Culture & Society*, Vol. 10, no.1 (January 1988), pp. 41–60

Coldstream, John (ed.), *Ever, Dirk* (London: Phoenix, 2009)

Cotton, Bill, *The BBC as an Entertainer* (London: BBC, 1977)
Double Bill, (London: Fourth Estate, 2000)

Cryer, Barry, *You Won't Believe This But . . .* (London: Virgin, 1998)
Pigs Can Fly (London: Orion, 2003)

Dunn, Kate, *Do Not Adjust Your Set: The Early Days of Live Television* (London: John Murray, 2003)

Fisher, John, *Funny Way to be a Hero* (London: Frederich Muller, 1973)
Tony Hancock (London: Harper, 2009)

Foster, Andy & Steve Furst, *Radio Comedy 1938–1968* (London: Virgin, 1996)

Frith, Simon, 'The pleasures of the hearth: the making of BBC light entertainment,' in Tony Bennett *et al* (eds), *Popular Culture and Social Relations* (Milton Keynes: Open University, 1983)

Gambaccini, Paul & Rod Taylor, *Television's Greatest Hits* (London: Network Books, 1993)

Gillett, Philip, *The British Working Class in Postwar Film* (Manchester: Manchester University Press, 2003)

Gilliatt, Penelope, *To Wit* (New York: Scribner, 1990)

Grade, Michael, *It Seemed Like A Good Idea At The Time* (London: Macmillan, 1999)

Greene, Hugh Carleton, *The BBC as a Public Service* (London: BBC, 1960)

Hildred, Stafford & Tim Ewbank, *Sir David Jason* (London: John Blake, 2010)

Hudd, Roy, *Roy Hudd's Book of Music-Hall, Variety and Showbiz Anecdotes* (London: Virgin, 1994)

James, Clive, *Clive James on Television* (London: Picador, 1991)

Jeffries, Stuart, *Mrs Slocombe's Pussy* (London: Flamingo, 2000)

Kumar, Krishan, *The Making of English National Identity: Englishness and Britishness in Comparative and Historical Perspective* (Cambridge: Cambridge University Press, 2003)

Lewis, Roger, *The Life and Death of Peter Sellers* (London: Century, 1994)

Lewisohn, Mark, *Radio Times Guide to TV Comedy* (London: BBC, 1998)

McCann, Graham, *Cary Grant: A Class Apart* (London: Fourth Estate, 1996)

'Why the best sitcoms must be a class act,' *London Evening Standard*, 21 May 1997, p.9

'An offer we can refuse,' *London Evening Standard*, 2 December 1998, p.8

Morecambe & Wise (London: Fourth Estate, 1998)

'Sit back and wait for the comedy,' *Financial Times*, 24 November 1999, p.22

'Half-man, half-desk: the secrets of a talk-show host,' *Financial Times*, 8/9 April 2000, p.viii

'Don't bury your treasures,' *Financial Times*, 28 June 2000, p.22

'Nocturnal transmissions are a turn-off,' *Financial Times*, 8 May 2002, p.18

'You never had it so good or so funny,' *Financial Times*, 13 November 2002, p.17

'How to define the indefinable,' *Financial Times*, 20 March 2003, p.14

'Bob Hope: The master of special delivery bows out,' *Financial Times*, 29 July 2003, p.15

'Steptoe and Son,' *British Comedy Greats,* ed. Annabel Merullo & Neil Wenborn (London: Cassell Illustrated, 2003), pp.157–161

Frankie Howerd: Stand-Up Comic (London: Fourth Estate, 2004)

(ed.) *The Essential Dave Allen* (London: Hodder & Stoughton, 2005)

Spike & Co. (London: Hodder & Stoughton, 2006)

Fawlty Towers: The Story of the Sitcom (London: Hodder & Stoughton, 2007)

Bounder! The Biography of Terry Thomas (London: Aurum, 2008)

McFarlane, Brian, *An Autobiography of British Cinema* (London: Methuen, 1997)

The Encyclopedia of British Film (London: Methuen, 2005)

Miall, Leonard, *Inside The BBC* (London: Weidenfeld & Nicolson, 1994)

Midwinter, Eric, *Make 'Em Laugh* (London: George Allen & Unwin, 1979)

Muir, Frank, *Comedy in Television* (London: BBC, 1966)

Murphy, Robert (ed.), *The British Cinema Book* (London: BFI, 2001)

Nathan, David, *The Laughtermakers* (London: Peter Owen, 1971)

Parkinson, Michael, *Parkinson* (London: Elm Tree, 1975)

Pedrick, Gale, 'Laughter in the Air,' *BBC Year Book 1948* (London: BBC, 1948), pp.53–6

Plomley, Roy, *Desert Island Lists* (London: Hutchinson, 1984)

Priestley, J.B., *Particular Pleasures* (New York: Stein & Day, 1975)

Richards, Jeffrey, *Visions of Yesteryear* (London: Routledge, 1973)

Films and British National Identity (Manchester: Manchester University Press, 1997)

Silvey, Roger, *Who's Listening? The Story of BBC Audience Research* (London: Allen & Unwin, 1974)

Sloan, Tom, *Television Light Entertainment* (London: BBC, 1969)

Stone, Richard, *You Should Have Been In Last Night* (Sussex: The Book Guild, 2000)

Street, Sarah, *British National Cinema* (London: Routledge, 1997)

Took, Barry, *Laughter in the Air* (London: Robson/BBC, 1976)
  'Whatever Happened to TV Comedy?' *The Listener*, 5 January 1984, pp.7–8, and 12 January 1984, pp.8–9
Tynan, Kenneth, *Profiles* (London: Nick Hern Books, 1989)
Viner, Brian, *Nice To See It, To See It, Nice* (London: Simon & Schuster, 2009)
Watt, John (ed.), *Radio Variety* (London: J.M. Dent, 1939)
Wheldon, Huw, *British Traditions in a World-Wide Medium* (London: BBC, 1973)
  The Achievement of Television (London: BBC, 1975)
  The British Experience in Television (London: BBC, 1976)
Whitfield, June, . . . *and June Whitfield* (London: Corgi, 2001)

Index